GOSPELS AND GRIT:
WORK AND LABOUR IN CARLYLE, CONRAD, AND ORWELL

Gospels and Grit

Work and Labour in Carlyle, Conrad, and Orwell

ROB BRETON

UNIVERSITY OF TORONTO PRESS
Toronto Buffalo London

© University of Toronto Press Incorporated 2005
Toronto Buffalo London
Printed in Canada

ISBN 0-8020-3888-3

Printed on acid-free paper

Library and Archives Canada Cataloguing in Publication

Breton, Rob, 1965–
Gospels and grit : work and labour in Carlyle, Conrad and Orwell/Rob Breton.

Includes bibliographical references and index.
ISBN 0-8020-3888-3

1. Carlyle, Thomas, 1795–1881 – Criticism and interpretation.
2. Conrad, Joseph, 1857–1924 – Criticism and interpretation.
3. Orwell, George, 1903–1950 – Criticism and interpretation.
4. Work in literature.   I. Title.

PR830.W63B74 2005   820'.9355   C2004-906490-8

University of Toronto Press acknowledges the financial assistance to its publishing program of the Canada Council for the Arts and the Ontario Arts Council.

This book has been published with the help of a grant from the Canadian Federation for the Humanities and Social Sciences, through the Aid to Scholarly Publications Programme, using funds provided by the Social Sciences and Humanities Research Council of Canada.

University of Toronto Press acknowledges the financial support for its publishing activities of the Government of Canada through the Book Publishing Industry Development Program (BPIDP).

To my wife, Lindsey McMaster, and our daughter, Liv, for showing me that labour too can bring joy.

Contents

ACKNOWLEDGMENTS ix

Introduction 3

1 Thomas Carlyle 34

2 Joseph Conrad 94

3 George Orwell 150

Epilogue: Postindustrial and Postmodern Work 212

WORKS CITED 227
INDEX 239

Acknowledgments

Many have helped me write this book, and in many ways. I owe a tremendous amount to family and friends, and to co-workers from workplaces of all descriptions. The work that went into this book began a long time before I started writing it.

Among the many people at the University of British Columbia to whom I owe particular gratitude I must first thank Jonathan Wisenthal. Not only did Professor Wisenthal teach me much about Carlyle, Conrad, Orwell, and many others, he also showed me what it is to be a real scholar and true original. He has been and continues to be a wise mentor and, beyond that, a friend. I also owe great thanks to Andrew Busza and John Xiros Cooper for their knowledge, patience, and guidance.

GOSPELS AND GRIT

'*Work.*' Not, work at this or that – but, Work.

Dr Arnold

To suggest that a creative writer, in a time of conflict, must split life into two compartments, may seem defeatist or frivolous: yet in practice I do not see what else he can do. To lock yourself up in an ivory tower is impossible and undesirable. To yield subjectively, not merely to a party machine, but even to a group ideology, is to destroy yourself as a writer. We feel this dilemma to be a painful one, because we see the need of engaging in politics while also seeing what a dirty, degrading business it is.

George Orwell

Introduction

In *David Copperfield* (1849–50) the fishy Uriah Heep attempts to defend his passive-aggressive villainy by explaining that he was taught 'from nine o'clock to eleven, that labour was a curse; and from eleven o'clock to one, that it was a blessing and a cheerfulness, and a dignity, and I don't know what all' (829). The dichotomous and checkered history of European work generally begins with the ancient Greeks disparaging work, understanding it as a necessary evil, unfortunate for slaves and antithetical to contemplation. Later, medieval Christians followed them and the ancient Hebrews by continuing to see work as a burden. Work was necessary because of original sin or to atone for original sin and score points towards salvation. It was treated as a punishing corrective to the body's urges. Luther and Calvin, however, began investing work with all sorts of value, though paradoxically advocating effort and renouncing the material gain that effort accrued. By the nineteenth century work had been lifted to the status of a Gospel and heralded as a blessing. Yet even then, according to Uriah, besides the epithet that 'Satan finds work for idle hands' lingered the opposite idea of 'in the sweat of thy brow shalt thou eat bread.'

The Victorian idea of work, following the ambiguous history of work suggested in the cursory survey above, was mostly split on secular grounds, arguably making the ways work was conceived, perceived, approached, and defined more radically divided than at any other period of time. Early Protestantism treated work – the origin of economies and social organizations – as a fiat to withdraw from the economic society. This paradox was only amplified as work became a moral imperative and a substitute for religious scepticism in the midst of rapid industrial expansion and demographic relocation. On the one hand, the most ardent and admired cultural critics and the most popular mythologies promulgated work as a value in itself. Full engagement was said to entrain self-definition, stabilize and satisfy the ego, form and affirm it, generate well-being, foster a sense of fulfillment and individuation, and lead to harmonious social integration. Though the idea that work constructs identity is far from a metaphysical notion, it retained its religious and especially Protestant overtones of signifying virtue, of dignifying or ennobling the practitioner no matter how humble its nature might be. Intrinsically valuable, independent of its product, and embedded in non-economic imperatives, or part of the 'moral economy,' it was also said to nurture ideas of mutual obligation and leave behind beauty, the integral workmanship of the craftsperson. The hard worker is morally superior to the idler, the craftsperson more trustworthy than the careless. Passages in life and adulthood are marked and certified by Work. More than anything, the dominant nineteenth-century Gospel of Work was written to counter economic, rationalistic thinking: to provide alternative concepts to self-interest, utility, and maximizing not found in the rising science of economics. Work as a way of life, for its own sake, was not an activity circumscribed by paycheques, contracts, or time.

On the other hand, the rationalization of work in the nineteenth century – widespread industrialism and the redefinition of work into a purely economic context, as the means for extrinsic gain – produced ideologies that assumed work could only be a curse. 'People work only to enjoy the leisure that follows,' argues the emergent rationalist and expert behaviourist. Subsequently, the same critics and popular discourses idealizing work had to revile it in its prevailing shape. What we today call de-skilling, repetition, boredom, degradation, and alienation; clockwork over task-based work and the systemization of conduct; the growing separation between manual and mental labour, the division of labour, and the fragmentation of knowledge about production; the demarcation of 'work' and 'life' (with the relations of production, however, continuing to be imprinted on and to organize life outside of the workplace); the instrumentalizing of worker into or as subordinate to machine; and the ideological diffusion of the theory of disutility – all fitting under the rubric of rationalism – could not be a blessing or lead to well-being. For radically traditionalist thinkers reacting to modernity – for Thomas Carlyle then, Joseph Conrad and George Orwell later – only the rationalization of work made it an absolute curse. For them this brand of work was contrary to both intrinsic satisfaction and the hard toil that produces a sanctifying sweat on the brow. I refer to it, judged in this way, as *labour*, though I maintain that 'labour' has other meanings as well. Nothing in the bifurcation of this Gospel of Work and this censure of modern labour is inherently a paradox or a prima facie contradiction, except when one is asked to Work for intrinsic gains under the conditions of modern labour. Only the treatment of work as if outside the realm of objective labour, necessity, or economics in general – when extracted or represented as if extractable from society – leads to contradictions.

The Victorian Gospel of Work that has its roots in Romantic critiques of industrialism and their various histories in eighteenth-century German and French thought should not be confused with the rhetoric of a work ethic sponsored by managerial classes profiting from industrial activity. Nor should it be reduced to Puritanism or a Protestant work ethic, though echoes of both can be found in it. The historical trajectory of Puritanism and Protestantism is more directly oriented towards the world of competitive business and individual success than it is to a largely conservative anti-utilitarian or organicist ethic addressed primarily in the direction of the working class. The work ethic of the rising capitalist class, generally speaking, was concocted only to motivate factory workers, mitigate guilt for the profits low wages generate (a rationalization of its own), or to defend, increase, and guarantee its own success while presenting a moral and cultural challenge to a befuddled aristocracy. Even if the Gospel of Work that sermonized work for its own sake or as a confirmation of (usually masculine) identity provided crucial support for employers, as it continues to do today, the utilitarian concept of work (not to mention the work itself) had nothing to do with intrinsic value. Accepting the tenets of classical economics, and especially the hedonist account of human nature underlying the theory of disutility, manufacturers propelled in part by the schema of utilitarian values accepted that work was undesirable and intrinsically unrewarding, that wages buy out disutility. Under normative economic theory, wages justify egregious working conditions as workers are *supposed* to despise work. Instead of encouraging the obstinacy of the craftsperson periodically idealized by the Gospel of Work, extrinsic rewards were offered to induce obedience to the industrial subdivision of labour, to scientific and hierarchical management, to work rationalization. For the white-collar bourgeoisie themselves, who compartmentalized their ideas concerning industrial work, work meant individual striving for success, deferring gratification, and strictly dividing and privileging public work over private life and earned over inherited income. Insofar as bourgeoisie promotes the value of work (for dubious reasons) and assumes that, by nature, 'man' only works in order to afford leisure (the theory of disutility), its contradictions are more blatant, twisted, and ideologically loaded than the incongruities I focus on in this study between moral Work and economic labour. There are, however, many points of contact between the bourgeois, managerial, or capitalist work ethics and the Gospel of Work according to Carlyle, Conrad, and Orwell. The bourgeois valuation of both a traditional Gospel of Work and rationalized labour further complicates and expands the multiple, competing concepts of work in this period.

The idea of a single, unified Gospel of Work shared by all Victorians is grossly inadequate. Just as work ethics need to be sorted into career ethics, Smilesian ethics, performance ethics, and so on, Gospels of Work have to be disentangled. The work gospel of the middle class, of the working class, or of the titled, if indeed they had one, must also be distinguished from the gospels said unto the classes. Certainly the middle-class idea of self-reliance, independence, and the entrepreneurial spirit was not intended for the ears of the working classes. I am primarily interested in the 'radical conservative' or traditionalist Gospel of Work epitomized and embodied by Carlyle, Conrad, and Orwell. The dominant discourse in this very Victorian Gospel ascribes and prescribes pre-capitalist Work to the working class. Here the working class, primarily, is seen to be absorbed in the fruitions of nonrational work, of effort in itself, of work for its own sake. Here also, work rationalization, the theory of disutility, and the principles of the economic are generally denied or condemned. Work is simply a moral imperative. But a second discourse materializes in between appeals to the intrinsic value of work. This point of view deals pragmatically with modern working conditions and is fully consistent with the logic of rationalist capitalism. It is addressed to the middle classes and in turn addresses the specific, concrete, historical, objective conditions of modern work. Here the same speakers might mediate on behalf of those who labour, insist on 'sound economics,' on fair wages and regulated working conditions, but they also accept the structure and practice of the economic on its own terms. 'Inside the Whale' of rationalism they struggle, but they also concede to the reality and size of the beast. The traditionalist (or nostalgic), conservative (or reactionary), organicist (or authoritarian) ideology shares the page with an equally liberalist orientation towards the inevitability of market practices. I examine these modulating approaches to work and the discursive shifts that take place between them depending upon the implied audience, or more exactly, the social class being held in representation.

The anti-visionary discourse reflects what Walter Houghton in 1957 called the English 'PRACTICAL BENT of mind': 'deep respect for facts, pragmatic skill in the adaptation of means to ends, a ready appeal to common sense – and therefore, negatively, an indifference to abstract speculation and imaginative perception' (110). The expression of that pragmatic bent – not quite a Gospel of Practicality or the liberal Gospel of Autonomy but indeed the logic of efficiency and *labour* – is kept far away from the Gospel of Work, even when the two discourses are in the same book or on the same page. The Gospel of Work is treated as a point of transcendence, a mythical moral economy to withdraw into and thus bypass the real properties of society. The contradictions between a language accommodating modern economic modes and relations and sermons spreading the Gospel of Work remain nondialectical: neither of the two discourses is qualified or challenged by its opposite. They exist side by side, or on paths set for a collision, but they do not encounter each other. One, responding to economics, complies with and participates in the economic-as-is; the other, responding to economism, to the exaggerated application of economic laws to every nook and cranny of society, idealizes Work. As antinomies they rest peacefully, but unless kept separated, the dialectic suppressed by isolating one from the other, they would either cancel each other out or undermine the cautious gradualism of the liberalist strategies and the distant utopianism of the conservative Gospel. The unified apotheosis of Work promulgated at one moment, and the radical restructuring of the economic that it implies, is thus cut off from the historical denial of that inviolability at another by the British 'practical bent of mind.' The potentially catastrophic collision between the idea of Work and the economic function of work is displaced by a series of structural dislocations and discursive dissonances. On the one side is the Gospel of Work, the ultimate expression of nonrationalism; on the other side is the logic of rationalism, of the real conditions and economic imperatives that are part and parcel of daily existence. Neither side of the opposition – when divided along the lines of the celebration of work's intrinsic values and the act of working the system for short-term extrinsic ends – is in itself wholly objectionable. Only the refusal to oppose the two sides to each other raises immediate questions. Bringing the two sides into contact would expose inescapable incompatibilities and demand a resolution that the writers discussed in this study are unwilling or unable to provide.

It is at this point that the special relationship between Carlyle, Conrad, and Orwell, the subjects of this study, might begin to make itself clear. All three are deep-seated traditionalists and part of a very British tradition of radical conservatism. In their respective eras they best represent a dichotomy between an almost revolutionary plea for a return to pre-capitalist values and 'unromantic,' 'practical' approaches to the business at hand, whether it is national, colonial, or individual. This latter discourse is adamantly anti-revolutionary. Infusing both fictive and nonfictive writings with politically charged social criticism approximately fifty to sixty years from each other, beginning with Carlyle around 1830, each reproduces for a generation seductively compartmentalized versions of 'common sense': a wholesale condemnation of the 'system' and a no-nonsense attitude towards its usefulness. These crosscurrents are certainly not endemic to Carlyle, Conrad, and Orwell, but these writers uniquely concentrate the dichotomy in a discussion of work (both a Gospel and the nitty-gritty of it). They also have a pronounced and consistent way of describing working-class culture that entirely contradicts their economic discourses. Others can be said to share this bifurcated habit of mind – indeed this project attempts to illustrate various stages in the nineteenth and twentieth century where Work and economics are polarized – but rarely with the degree of separation Carlyle, Conrad, and Orwell impose between Work and the economic. On the one hand we hear an unqualified veneration of Work and an accompanying suspicion of its organization, its economic function; and on the other hand we hear the down-to-earth accounting of the pragmatic realist.

All three 'seers' – Carlyle is still known as the Sage, E.M. Forster calls Conrad 'the mystic,' and even Orwell's contemporary critics such as Christopher Hitchens continue to perpetuate his reputation as prophet – were preoccupied with the past, with the way things were. They all had experienced direct contact with physical labour, though they wrote about it and idealized it after the fact. Moreover, the work they experienced was far removed from reminders of the market, or so they would later have it: lost worlds onto themselves where Cobbettian cottage economies, pre-industrial sailing ships, and constructive challenges to primitive, manly endurance seem to constitute the only reality. Indeed, stonemasonry, sailing, or *plongeur* work and tramping can be seen as pre-capitalist or marginalized from modern economic practices. The work Carlyle, Conrad, and Orwell represent and which they associate with the past, though also with the finest contemporary Worker, reflects something in their personal histories, even if they were never exactly or wholly integrated in the esteemed world of Work for which they stood.

Thomas Carlyle was born in a small market village – a population of 1,198 in 1795, the year he was born – in the Dumfriesshire community of Ecclefechan, Scotland, where agriculture and small trade (weaving, clog and hat making) made up most of the village economy. He was a workingman's son. James Carlyle was a stonemason who built his own home and turned to farming, the life of his parents, in times of need. Two of his four sons would never attend university, remaining rather on the farm. Thomas Carlyle was to create for himself a very different life than his father's. He went to Edinburgh University, studied continental philosophy, and then moved to England to eventually become a professional writer, though he never relinquished the lessons of austerity and hard work he himself associates with his father in *Reminiscences* (1881). This process of displacement nonetheless must have problematized his sense of identity; it was to be complicated in other ways as well. The Carlyles were of 'peasant stock' but had servants. Although 'they were to know real hardship,' as Ian Campbell documents, they were also to know 'moderate prosperity' (2). In a sense Carlyle grew up across or between class lines, just as he came to be positioned ambiguously between rural and urban worlds and, perhaps most important, between Scottish and English nationalities. I do not want to reduce Carlyle's prose to a kind of class-determinism or in fact devote too much attention to biography. I only want to suggest that his ambiguous social position contributed to an ambiguous but overdetermined pronouncement of traditional Englishness and traditional English values. Carlyle would feel and respond to dual pressures of pastoral traditionalism and matter-of-fact pragmatism. But as an 'English' writer of an indefinite social world he would establish himself by associating England with extremely rigid principles and permanent values.

Joseph Conrad's socially mixed background is more complex than Carlyle's, with family roots in the *Szlachta*, the Polish gentry of the day, and, on his mother's side of the family, in the moneyed class. Conrad's father, Apollo Korzeniowski, was, after the Russians had sequestered his estate in 1859, an aristocrat without lands. In 1857 Konrad Korzeniowski was born into a former region of Poland then under Russian rule. Because of his father's anti-Russian political activities the family was exiled to northern Russia in 1861. After his parents died of tuberculosis, Konrad went under the tutelage of his anti-insurrectionist and tradition-conscious uncle, Thaddeus Bobrowski. Bobrowski would be Conrad's caretaker for the next twenty-five years. At the age of seventeen, Conrad escaped the political confusion and disorder that had surrounded him from birth to become a sailor. At sea he would experience a traditional order of work and rank, swiftly climbing the chain of command of the French Merchant Marine and then the British Merchant Navy to eventually captain his own ship.

As with Carlyle, then, Conrad's early years before becoming a professional writer included a diverse set of social influences and a tremulous social designation but were anchored by the idea of intrinsically valuable, traditional work. Bobrowski eventually allowed Conrad to go to sea in order to overcome his sickly demeanour and so that he would learn discipline, demonstrating his belief that through work (not its extrinsic reward) one triumphs over individual or social obstacles. It was a lesson Conrad would dramatize in many of his major novels. However, commenting on Conrad's introduction to sailing, Zdzisław Najder confirms that 'Konrad was not sent to toil as a common sailor ... the sober-minded Bobrowski saw him as a sailor-cum-businessman who would combine his maritime skills with commercial activities' (37). Like Carlyle, Conrad was only tangentially related to the world of Work, just as he was ambiguously tied to any specific social class, and, again most important, was always considered by himself and others somewhat of an outsider to England.

Again, I am not writing biography or suggesting that early personal history determines future character. I only want to point out a pattern of influences that initiated Carlyle and Conrad into the non-economic values of work, though neither of them exactly lived by physical work or were wealthy enough to ignore real economic need. Both Carlyle and Conrad would later describe the ideal worker as able to exist on the non-economic features of work alone. They would both develop an interpretation of Englishness that contrasted with the indefiniteness of their social positions and yet at once reflected their pre-English roots *and* their understanding of what the English valued most about England, including a traditionalism established through definitive hierarchy and class functions. Conrad would in fact construct Englishness from a perception of the institution, sailing, that allowed him to become a British citizen. (He also, one might add, understood Englishness from reading Carlyle, having taken up *Sartor Resartus* [1833] to learn the language.)

At first, grouping George Orwell – socialist, champion of 'rebels,' and according to George Woodcock, an angry liberal in the tradition of Dickens – with Carlyle and Conrad may seem peculiar; however, I hope to trace a particularly thick thread of continuity between the trio by analysing their attitudes towards work. Orwell's biography is as involved as Conrad's. He famously described his family as 'lower-upper-middle class.' In 1903, when Eric Arthur Blair was born in Motihari India, Orwell's father was a relatively well-to-do civil servant. But as Orwell himself was to point out, 'People in this class owned no land, but they felt that they were landowners in the sight of God and kept up a semi-aristocratic outlook by going into the professions and the fighting services rather than into trade' (*Road* 108). Orwell's sense of transgressing classes leads Terry Eagleton to see him as a self-fashioned émigré. He in fact never ceased thinking in terms of a classed society and himself – though he was a lot more inconsistent here – as its observer, not quite fitting in.

When Orwell came to England as a one-year-old with his mother, the Blairs were comfortably middle-class, despite Orwell's later claims that they did not have the money to match their bourgeois aspirations. Bernard Crick suggests that the Blairs may indeed have had 'lingering aristocratic pretensions' (*Life* 53), and perhaps it was those pretensions that saw Orwell to Eton. Orwell's great grandfather Charles Blair had married into the aristocracy, having made his own wealth from owning plantations and slaves in Jamaica. But Orwell was not to follow Eton with Oxford or Cambridge, choosing instead to return to India to become a member of the Indian Imperial Police. This was to give him insights into the lives of the poor, and returning to England he adopted a life in close proximity to the destitute and to working-class culture. Orwell, like Carlyle and Conrad before him, lived on the periphery of working-class life, never quite part of its daily physicality: all three were onlookers with varying degrees and kinds of personal contact. Orwell famously submerged himself into working-class life, usually surfacing back to his bourgeois roots to write. Carlyle and Conrad knew of physical work from further distances. They all, however, experienced work as something to visit, to participate in at will or by choice. Though for all of them the struggle to make money dominated a large part of their professional lives – Carlyle and Orwell finding themselves as unhappy schoolteachers before becoming writers, and Conrad often finding himself in debt – venturing into the world of physical work and of working-class culture was primarily experienced as a retreat from the modern world of economic ubiquity. Work was an escape from the confusion and instability of modernity, as it often is in their writings. Work was also a way to overcome feelings of exclusion and alienation, again as it often is in their writings.

The tendency to project Romantic sensibilities onto the real social world and to doggedly face down capitalism and poverty by appealing to the supposed warmth, camaraderie, physicality, and pre-industrial values of working-class culture is not born solely from personal circumstance. But the conditions were evidently at play for a radical conservative idealism to take firm root. Though without doubt wide variations of temperament, style, and political outlook are to be found among Carlyle, Conrad, and Orwell, each would make a religion of work – of the traditional work of a working-class culture they lived with or chose to encounter – while challenging a world turned mechanically rationalistic. All three of them would cast themselves in the role of the noble caretaker looking out for the well-being of the worker (and be appalled or at least shocked at the idea of a politically active worker). This noblesse oblige that wards off disorder, from their own expatriated view, was the quintessence of Englishness.

As said, Orwell saw himself as an outsider, not only from the English literary tradition, but also from each class of English society itself. For Orwell, to be a true English subject was to be an outcast, economically or politically. Modest origins seem to have led Carlyle to consider himself an outsider and to play the role of the loner while attending Edinburgh University, a feeling that would only increase when in England. A.L. Le Quesne argues that Carlyle's 'national and social origin ... contributed to making him a maverick and an outsider in the English literary world' (2). The same has been said of Conrad, who was not only Polish but a bona fide merchant sailor, not the typical nurturing ground for the English novelist in the 'Great Tradition.' That outsiders to Englishness, or self-declared independents, would become the dominant voices in their generations to demand a return to traditional English values and to embrace the nostalgia of a paternal Merrie England ought not to be surprising. Theories of imitation in which the excluded or those with a sense of exclusion and marginality are led to exaggerated amplifications of the hegemonic ideology, or what is perceived to be the cherished historical identifiers of the dominant group, have circulated broadly among disciplines since Freud. With the self-labelled status of the 'outsider,' anxieties of identity might propel one to an overstated appreciation for what one 'naturally' lacks in order to come to terms with those feelings of alienation and instability. Today post-colonial theory suggests that 'the mimetic or narcissistic demands of colonial power' reap from the colonized peoples an imitative Other (Bhabha 34). Though post-colonialists take the idea of imitation beyond the idea that colonized peoples adopt and adapt to the ruling class in order to suggest that in the act of mimetic reproduction lies contestation and opposition, as imitation becomes mimicry and thus parodies authority, this cannot be said of Carlyle, Conrad, and Orwell. They more likely felt the pressure to replicate and champion their ostracizing 'hosts' from within, disparaging only what the English had become, not who they 'were.' Carlyle and Orwell in particular wrote about Englishness and the English character as anti-modern, as maintaining traditional work values despite modernity. Marshalling a national tradition around a history from which one feels disconnected, in this case a projected English tradition of the place of work in a beloved past, perhaps relates to a desire to assimilate. Taking up the mantle of the Jeremiah condemning modern economic relations manifests a feeling of alienation, but doing so by playing the present off the past asserts intimacy with the never-changing 'people.' A sense of being intrinsically uprooted, excluded, or marginalized from 'the people' – from rural life, sea life, or the life of the poor – might also have led Carlyle, Conrad, and Orwell to commit themselves to the rituals of anti-intellectualism and disinterested work. Or perhaps the special status of the writer who characterizes a tradition but feels removed – distanced, out of touch, as an observer and not a participant – from that tradition leads to inflated and embellished representations of the past and how it *worked*, recapturing the essence of participation. In any case, notwithstanding their learned philosophies and social critiques, one reason why Carlyle, Conrad, and Orwell appeal to Work may be in order to stabilize a sense of identity made indefinite by feelings of displacement.

At the same time, however, Carlyle, Conrad, and Orwell characterize Englishness as commonsensical, in the sense of being fundamentally pragmatic. They all took for granted an anti-romantic sensibility that denies and defies the traditional values they themselves associate with Work. Carlyle, Conrad, and Orwell had their own economic exigencies to manage, as do 'the English people.' It is the rupture and defensive compartmentalization in this characterization of standard Englishness as articulated through modes of work that this book examines. I have no aspirations to offer an exhaustive or totalizing account of Work Gospels, Englishness, working-class culture, or Carlyle, Conrad, and Orwell. Rather I offer a perspective, Work and the economic, within which these and other interests can be both interrelated and examined separately. To do so, I frequently consider other writers who are relevant to and who further my discussion of Carlyle, Conrad, and Orwell. I am of course more interested in the continuities among Carlyle, Conrad, and Orwell, expressed most clearly in their treatment of work, than the discontinuities. The major force in the development of English social criticism that they can be taken to represent does not seem to include a mechanism to correct itself despite constant historical change and their awareness of it.

It is one thing to conceive of work rationalization and economism as exploitative and perverted, an unforgivable and non-negotiable ideology of optimization. But it is another to treat economics and the realm of necessity as opposing terms to Work. The complete division between economics, the historical society, and Work, an ethical estrangement from society, is fundamentally dissimilar to and much more problematic than the ancient or classical division of contemplation and necessity. As with contemplation, Work can only take place in the realm of freedom, as if outside of an economic context – but work is the very foundation of the economic context. Withdrawing into plain and simple work, made possible by the undialectical split between Work and the economic, leads to the paradox of advocating and representing the intrinsic values of Work in the conditions of industrial and instrumental rationalism and the context of necessity, to overlooking class when class – working-class and bourgeois experience and perception – is most relevant. The ideology of Work is ultimately amenable with the strictures of rationalism. Carlyle, Conrad, and Orwell will struggle with the Ideal and the real; it is in fact a common theme in many of their writings. However, moral Work and pragmatism, the Ideal and the real, are not brought together in a way that would allow a dialectical and polemical confluence.

The dualism between Work and labour has many forms. The list below is incomplete; it provides examples of how I express the disjunction or describes some of the shapes that the disjunction actually takes. This set of opposites is not meant to either confirm or challenge binary structures, but rather to offer ways of considering a split in the perception of work: the discontinuous thought, discourse, and representations of a particular group of English writers as they react to work rationalization.

Nonrationalism and Work	**Rationalism and Labour**
Work	Economics
Homo Faber	*Homo Economicus* or *Homo Laborans*
Realm of Freedom	Realm of Maximizing or Realm of Necessity
Idealism	Materialism
Moralism	Pragmatism
Form	Reform
Finality	Conditionality
Totality	Variability
Withdrawal	Concession
Abstractness	Concreteness
Generality	Specificity
Intransitiveness	Transitiveness
Art	Sociology
'Culture'	'Society'
A Priori	A Posteriori
Wisdom	Logic
Subjectivity	Objectivity

The subjects of my study are not locked into polarized habits of mind, but they do oscillate between withdrawing into Work and its world and cautiously prosing on economic reality as the only conceivable reality. The glitches and silences in their texts, the fissures resulting from the division between Work and economics, reinforce a disengaged moralism: the idea that the individual can and must overcome the prevailing social formation. I call this 'moral individualism.' If a worker gleans the values of Work from labour periodically represented as unremitting, ubiquitous rationalism – in need of an economic discourse – then it is as if the worker's volition has enabled a withdrawal from objective reality to the quarantined hallowedness of Work by exploiting the division between Work and the economic. This worker works as if independent of economic rationalism. In other words, the space between Work and labour evidences the ordering and writing of subjectivity as if disconnected from the production process, even though that process is often written as an all-determining rationalism, the 'real' to be at best whittled away through prudent gradualism. Work becomes simply an act of the will, performed for its own sake, and the issues of economic need and desire, not to mention structure, are compartmentalized as if Work and economics were entirely unrelated. The split and the lack of any middle ground between the split ensures that the problems raised by the impasse between a Gospel of Work and a sociology of labour do not surface. Meanwhile, the agency of the subject slips into a methodological moralism, which in its own way endorses orthodox capitalist logic. Carlyle, Conrad, and Orwell are, essentially, emotionally conservative. This brand of conservatism, however, they dissociate from the aristocracy, or align with 'the English people.' But as Carlyle, Conrad, and Orwell embrace the idea of moralism (moral individualism), they move towards validating the central tenet of liberal theory: the inherently free individual's ability and duty to construct his or her own reality. English liberalism often expresses this as a right to construct reality. All three vehemently maintain that liberal laissez-faire has corrupted society. But by simultaneously maintaining that individual morality supersedes or ought to supersede society, Carlyle, Conrad, and Orwell pull back from attacking liberalism and lend themselves out to the economic status quo.

This belief in the sanctity of the inner, inviolable self underlies most underdog narratives in which ostracized and alienated subjects find happiness by joining and excelling in the very societies that were so corrupt as to reject them in the first place. In many ways it also corresponds to Protestantism and the ideology of self-sufficiency. But to be clear, it does not explicitly ratify the rationalist doctrine of self-interest. According to classical and neoclassical economic theory, the maximizing economic agent, sanctioned by the title of a rational agent, is driven by self-love. The inherently moral individual is driven to withdrawal, to be the loner, ultimately joining society only at the final moment or in the final analysis. The way in which the stable, uncomplicated bourgeois ego in the mythology of the self-made man is said to create an unselfish society because he has recourse to an inviolate *caritas* is suspiciously similar to the isolated, integral, autonomous self seemingly stepping at will from the rationalist world in which he or she participates into the world of Work. Both narratives might be read as versions of a *Tom Jones* (1749) noble-by-birth story, claiming the moral high ground of an innate goodness. But in our version of the working-class underdog, workers are governed by a deeper meaning of self-sufficiency than the rationalist maximizing that lies behind middle-class individualism. Work in itself, for reasons that are non-economic and even countereconomic, is considered sufficient. The workers themselves are thus content with their work ladders. They do not find or desire a social equivalent, and their participation in the economy is rendered invisible.

The mythology of the underdog in this case, inextricably bound to male-centred ideologies of toughness, of persevering through harsh conditions, corresponds to the treatment of Work (albeit in fact regular, everyday work) as if separate from its context and its effects. Work is removed from the world of rationalized labour and modern economics, the exploitation of labour and capitalist gain. Workers are told to perform sacred Work in the conditions of labour, when their labour power, represented as the intrinsic value of Gospelized Work, generates extrinsic profits for hidden capitalists. The paradox of withdrawal, treating work as the means to evade, surpass, or transcend rationalism, can come close to sanctioning back-door exploitation. The intermittent denial of the economic function of work also denies or dismisses necessity. Economic need becomes swept up with counter-Work, greed, or economic bamboozling. The utopian outlook would obviate the same pragmatic economics that dominate during the intermittent denials of Work. That pragmatism, the discourse of labour, also has its attendant narratological configuration, a pragmatic realism. The pragmatic realist negotiates his or her day-to-day existence without reference to the non-economic rewards underlined by a Gospel of Work. Steady employment, wages, and a decent standard of living are all that his or her labour represents. Referring to Carlyle and the critique of capitalism in *Past and Present*

(1843), Georg Lukács identifies the schizophrenia of the Carlylean subject – realist and moralist – I try to understand. He argues:

> In such accounts it is shown, on the one hand, that it is not possible to be human in bourgeois society, and, on the other hand, that man as he exists is opposed without mediation – or what amounts to the same thing, through the mediations of metaphysics and myth – to this non-existence of the human (whether this is thought of as something in the past, the future or merely an imperative). (*History* 190)

Pragmatism does not always go so far as to insist on the impossibility of humanity under rationalism, but it does concede to, work within, the conditions of labour. Its moral opposite does not always 'oppose this non-existence of the human.' More often than not, it simply ignores, bypasses, surpasses, or is otherwise cut off from the politics of everyday economic life.

That the idealization of work reaches its zenith at the very moment when industrialization loomed largest, when the machinic systems of work rationalization threatened to become the values of the economic and social world, is both understandable and remarkable. Such a threat would provoke a reactionary outcry, the retreat into a traditional world; but validating a rhetoric of the intrinsic value of activity and duty when the only available work for the working class, for those who were actually doing work, was void of any potentially intrinsic value demands scrutiny. The tendency to buffer moral Work from the exigencies of labour is not peculiar to England: Emerson, the transcendentalists, and Tolstoy do the same. What is startling about the English situation is that it took place at the height of industrialism, in the most soot-covered streets. To withdraw into hard effort, into mind-numbing and exhaustive toil, can be read as a noble gesture to overturn modern capitalist relations, to turn back time. But such an entreaty also greases the machines of rationalization in a way that withdrawing into something noncorporeal or entirely bohemian does not. When valorizing work, the experiential features of labour are concealed in the same way that liberal ideologies conceal the labour of the working classes in order to insist on the naturalness and ethicalness of middle-class ascendancy. In both bourgeois and moral representations of work, volunteerism, hobbies, and appeals to intransitive work – '"*Work.*" Not work at this or that – but, Work' – occur at an astonishing rate. I am not interested in flogging the Work high horse, but in understanding the implications, effects, and significance of dividing moral Work from economic labour, generalizations from specifics, or vision from action. I am interested in the different and often contradictory arguments raised about Work and labour according to or depending on the class being addressed or considered. If, as Lukács said, 'the essence of praxis consists in annulling *that indifference of form towards content*' (*History* 126), then what is the essence of the indifference?

Discussing ideologies of work, I also find myself inevitably drawn into a debate over working-class culture and working-class agency. On one side of the debate, led by E.P. Thompson, is the recognition that the British working class played a role in determining its own history; that the object of the social sciences and the humanities is not simply to categorize the systems and structures of social life that construct the subject. Systems and structures and their shaping power are not denied, but the extant individual is seen to negotiate them. On the other side are Althusserian 'structuralist Marxists' such as Perry Anderson. They accuse the 'culturalists' of abandoning materialism and indeed Marx; they treat working-class subjectivity as a constructed abstraction or byproduct of history. The historical process is unaffected by the individual subject. Though fewer and fewer in this debate are willing to dichotomize materialism and agency, conditioning and freedom, accusations of essentialism or functionalism are central to the businesses of cultural theory.

The British tradition of cultural studies is no doubt related to the antirationalism it interprets and the hyper-utilitarianism it dissects. But instead of elevating culture above society or reducing 'materialism' to 'determinism,' to indoctrination, and treating structure as a unitary, inescapable machine turning out predictable constructs, the study of culture and materialism has to include an account of the economic decisions people *have* to make in order to survive. Treating materialism as an insurmountable, totalizing matrix or agency only as the refusal of the matrix has in common with the dichotomization of Work and economics the tendency to ignore basic needs.

This is where the most important contributor to recently inform the debate between materialism and culture, Pierre Bourdieu, comes in. In *The Logic of Practice* (1980), Bourdieu searches among workers or working classes for signs of 'the logic of costs and benefits, including the costs of transgressing the official norm and the gains in respectability accruing from respect for the rule' (17). This practical logic is not a finalist or mechanistic economism because it does not correspond to narrowly understood economic interests, a profit motive for example, but to a general optimizing strategy of which economic strategies are but one among many. But Bourdieu also accepts that the act of sociological interpretation imposes an organizing principle on human actions that 'may have, strictly speaking, neither meaning or function, other than the function implied in their very existence, and the meaning objectively inscribed in the logic of actions or words that are done or said in order to "do or say some thing"' (18). Bourdieu does not reduce materialism to ideological prescriptions, a materialism cut off from the material word. His concept of the *habitus* implies a new materialism, 'a practical relation to the world' – 'the preoccupied active presence in the world through which the world imposes its presence, with is urgencies, its things to be done and said, things made to be said, which directly govern words and deeds' (52). The *habitus* initiates an internalized logic that generates and organizes practices or dispositions in a nonmechanical manner, creating nonmechanical behaviour. Bourdieu locates a midway point between the spontaneous subject and the automaton, one where responding to the demands of necessity is a primary determinant. Determinism and freedom or the individual and society are effectively de-dichotomized.

Despite Bourdieu's guarantee that he is not whittling away at the concept of 'freedom,' that he is in fact disputing rational theory, he often appears to give little more than lip service to the possibility of the non-economic. The Bourdieusian *habitus* turns out to be little more than a Veblenian world of ubiquitous conspicuousness. Bourdieu holds that 'Even when [sub-proletarians] give every appearance of disinterestedness because they escape the logic of "economic" interest (in the narrow sense) and are oriented towards non-material stakes that are not easily quantified, as in "pre-capitalist" societies or in the cultural sphere of capitalist societies, practices never cease to comply with an economic logic' (122). All items of ritual or culture, all seemingly spontaneous behaviours, have a material base, are an investment of one sort or the other. The non-economic ideas associated with Work – honour, loyalty, prestige, identity, activity, strength – undoubtedly have an economic side, but it is not the economic calculations of the workers that are most prominent when Work comes into play or its ideology is appealed to. Bourdieu's theory directs attention away from the adherents of Work who have the most interest in disseminating the ideology of disinterestedness, of the non-economic. He is right to abandon economic/non-economic antimonies and to acknowledge that 'Only a virtuoso with a perfect mastery of his "art of living" can play on all the resources inherent in the ambiguities and indeterminacies of behaviours and situations' (107). And he is most right to resist the idea that 'Practical logic has nothing in common with logical calculation as an end in itself. It functions in urgency, in response to life-or-death questions' (262). He also shows that without economic advantages, without knowledge about the economic that can only be amassed by having power over the economy, it becomes proportionately difficult to maximize one's economic advantages, or even be a 'rational' economic agent. But his working classes are seen as problematizing the rituals of their own invention, squeezing the economic from practices they created to counter 'economic man.' Not only do all practices experienced as disinterested conform to rationalist maximizing, ultimately in step with a vaguely defined super-economic optimizing strategy, but the pre-capitalist activity of the working classes is understood solely as the practical logic of the working classes – not the practical logic of the ideologies themselves. Finally, it is not obvious that the doxic mode of working-class logic precludes a revolutionary consciousness; attempting to further one's interests, even if it means conforming to practices (or the language) of the economic ruling class, *can be* political or subversive in its own right.

Bourdieu's work nonetheless informs this study, though the main theories and definitions of work I draw on reach back to Hannah Arendt, Raymond Williams, and Max Weber. In *The Human Condition* (1958), Arendt defines 'labour' as activity directed to satisfy biological needs and 'work' as producing objects that outlast the productive activity and that lend continuity to existence. They form the basis of my use of the terms, though I use 'Work' and Arendt uses 'labour' to denote self-objectification (Marx's concept of alienation is based on the idea that the worker feels lost when the self-imprinted object is taken away from him or her, the creator) and the way that the cycle of toil and rest can be a trans-economic, intrinsically rewarding sensation. Still, her social critique and the anti-rationalism I focus on both lament the disappearance of 'work' products, products transcending consumption. Arendt writes, 'The industrial revolution has replaced all workmanship with labour, and the result has been that the things of the modern world have become labour products whose natural fate is to be consumed, instead of work products which are there to be used' (124). More explicitly than her, I use 'labour' (outside of its meaning as the antithesis of satisfying work) to mean conventional economic activity (she uses 'labour' to mean answering necessity and ensuring survival, but not necessarily in an economic context) and use 'Work' with a capital 'W' to refer to activity understood to be intrinsically satisfying and treated as if outside of an economic context. I use a lower-case 'work' to indicate work disendowed of any special meaning.

My definitions of Work and labour also correspond with Williams's analysis, in his eponymous book, of how 'culture and society' have been misdefined. In this way I am undeniably in the currents of the 'Culture and Society Tradition.' 'Work' I associate with his understanding of the misused word 'culture,' suggesting that it is a most significant example of such an attitude towards 'culture':

> an abstraction and an absolute: an emergence which, in a very complex way, merges two general responses – first, the recognition of the practical separation of certain moral and intellectual activities from the driven impetus of a new kind of [industrial] society; second, the emphasis of these activities, as a court of human appeal, to be set over the processes of practical social judgment and yet to offer itself as a mitigating and rallying alternative ... Further ... in the formation of the meanings of *culture*, an evident reference back to an area of personal and apparently private experience, which was notably to affect the meaning and practice of art. (xvi)

I treat 'Work' as almost synonymous with Williams's critique of 'culture,' that is, a point of transcendence from the nitty-gritty reality of economic life. The fascinating aspect of work, however, albeit represented as Work, and unlike 'culture' per se, is that it is the root and substructure of economic reality. I also argue that, while holding 'Work' in abeyance, the writers I discuss – and they are often the same writers he discusses, apart from Conrad – also tackle 'society,' economic reality, and the realm of necessity. Those pragmatic economics are a complex – corporatist and liberalist at points, reformist and activist at others – mixture of right- and left-wingery, but nonetheless saturated in 'society.' In terms of the tradition Williams identifies, they are kept compartmentalized from the discourse of culture (or Work); the gradualist or conformist approach to economics could never lead to Work. Like Williams, I believe that a general theory of work (his is a general theory of culture) should include grasping the relations between Work and labour (or culture and society) as *a whole way of life*.

From Weber I am borrowing a concept of rationalism. Weber uses the term broadly, but his distinction between formal and substantial rationality is central to my discussion of anti-rationalism. In Weber's sense, an action is deemed formally rational if it is an efficacious means to a premeditated end and is governed solely by that end. I follow his use of the term 'substantive rationality' to identify rationality from the point of view of an ethical end, which entails ethical means. From the point of view of formal rationality, equality, fraternity, community, and job satisfaction are non- or even irrational values. Modern, formal rationalism emphasizes a doctrine of instrumentality, systemization, and quantitative pursuit. It abolishes religious and customary restraints but stresses impersonal legal controls over any deviancy that might interfere with the predictability of society. Society is to passively await the benefits supposed to accompany the maximizing of personal wealth. It means economic preoccupation, ascetic self-control, and technological control over nature. Rationalism goes hand in hand with the model of free-market exchange: the deliberate pursuit of individual gain without interruption from the field of ethics, the restraint of emotions, the confusion of caprice, the ambitionless continuity of tradition, or the 'irrationality' of ideology.

In my study, rationalism is also an approach to work in which work is only the means to production and extrinsic maximizing or compensation. Workers are often the means themselves, a paradigm that keeps formal rationality irreconcilably at odds with substantive rationality. Economic rationalism may have begun in the eighteenth or even the seventeenth century, but it was not until the growth of the study of political economy in the nineteenth century that it became systematically accepted. Although Weber introduces the work ethic as part of the trend towards rationalism and the rationalization of work, the work ethic in the anti-utilitarian tradition is formally nonrational. It has nothing to do with extrinsically oriented strategies of exchange. It is substantively rational in that it is first and foremost to engender a moral end, personal stability, or community commitment: it expresses a traditionalistic resistance to the rationalization of work. Weber thinks only of the capitalist, the 'self-made man,' when he links rationalism to *the* work ethic. Such a unitary work ethic, however, is not likely even within the capitalist class or its understood Protestant/Puritan innovators. I have little more to say about Weber's (or Tawney's) thesis on the relationship between Protestantism and the origins of capitalism, because the idea of a unitary work ethic seems too monolithic and the idea of its determining power seems too isolated to support a theory on the origins of capitalism. Though I will argue that Protestantism and Puritanism play a part in the origins and schizoid development of Carlyle's and Orwell's thought, the Gospel of Work (and capitalism) would have risen and did rise independently of a Protestant ethic.

As a sociologist, Weber simply reports on modern rationalization. But one is not remaining entirely neutral if one sees capitalist rationalism as an 'abomination to every system of fraternal ethics' (*Economy* 1: 637). Weber's concern was over the disjunction between formal and substantive rationality – that is, a modern indifference to substantive ends. Still, Weber only challenges unchecked rational*ism*. He recognizes the benefits of modernizing and the futility of acting as if the overturning of modernity would ipso facto increase human happiness, justice, and comfort. Carlyle, Conrad, and especially Orwell make the same recognition, but the compliance with and rejection of modern rationalism are not organized by an attempt to explain it as with Weber's thesis.

Weber's analysis of rationalism best lends itself to my argument in its intersection with Karl Marx. Marxists generally hold that the rationality of individual economic agents attempting to maximize profits conflicts with what is rational for the capitalist system as a whole (Glyn 107). Private ownership inevitably leads to the malfunctioning of capitalism itself. Weber emphasizes that what is formally rational for economic agents is not rational for those same agents in terms of their lives as a whole. The 'early Marx,' who looms throughout my pages, approaches rationalism from both a structural and a moral perspective. If I at points seem antagonistic towards Marx it is only because any discussion involving Work and labour has to respond to him and move outwards from him. His criticism of Hegel's 'universal notion of work' (and of nonmaterialism in general) could model for my criticism of the withdrawal into the Gospel of Work. His concept of alienation (essentialist, for one has to be alienated *from* something and for Marx it is the species essence, *homo faber*), the estrangement of people in competition with one another or of people separated from the products they invest themselves into, could model for my criticism of pragmatism. That alienation is endemic to the relations of private property, to the division of labour, to the stupefaction of the industrial worker, and to capitalist instrumentalism, goes far to dialectically oppose Work and labour, to confront Work with labour. His inversion of the intellectual hierarchy between thought and action, the model of materialist dialectics, is implicit in my critique of the glaring absence of praxis and dialectics from Carlyle to Orwell. His assertion that it is not (individual) reason but (communal) work that distinguishes human and animal (and subsequently that there is a need to separate work from private rewards and turn it into an end in itself) is behind my sympathy for the anti-rationalist tradition. His critique of political economy – that it shapes, accelerates, and legitimizes industry and not only theorizes upon it – is central to my argument about the relation of theory to economic behaviour, as is some of his work on the ideological content of morality, a product and reflection of social structure. My critique of the ideology of 'only connect' – the passion and the prose, the Ideal and the real – in so much of English literature ultimately comes from Marx's insistence on seeing society in a dialectic totality.

Arendt criticizes Marx on the basis 'that in all stages of his work he defines man as an *animal laborans* and then leads him into a society in which this greatest and most human power is no longer necessary. We are left with the rather distressing alternative between productive slavery and unproductive freedom' (105). Such criticism is unfounded because Marx does not define man as *animal laborans* but as *homo faber* reduced to *animal laborans*. Marx was looking forward to a time when economic necessity would no longer be the reason we work, not to a time when people no longer work. In *The German Ideology* (1846), he imagines when everyone would be free 'to do one thing today and another tomorrow, to hunt in the morning, fish in the afternoon, rear cattle in the evening, criticize after dinner ... without ever becoming hunter, fisherman, shepherd or critic' (160). Behind Marx's future society, in fact, is not idleness, but the productivist illusion common to the age he inhabited, the assumption that society under the realm of freedom would see more material production than all previous societies, that social and material progress were twinborn. Still, he always emphasizes the all-important question about how a society achieves material progress. Concluding his prognostication of a plentiful future, he contrasts it to the rationalist bent for specialization and especially the definition of self through employment: 'This fixation of social activity, this consolidation of what we ourselves produce into an objective power above us, growing out of our control, thwarting our expectations, bringing to naught our calculations, is one of the chief factors in historical development up till now' (160). The young, visionary Marx does not let go of economics when articulating the promises of Work, always seeing Work and labour as clashing, contradicting forces.

My grievance with Marx in this study has to do with his abandoning a model of Work as he moved towards *Capital* (1867). Though alienation from intrinsically oriented Work is always implicit in his later writings, he increasingly treated work in a narrowly economic sense as solely a matter of labour power and so forth. He implicitly contradicts himself by suggesting all morality is sheer ideology and bourgeois mystification. 'Morality,' for the young Marx, includes nonalienating Work. By taking for granted that the economic was a first-order activity given to fixed laws, his ideas mirror the political economy of his day. I am not suggesting that Marx-as-scientist was unimportant. Ron Bellamy makes the point that David Ricardo shows a lack of a scientific curiosity by accepting the idea that capitalists get the profits of labour power as a matter of course. But since 'science requires an answer to the question: Why and how do they get it' and Marx asked that question through his queries into labour power and surplus value, Marx was the better scientist (44). My complaint is that Marx the scientist divorces himself from Marx the moralist, creating a separation remarkably similar to the one central to this study, except that Marx retreats into abstract economics, not abstract Work. Thompson suggests that Marx's economism, and the treatment of 'Marxism as Science,' places Marx and Marxism beside Utilitarians, Malthusians, Positivists, Fabians, and structuralist-functionalists (*Poverty* 360). All fetishize science, but in the case of Marx and Marxism, this undermines the anti-rationalism in work and economics that the Marxist state would be based upon.

Lukács might provide the needed link between anti-rationalism and economics, between the spiritual ideal and the real, between Marxism as a religion and as a science – a conflation that enables praxis. Eagleton links Lukács's anti-scientism to Williams, to the emotionally driven cry for a synthesis of culture and society, though not appreciating that they share a 'theoretical idealism' and 'aesthetic predilections' (*Criticism* 36). Lukács emphasizes the different ways classes relate to objects and reality. The worker sees the object as knowable, as a process, as something built (in turn leading to a consciousness of the world, to history as something built). The bourgeoisie sees the object as a mystery, as static, as if capitalism itself were eternal (a 'rationalism,' Fredric Jameson adds, that 'can assimilate everything but the ultimate questions of purpose and origins' [*Form* 185–6]). Lukács ties life experience to perception in such a way as to suggest that vital art and meaningful notions of culture, even notions of Work, express a social process at every level. Behind my critique of the separation of Work and society lies his theory of art and society, just as his analysis of reification informs my own anti-rationalism.

I am limiting my study to a critique of the rationalism emerging out of nineteenth-century industrialism and economism, but rationalism is to be found well before that. Though John Ruskin castigated Renaissance rationalism, today the Enlightenment receives the brunt of the attack. Implicit in my study, then, though by no means central to it, is a critique of the Enlightenment. I follow, in this critique, Max Horkheimer and Theodor Adorno: 'The prognosis of the related conversion of enlightenment into positivism, the myth of things as they actually are ... and that which is inimical to the spirit, has been overwhelmingly confirmed' (x). That the Enlightenment brought on an administered world can be seen in a hodgepodge of changes leading into the nineteenth century. The development of a linear, highly regulated, and rule-governed menu or the specialized rooms that replaced large medieval halls, for example, can and have been attributed to the Enlightenment fetish for structure. Roland Barthes and Michel Foucault have argued that rational management led to the ordering of everything from religion to the body and sexuality. Victorian liberals such as Leslie Stephen, in *The History of English Thought in the Eighteenth Century* (1876), and John Morley, in *Critical Miscellanies* (1886), approvingly trace Enlightenment scepticism to laissez-faire doctrine, ratifying the rationalism (whether it be in work, human reason, or the free market) at the core of the ideas.

At the same time, Gerald Graff correctly argues:

> The 'reason' of most classical, Renaissance, and Enlightenment thinkers is moral and evaluative *and* objective. It bears little resemblance to the value-free, instrumental, purely calculative reason of positivistic science and industrial engineering. This change in the concept of reason reflects a transformation of the structures of social authority in which reason (and other concepts denoting authority) seem, in the eyes of many, to have been objectified. (28)

The bandwagon demonizing the Enlightenment has left. 'Man' was thought to have an unalterable nature well before it. Anthropocentrism, as an alternative to a God-centred universe, is in itself quite defensible, as long as it is the valuation of reason and not rational*ism* (or solipsism). Centres are also in themselves far from inherently evil. Marx implies that work is the centre of 'man,' a social species. And many have connoted that work, or making things and seeing in oneself the power to make things, is a healthy centre for human beings, insofar as it was the first step towards breaking a slavery to mysticism and gods (as the makers of all things).

I am also indebted to two recent anthologies on work and its cultural significance: *The Voice of Toil: Nineteenth-Century British Writings about Work* (2000), edited by David J. Bradshaw and Suzanne Ozment, and *The Oxford Book of Work* (1999), edited by Keith Thomas. Both these collections bring out an enormous diversity of attitudes surrounding work. The editors divide the texts into strikingly different and contradictory sections. The same writers who show up in one section will often strangely reappear in other juxtaposed sections, and this is what interests me. Aside from the anthologies, only a small handful of books have tackled literature and work. In *Work in the English Novel* (1985) Ruth Danon traces the development of a 'myth of vocation,' the non-Weberian Gospel of Work as self-prescribed to the middle class, in Daniel Defoe, Charles Dickens, and Thomas Hardy. I myself am more interested in this myth as directed towards the working class. In *Man and Work* (1976) David Meakin historicizes the varying meanings of work. Though mostly a survey of literature and work from the Greeks to the modern age, incorporating writers from many countries and many literary traditions, he correctly understands and treats work as presupposing 'revised notions of art, community, of culture in the very widest sense' (17). He also very neatly identifies two work ethics: the cult of productivity, economic competition, and its basis in the Protestant work ethic on the one hand, and a 'very different, life-enhancing ethic' on the other (41). This is a fundamental distinction and one I rely upon heavily. Meakin basically divides his figures into group A or group B depending on whether they have a Protestant ideology or a socialistic one. But the same writers who fit into his group A and conform to the economic status quo could equally fit into his group B, depending upon the audience they are addressing or considering. Meakin also places too much emphasis on Protestantism. The Protestant work ethic was self-addressed, a way for the middle class to identify the social and psychic development of the middle class. Addresses to working men, invocations to Work, and there are many of them, generally do not stress a 'calling' or the virtues of self-help, self-reliance, freedom, frugality, autonomy, and acquisitiveness. The literary history of work, including representations that conform to orthodox economic practices, goes far beyond the ideology of Protestantism.

Another book on British attitudes towards work is Martin J. Wiener's *English Culture and the Decline of the Industrial Spirit, 1850–1980* (1981). Wiener explains the economic decline of England after the Industrial Revolution by showing that 'culture' contained capitalism, that ideologies of Progress and economic endeavours for dominance were successfully frustrated and ultimately overturned by an aristocratic tradition, by the self-gentrification of the bourgeoisie. The conspicuous relaxation and early retirement of English entrepreneurs, their attempt to live and act like the aristocracy (for what ought to be considered as the capital of prestige), led, Wiener argues, to the demise of the industrial or entrepreneurial spirit. To accept this thesis, however, one has to deny or minimize more obvious factors leading to the decline of British economic hegemony, such as the collapse of its empire or the effects of the Second World War. One also has to ignore the middle-class values of business and ascendancy in say Dickens or Carlyle, and focus only on the cultural or aesthetic rejection of industry (which must have been substantial in the first place in order to garner a reaction). Wiener dichotomizes culture and the industrial spirit in the same way that Carlyle does but then ignores the latter and grants a level of success to 'culture' that acts to reduce the human violence of 'the industrial revolution' to a blip.

I myself make four major, interconnected arguments: one, about the anti-rationalist or anti-utilitarian tradition; two, about the relationship between economic theory and culture; three, about the construction of working-class culture; and four, the most important, about the non-dialectical division between Work and its economic function. The anti-rationalist tradition refers to an inheritance from Romanticism and the visionary, traditionalist reaction to industrialism and economism born in the Victorian period. Its thinkers are violently opposed to rationalism in work or society: to impersonal theories or laws, to systematic controls, to statistics, to specialization, and to the ordering of the world into a functionalized, calculable, consistent means towards a substantially unclear but maximized end. Yet the discourse of anti-rationalism is not made to oppose an alternating discourse fully compatible and often complicit with the industrial or entrepreneurial spirit and the economy-as-is. The way in which Work is isolated from economics allows for the representation of a moral, independent individual in the midst of an immoral and deterministic world. In the history of the reaction to multiple waves of rationalism is a ferocious privatism – one that treats both individual and collective work as a private experience and a non-economic activity – but also the famous British pragmatic bent. It is a history of not connecting its moral and practicable instincts, despite initiating the dogma of 'only connect.'

My second objective is to show that there is some direct correspondence between a prevailing economic theory and culture, though I am not especially interested in the chicken-and-egg question of which came first. All the economic theories taking precedence in the periods I am discussing adopted a model of rationalism that assumed human beings are naturally driven to maximize their self-interest. The reaction to it from the anti-rationalist tradition is negative to say the least. But in these sections of my study I am interested in showing the fusion of specific economic theories and society, the formation of economic cultures, that provokes the protest. Classical and neoclassical economics, political economy, and economic schools and disciplines that grew simultaneously with the rise of quantifiable labour all define the maximization of self-interest as normative or 'rational.' Modern decision theory continues to disregard nonmaximizing economic activity that attempts to achieve only satisfying results (e.g., profits), dismissively referring to it as 'satisficing': it is not considered a rational choice. Economists who follow the classical schools are generally willing to admit that satisficing takes place but do not include it in their models. I argue – following Richard Biernacki and others – that the models themselves have an impact on culture, on the behaviour of economic agents: that theories are normative as well as descriptive. The economic theories I investigate, themselves shaped by dynamic cultures – from technology to politics to the arts – generate, shape, develop, and legitimize theories of *homo economicus* that neuter subversive ideas about social organizations and privilege the importance of economic man, his reason, in order to justify and serve the ascendant or dominant capitalist class. The radical conservative element reacts to rationalist theories through the anti-rationalist concept of work for work's sake and a defence of working-class culture. But it also comes to terms with rationalism and concedes to rationalist theory, in part to respond to immediate crises or address everyday economic life, and in part because it is the most immediately available economy. In either case, the response is shaped according to undisputed presuppositions of labour and its field of possibility.

The economic theories I examine, hedonist at root, consider it axiomatic that people prefer leisure to work (why wages are called 'compensation'). They cannot account for the desire to work for non-economic reasons, the widespread resistance to retirement, or the nonemployment activity we might do with zeal – housekeeping, childrearing, volunteering, or gardening and such – but would not do for pay. They cannot account for the fact that there is no relationship between the amount of disutility, the degree of undesirability in the work activity, and the size of the economic reward. By arguing that work is a disutility, they deny that the context, structure, or organization of work is the disutility. They also argue that a rationalized workplace is acceptably alienating. These theories refuse to accept that people act nonrationally, without self-interest, without a goal: that people buy flowers for the hell of it. If we do, it is deemed a second-order activity. Finally, they deny that ideology and collective forces manufacture desire (the leisure that supposedly drives us unwillingly to work), work ethics, or the maximizing strategies and conduct of economic agents. Economic agents might strategize, but such strategies are governed by patterns of perception and action indoctrinated into the agents by culture, to which economic theory is a large and weighty contributor.

My third objective is to trace the construction of working-class culture as developed by nonworking-class writers. From Carlyle to Orwell a narrative of resigned servility, economic simplicity, political docility, and general passivity has been thrust upon the working classes, playing down the rise of an autonomously organized working-class politics that explicitly positions the Gospel of Work against the real properties of labour. There are obviously many different representations of working-class culture by the nonworking classes. P.J. Keating identifies six types of working-class characters in the Victorian novel alone (26–7). Most of those novels were written by and directed at the middle class, though religious and temperance tract societies directly targeted the poor. The influence of the conservative, 'reactionary' tradition – Carlyle, Ruskin, Conrad – on middle-class, liberal values cannot be underestimated. The representation of the working class finding relief under an imaginary, feudalistic shield of those who know best, the metaphor of the familial society, is challenged only by the working class itself.

Though the working class often stands for 'the English People' and thus are said to have the attributes of Protestantism – self-reliance, John Bull volition, an intuited sense of right and wrong, etc. – autonomy is not the characteristic it is *shown* to have. Against the backdrop of true paternalism, the honourable and loyal guides of the self-fashioned aristocratic stereotype, it is fast to compliance, humility, and cheerfulness. Always a bit rude, rough, earthy, corporeal, gregarious, and beery, it is also doggedly conservative, reverent, ready to please, and simple. It is nonviolent, as long as it is under a protective umbrella. Scenes of working-class life that depict sordid poverty, abject brutality, and a lack of vitality, gay banter, and playfulness point to the absence of what ought to be there, what is inherent in the group but under assault by urban and industrial coldness. The working class is nonrational, only becoming irrational or violent when pushed too far by bourgeois rationalism. Above all the working class is characterized by its love of work for work's sake; if not, that devotion to work and that natural affinity to it are retarded, again, by rationalization. Part of the plight of the working-class underdog that we will see over and over again involves wresting intrinsically valuable Work from objectively alienating conditions. Finally, despite the ability to find value in industrial bleakness, the working class is constantly represented as having a tragic sensibility, a fatalistic attitude towards its place in the world. Orwell differs from Carlyle and Conrad by also, when in his 'economic mode,' representing the working class as entirely preoccupied with and resigned to day-to-day economic survival. But whether life is a struggle for super-economic or purely economic reasons, Orwell's ideal working class never thinks in terms of a revolutionary or even a reformist struggle – struggling *for* justice as opposed to struggling *through* injustice.

The fourth objective of this study – to theorize on a set of disjunctures under the rubric of Work and labour and to contextualize two distinct discourses that displace and would deform each other – I have already described. I disagree with Jameson that 'the production of aesthetic or narrative form is to be seen as an ideological act in its own right, with the function of inventing imaginary or formal "solutions" to unresolvable social contradictions' (*Political* 79), but only insofar as one is more likely to find a lacuna than a 'solution' (however forced) to those social contradictions, at least in the texts and contexts in which I am engaged. There is no solution or resolution available in these narratives of work given the conservative aversion to radical action or radical theory. Orwell epitomizes the work/labour split, though he has moments when he writes dialectically. He also more than most seems to recognize the contradiction in his approach: that 'George Orwell' was born of a tension, that 'A humanitarian is always a hypocrite' (*CEJL* 2: 218). But Orwell, for the most part, swings harder and faster between gospelizing work and pragmatically acquiescing to the world-as-is than those before him. Perhaps more fervently than most of his predecessors, he articulates a belief in moral change, that one has to change or perfect oneself before one changes or perfects the world, or despite the increasingly imperfect world. What makes Orwell so strange, why he epitomizes the split, is that he, swinging in the opposite direction, also redresses that very aspect of moralism, as in his essay on Dickens, and because he virtually personifies defeatism, economic fatalism, or what I call pragmatic realism. I bring him up throughout the following pages in order to establish his central place within radical conservatism.

The focus of this study is on nonworking-class representations of the working classes at work, in response to the rationalization of work. My readings of the texts in this study are for this reason very specialized, though I hope it becomes clear that to separate Work from labour has far-reaching implications. From my understanding of the way in which work is treated I arrive at my version of the text. This inevitably cuts short other possible readings of the texts, and other genuine meanings, but allows me to make connections between texts and organize them into categories that would not otherwise seem obvious. Because I begin with the assumption that there are innumerable ways to arrive at meaning, I do not assume that these categories are in any way waterproof. As I only examine instances where Work gets separated from its economic meaning, I have also left out a number of writers who often come up in literary discussions of work, such as Thomas Hardy, Bernard Shaw, and Henry Green.

I am interested in a distinctive rhetoric of Work, albeit one that originates from fictive and nonfictive sources. Though one might think that there would be substantial differences in representations of work depending upon whether the text is an essay or a piece of fiction, to my surprise I found that there was not. It might seem likely that nonfictive prose would more easily accommodate a discourse of labour whereas fiction would lead to Romantic visions and articulations of Work. But I found no such consistency. Though I explore the language of labour and Work in each of the main chapters in order to illustrate that form and content do indeed coincide, that what is being said about Work or its economic implications corresponds to how it is being said, Carlyle, Conrad, and Orwell are as likely to use the rhetoric of Work when writing nonfictional prose as Conrad or Orwell are of assuming the grammar of labour when writing fiction (Carlyle would never admit to writing fiction). Stylistically they are worlds apart. Fiction or nonfiction is not a determining factor in what gets represented; taking the position of the participant or observer, on the other hand, is. As I imply above, Carlyle, Conrad, and Orwell were both participants and observers of the culture they admired. When representing Work, Carlyle, Conrad, and Orwell take on the role of the participant, if not workers themselves then the spirit of the Worker. When documenting a world contained by economic reality, they speak as observers, detached and distanced from the world of Work. Inflections between the voice of the observer and of the participant occur as frequently and dramatically in fiction as in nonfiction.

Though I am also interested in the supposed Work of writing itself, mostly I examine how Carlyle, Conrad, and Orwell relate the pleasures and virtues of Work to the working classes while reserving a language of labour for the nonworking classes. I argue that in this way they reproduce and manifest not only a literary but a reoccurring historical tendency as well, though the designation of 'class' may fluctuate. The working class, it seems, enjoys a special knowledge of Work but is particularly oblivious to the world of labour. It is primarily to interrogate this myth that at various points I also examine the working class representing itself at work, representing its own culture.

CHAPTER ONE

Thomas Carlyle

One of the more curious conventions to take hold of the Victorian middle-class imagination involved a sort of mapping or social explorationism: touring or 'going down' among the lower classes and reporting back to the world above on the squalor and hardship faced in London's East End or Manchester or any other 'underworld' in the UK. Henry Mayhew's and Charles Booth's voyages are perhaps the best known, but before Orwell did it almost fetishistically, everyone from the busybody philanthropists Charles Dickens derides to Bernard Shaw and Beatrice Webb did it, including Dickens; even Andrew Ure, the manufacturer, did it (though he, perhaps in response to the reformist message it usually conveyed, found the industrial towns of England to be very pleasant indeed [17–18]). In *Past and Present* (1843), Thomas Carlyle himself demands his readers to 'Descend where you will into the lower class' (9). Whether it suggests a localized colonial spirit or a challenge to the aristocracy's claim of having a special relationship to the poor, the combination of vivid description and personal reflection helped shape the 'Condition-of-England question,' a phrase among many others Carlyle inadvertently coined ('Chartism' 168). The directness of 'Chartism' (1839) and *Past and Present*, or the Condition-of-England question in general, adumbrating much in realism and naturalism, marks a distinct break with the social criticism of the self-exiled, hyper-subjective Romantics. Notwithstanding attempts at cultural homogenization and sanitization, the almost paternal form of the research, however, nearly always conveys modest prescriptions for change.

Though Orwell would establish himself as *the* writer who descends into the lower classes, he never admired Carlyle: the overblown style, power worshipping, or the organicist authoritarianism. Yet both writers precipitate support from the political left and right, a detail of more than trivial importance. They both promote activism, but are suspicious of radical action; appeal to tradition, manliness, and simplicity; are ironists but not cynics; oscillate between speaking on abstract and concrete matters; and write about the virtues of Work in periods of high unemployment and job insecurity. They both complain that governments, official institutions, 'extreme' social critics, and modern societies in general lack soul. Thus they are both reluctant to come to terms with modernity, retreating to and ensconcing themselves in conservatism, nature, and the past. They also depict a working class that does the same. Yet they both, in alternate discourses, grudgingly accept modern society and cooperate with its demands. But Orwell did not admire Carlyle. The trajectory from an outspoken Carlyle to an outspoken Orwell, himself brimming with Victorian values, reveals a shift in foundational assumptions about final and contingent knowledge, though the basic division between moralism and pragmatism remains firmly intact. At the same time that Carlyle's rhetoric of Work is final, complete, and evangelical, a great deal of interpretive work, circumspection, and equivocation – a discourse of labour – takes place as well.

Carlyle speaks of Work as if with a single vision of it, of *the* work ethic, of the opportunity for self-realization, and of non-economic imperatives. But he also recognizes class, class struggle, wages, Corn Laws, and the need for legislation almost as if he recognized a difference between 'Work' and 'labour' – almost as if he accepted that the idea of any final pronouncement is unfeasible when measured against concrete experience. Carlyle's treatment of work, the double theses embedded in *Past and Present*, will be the main subject of this chapter. A simultaneous but undialectical confirmation of spiritual and material values, of 'culture' and 'society,' or of *homo faber* and *homo economicus* sets up a tremulous balancing act for the (S)age. In his a priori, intransitive, generalizing voice, Carlyle echoes both humanistic and theistic doctrine, interchangeable despite their original opposition. In his concrete, transitive voice he subordinates human nature to a human condition, philosophy to history, and the Gospel of Work to the matter of wages.

My intent is not to further denigrate Carlyle's reputation, battered as it has been by the treatment of the *Latter-day Pamphlets* (1850) as the Carlyle on-tap. Rather, I want to identify and examine the suppression of a dialectic between Work and labour that acts to structure Carlyle's thought. As E.P. Thompson suggests,

> The mistake, today, is to assume that paternalist feeling must be detached and condescending. It can be passionate and engaged. This current of

traditionalist social radicalism, which moves from Wordsworth and Southey through to Carlyle and beyond, seems, in its origin and its growth, to contain a dialectic by which it is continually prompting revolutionary conclusions. The starting-point of traditionalist and Jacobin was the same. (*Making* 378)

This explains why 'Wherever the traditionalist Tory passed beyond reflective argument about the factory system, and attempted to give vent to his feelings in action, he found himself forced into an embarrassing alliance with the trade unionists or working-class Radicals. The middle-class Liberal saw in this only evidence of Tory hypocrisy' (*Making* 379). Yet a nondialectical allegiance to spiritual (moral) and material (pragmatic) values also finds Carlyle, a Tory par excellence, objecting to the domination of political economy and the spiritual malaise of the age, but embracing industry, a liberal invention. Though Carlyle denies it, industry is genealogically tied to political economy, rationalized work to rationalism. 'Such is the factory system, replete with prodigies in mechanics and political economy,' says Ure, Gospelizing industrialism (18). The moral Carlyle attempts not only to reintroduce feudalistic working relationships and disengage industry from political economy, but to reappropriate the concept of rationalism from the clutch of economics. This ends in his assigning rationality to spiritualism, an act only possible in an era dominated by the language of instrumental reason. At times, Carlyle seems as if he would be the last Victorian to embrace rationalism or its language, but when illustrating the validity of life beyond the economic, he frequently adopts the terms most convenient to political economy and most credible in a vaguely secular society that seeks the certainty of noncontingent, *temporal* knowledge.

In this chapter I am interested in Carlyle's attitude towards work but also in lasting echoes of Carlylean work from the 1840s to the 1860s. Specifically, I am looking to see his practice of divorcing work from its economic counterpart, when surveying the working class, reproduced in the Victorian novel. I mostly focus on Charles Dickens and Elizabeth Gaskell. By doing so I do not mean to argue that they were the only ones to segregate representations of Work from representations of labour or that they necessarily did it more than others, but that they can be taken to represent some of the most important liberalist currents in Victorian literature nonetheless allied to Carlyle. Neither of them is exactly shaped by Carlyle's writings, but they nevertheless alternate between paternalistic and individualistic points of view, according to the class-based culture being described or directed, in a manner derivative of and deferential to Carlyle and his oscillations between an ideal past and an industrious present. I am also interested in the way in which the conservative tradition was challenged by Thomas Cooper, revived by John Ruskin, but then radically converted by William Morris.

In some ways the philosophy of work that was so openly received by such diverse Victorians as Dickens and Ruskin resembles the Marx of the same period, the 1840s. Both Carlyle and Marx conceive humankind in relation to material activity: in willed work human beings objectify or project themselves onto a creation and thus become real and knowable to themselves in a sense that exceeds basic materiality (corporeality). In this way, both reject the dichotomy that forever separates materialism from essentialism. The idea that work initiates a process of reciprocal alteration – the subject alters the world and the world alters the subject – firmly establishes the place of history in philosophy. They both would overturn the philosophical tradition that assumes the primacy of contemplation over activity. Marx and Carlyle, then, contribute to the secularization of the age, countering the idea that what humans do will never equal what the *Kosmos* will do – that which exists in eternity or beyond history. They also agree that industry manifests *homo faber*, that returning to a premachinic golden age is both impossible and undesirable, but that the relations and conditions of production in contractional/exchange systems alienate individuals from themselves and each other.

They also differ in many ways. Aside from the more obvious differences in their social visions, they differ insofar as Marx always emphasizes the idea that work offers humankind the opportunity to prove itself as a 'species being' whereas Carlyle, notwithstanding the hierarchical paternalism of his social vision, stresses that 'a man perfects himself by working' (Rosenberg, *Seventh* 60–1; Carlyle, *Past* 196). Though *Sartor Resartus* (1833) marks a movement from a Romantic to a social, historical, or 'Victorian' sensibility, work itself is principally treated in it as personal therapy. Work is Teufelsdröckh's answer to his own spiritual problems, such as depression and doubt. Even if Carlyle's despondency was brought on by an anomic epidemic and self-help is a public medicine, work's agency confirms selfhood regardless of society. *Sartor Resartus* might outline a path towards the 'NOT-ME' but it is not until *Past and Present* that Carlyle manifests an awakened public consciousness. To an extent, the shift parallels Marx's reworking of Georg Hegel. According to Hegel, saturated in Idealism, work is not a specific economic activity but the way in which the self shapes the world under the guidance of the spirit: a middle point between 'man' and the world. For him 'alienation' or self-objectification is the end of philosophy's interest in work. For Marx, 'self-objectification' is the starting point of philosophy. In history, objectification becomes 'alienation' and 'estrangement,' a reification largely endogenous to capitalism. Even though Carlyle's emphasis in *Past and Present* is elsewhere, on Work as a good in itself and on final knowledge, he pulls himself towards a materialistic theory and concrete subject matter. But only to an extent: the discourse of labour can be found only in pockets, compartmentalized and ghettoized.

A further point of divergence between Marx and Carlyle is that the latter finds work not only provides a mirror to selfhood, but also reflects the worker's bond to a cosmic, anti-historical determination. Philosophically, Carlyle is somewhere between Hegel and Marx. Marx sees history as the interplay of economics with other forces; Carlyle sees history as the interplay of the cosmos with other forces (including economics). As a result, Carlyle pushes himself away from material and towards axiological theory. In Carlyle, ethics govern social relations (and modes of production): modes of production do not govern ethics (or social relations). This opens up the way for Carlyle, and later for others, to construct the idea of the good industrialist, the Captain of Industry. Conclusive, universal ethics are readable despite material changes, he says; they are simply not being universally heeded.

In this way Carlyle's interpretation of work is principally anagogic. Beyond giving it a literal (production), allegorical (self-objectification), and moral (therapeutic and socially valuable) reading, he invests it with mystical and spiritual meanings. Productive work is 'appointed by the Universe' (*Past* 144) to bridge subject and object, the individual and the pantheistic external. The paradox in locating a transcendental order in work (albeit represented as Work) has a near parallel in archetypal/structural criticism and the paradox inherent in locating anagogic mysticism by the way of a very scientific orientation. Carlyle answers Victorian doubt with a philosophy of Work. Religion takes faith. Work demands that same faith because before work there is no way to know the object being worked upon. Work seems to be 'impossible' for the object of work is 'as yet a No-thing': one performs work 'for the Unseen' (*Past* 205). The religion of Work, then, does not directly counter either spiritual or material history. Through Work subject and object are grafted together, with the individual's part in a World Spirit becoming knowable because it is located in the material object of his or her work. Eloise Behnken points out that this is proto-existentialist reasoning insofar as the spirit cannot know itself unless it is translated into external works – that is, existence precedes essence (27). Though it is true that with Carlyle action precedes knowledge, the subject does not *create* selfhood or a purpose, she or he *finds* them. As with Hegel, the spirit is historical because human forces can and do frustrate it: history delays its predestined course. In Calvinist theology the Elect work because success at work is a sign of providential approval. Carlyle's Calvinist upbringing reappears in the idea of a world spirit vaguely dependent upon (or at least not independent of) human history. Through Work universal meanings and transcendental laws demonstrate themselves. Carlyle mixes the traditional idea of truth as revelation and the modern, productional idea that knowledge is limited to what humans make. Work compensates for the absence of God but also manifests God's presence, 'bodies forth the form of Things Unseen' (*Past* 205), in its elaboration of the ontological experience.

Both sides of this paradox lead towards a unified vision of Work as compulsory activity for spiritual gain. Carlyle compounds other paradigmatic meanings in his representation of work, such as the expression of cultural and national identity. It is his response to all forms of excess: to the excesses of Romantic self-consciousness, idleness, ennui, religious doubt, intellectualism, freedom, independence, social unrest, and so forth. But the point is that despite obstacles, he forges a coherent, final theory of Work: a *deus ex machina* in the playing out of a moral universe.

The greatest threat to that vision of Work is industrial capitalism and the social relations it produces. Marxists tend to argue that any intrinsic value gained from work is coterminous with the mode of production and the organization of working relations. Sociologists sometimes object to this formula by documenting subjective aberrations. Most work theorists today more and more treat aberrations as the norm. But all are suspicious of the promotion of work that takes place irrespective of its content and purpose. Carlyle's Gospel of Work is undoubtedly disturbed by industrialism, a word he coined in order to differentiate between an acceptable social fact (industry) and an unacceptable, asocial way of life. He speaks of 'Genuine Work,' of a golden age before the 'Steam-Demon [had] yet risen smoking into being' (*Past* 71). Yet Carlyle was not anti-industry, nor does he speak at length about the deplorable conditions in mines and factories (especially in comparison with Friedrich Engels, his contemporary). In 1842, a particularly gruesome parliamentary Blue Book made working conditions, not work, the subject of public scrutiny. In 1843, with *Past and Present*, Carlyle moves toward re-cloaking work.

Many Victorians were able to make the super-philosophical distinction between 'labour' and 'work,' even if they never articulated it as fully or as clearly as Hannah Arendt. In Arendt's *philosophical* distinction between labour and work, 'labour' denotes activity that satisfies biological need, sustains life, whereas 'work' organizes a social environment and aestheticizes. Her *super-philosophical* corollary is that labour in modernity is activity performed solely for extrinsic gain, money. 'Work' becomes the activity of the hobbyist, the artist, or the careful craftsperson focused on quality alone: it is that which both Carlyle and Arendt lament is being subsumed by a culture of labour, by profit seeking and advertising. But in an industrial society, 'labour' first and foremost means factory and machine work, the activity of the working class, and that which results in alienation. Carlyle's frequent failure to discriminate between labour and Work suggests a refusal to acknowledge industrial working conditions. Work for its own sake necessarily directs attention away from the real properties or conditions of production. His inclusiveness and intransitiveness also suggest an attempt to mobilize society towards productivity and to level working-class interests into the interests of the dominant class. Such a society could purport to achieve the coherency and solidarity previously thought unique to Christianity. As Gertrude Himmelfarb notes, before industry became widespread in urban England, it had 'been the poor who were blessed, who were of the kingdom of God. Modernity had changed that. Work was the new salvation, the source of "blessedness"' (206). Carlyle insists the aristocracy, the Captains of Industry, *and* labourers Work. That amounts to insisting labourers toil for extrinsic gain only, while defending low wages by affirming that work's reward is intrinsic ('labour' is not a good in itself). Though Carlyle argues in favour of fair wages and for better (paternalistic) working relations, he is ignoring or deluding labourers when he declares, 'Work, and therein have wellbeing' (*Past* 201). He is asking the labourer to find within himself the strength to glean the intrinsic values of Work from intrinsically (and extrinsically, the two are rarely separable) valueless labour. He desires the psychic health of labourers only insofar as it corresponds to social stability and precludes social and industrial disobedience. Besides 'Doubt, Desire, Sorrow, Remorse,' and 'Despair,' Work also stills the labourer against 'Indignation' (*Past* 196). He attacks Chartism and the nascent movement of working-class protest (as opposed to artisanal protest), especially because it focused on wages and piecemeal reforms but was not headed by a social vanguard. He slyly censures the negotiation of wages by conflating it with the calculation of statistics, a rationalist enterprise. He suggests that wages 'are but one preliminary item' leading to well-being, just as a utilitarian fetish of numbers is an incomplete and over-exaggerated explanation of what constitutes human motivation, justice, or happiness ('Chartism' 172). Carlyle speaks of Work as if it too did not contribute to labour, to the economic gain of capital or to the industrial conditions considered deplorable in his own day. The labourer would have needed an enormous moral – self-shaping – reservoir to accrue well-being. Carlyle, in a period of blatant industrial tyranny, assures all sectors of society that 'No man oppresses thee ... from all men thou art emancipated: but from Thyself' (*Past* 216–17). This is not the same Carlyle who argues 'without proper wages there can be no well-being' ('Chartism' 186).

By prescribing an almost unqualified therapy of Work and a uniform imperative, Carlyle preaches Work to labourers. He adopts a completely different discourse, one deploring how work has become laborious, when addressing the middle class or the aristocracy. By dividing a discussion of work from the issues of class he effectively wars against working-class consciousness and the need for reform. When he admits 'how much better fed, clothed, lodged and in all outward respects accommodated men now are, or might be, by a given quantity of labour' – obviously referring to the working class – it is from the point of view of a moralist complaint against the accompanying 'internal and spiritual' decay ('Signs' 227). In other words, instead of seeing the pragmatic value of food or clothes, regardless if they are mass-produced, he sees little victories in the working-class standard of living as contributing to the overall greed of the age. Regarding work, the only clear distinction he makes is between Mammonism and 'noble' or 'true' Work. The latter is 'sacred' 'were it but true hand-labour' because it posits faith in the Unseen (*Past* 202). Assembly-line work cannot be 'true' in that sense and labour does not have the opportunity to Mammonize, to hoard wealth. The negation of labour, of working conditions, expresses a steadfast commitment to categorical over conditional knowledge. Beyond that, by relating labour to blessedness, Carlyle validates obscene working conditions and the kind of alienation that accompanies the subdivision of labour and profits the capitalist class. Thompson makes clear that 'The first half of the nineteenth century must be seen as a period of chronic under-employment, in which the skilled trades are like islands threatened on every side by technological innovation and by the inrush of unskilled and juvenile labour' (*Making* 269). It is indeed troubling that the idolization and subsequent mythology of work, largely motivated by Carlyle, proceeds simultaneously to industrialism.

Such ironic timing, however, does not necessarily indicate bourgeois machinations. Placed in the context of the uber-rationalist/industrialist propaganda of the day, commemorating work acts as to inhibit the growth of industrial liberalism. Ure in *The Philosophy of Manufactures* (1835) recommends 'training human beings to renounce their desultory habits of work, and to identify themselves with the unvarying regularity of the complex automaton' (15). His arguments about the philanthropic effects of manufacturing are based on the idea that it is 'a blessing destined to mitigate, and in some measure to repeal, the primeval curse pronounced on the labour of man, "in the sweat of thy face shalt thou eat bread"' (17). Not unexpectedly, Jeremy Bentham also carried rationalist doctrine into the matter of work, arguing in 'A Table of the Springs of Action' (1817) that 'labour considered in the character of an *end*, without any view to any thing else, is a sort of desire that seems scarcely to have place in the human breast; yet, if considered in the character of a means, scarce a desire can be found, to the gratification of which *labour*, and therein *the desire of labour*, is not continually rendered subservient ... *Love of labour* is a contradiction' (104). Carlyle, effectively in a debate over human nature and its amenability to economic rationalism and industrialized work, responds by idealizing Work.

Even J.S. Mill, who protested against the one-sidedness of economic reasoning, scoffed at Carlyle's anti-utilitarian tracts. In Mill's words, the shortcoming of the utilitarian perspective, of Benthamism, was that it was 'cut off' from 'many of the most natural and strongest feelings of human nature' ('Bentham' 96). But speaking on Carlyle and the Gospel of Work, Mill sees straight through to the absent centre of Work, questioning the intransitiveness of 'Work for work's sake':

> Work, I imagine, is not a good in itself. There is nothing laudable in work for work's sake. To work voluntarily for a working object is laudable; but what constitutes a working object? ... [Carlyle] revolves in an eternal circle round the idea of work, as if turning up the earth, or driving a shuttle or a quill, were ends in themselves, and the ends of human existence. ('Negro' 27)

Here Mill's utilitarian instincts dominate and there is no talk of compromise, conflation, or connecting rationalist and nonrationalist principles. Work is the means par excellence that is justified by the end. Mill saw clearly that the Carlylean Gospel of Work directly opposes utilitarianism, that it counters every article in the utilitarian creed. His objection to Work is not that it ignores the objective process, the conditions of production, in its overvaluation of the subjective experience, but that it ignores the product, the only measure of value. Despite Mill's attempt to civilize utilitarianism, when its economic root is tabled, his loyalties to it become very clear.

The celebration of Work's intrinsic values is an implicit challenge to industrialism, a posting of its shortcomings, even if it is imminently redundant and highly suspicious. To collapse Work and labour into a sanctified Work is to confront and defy utilitarianism, *its* noncontingent, foundationalist assumptions and their cultural implications, and *its* objective to collapse all Work into labour, thereby arresting all meaningful satisfaction until after labour. Utilitarianism imposes a narrow definition on work: it is all labour, disutility. Carlyle does the same, but offers the opposite one that defines all labour as Work.

Political economy also identifies satisfactions and intrinsic needs as coming from beyond paid employment. Its parameters limit the cultural context in which activity, time, identity, and status (or subject-position) are defined and regulated, either as work or nonwork. Political economy makes a distinction between work and nonwork (for example, a hobby) that is not inherent in the activity itself but solely in the act of payment. Carlyle attempts to refashion the cultural contexts towards what inheres in the action. He attempts to elide the binaries set up by political economy between work and nonwork, labour and craft, or extrinsic and intrinsic need. The result is a unified vision of Work at a historical moment that ought to be impossible for a social critic with Carlyle's specific knowledge.

From its denigration of Romantic self-absorption *and* utilitarianism to its disparagement of democracy *and* the idle aristocracy to its recommendation for a satisfied working class *and* an industrious middle class, *Past and Present* attempts to define Englishness. Englishness is for Carlyle what England was in the past: a nation of feudalistic relations, paternalistic alliances between an aristocracy and a peasantry, and petrified social roles. To that end the book offers one of the first theories of work as the means towards social coherence via individual coherence. Conrad would later dramatize the idea that individuals who know only their work, are consistent and complete in it, harmonize with others who know only the same, the specific conditions or economic result of the work being inconsequential to the worker. The 'English people' for Carlyle are then those who live according to pre-industrial or bucolic values; that is, paternal classes and working classes all 'born Conservative' (*Past* 164). But *Past and Present* also attempts to replicate and confirm Englishness by way of a blunt pragmatism. Expediency and efficiency, evolution and progression, constitute Englishness. The 'English people' still comprise paternal and working classes, but middle-class Captains of Industry now occupy the positions of the nation's leaders. The working classes, by their faith in Work and its corollaries, are the means to maintain constancy. Meanwhile, as Carlyle was writing *Past and Present*, Chartists, a national group of working-class social agitators, were gathering. They had at that point brought their Charter demanding sweeping societal and political changes to parliament for ratification on two separate occasions, in 1839 and 1842.

Carlyle keeps recourse to both teleology and practicality even as he aggrandizes, for example, the Abbot Samson's work. The story of the Abbot provides a model for aristocracies, governments, and managers – for individual husbands and entire societies. Alternatively, it provides a critique of modern relations of production. To begin with, however, as R.E. Pahl makes clear, 'there was no pre-industrial golden age of satisfying work' (9). Reproducing the myth of Merrie England underlies an attempt to synchronize modernity with an invariant and thus superior past. It underlies an attempt to check the ever-transforming present by referring to an 'established' (invented) tradition (Hobsbawm 1–9). In Carlyle's parable, the Abbot creates an 'ordered world' out of 'chaos' through vigilance, a mission mentality, discipline, asceticism, and thrift. All his methods are a product of 'the work ethic.' Although it appears as a ruling-class or managerial ideology in which the worker internalizes a mandate to sacrifice his or her labour power for the 'greater good' of the company, as it certainly does today with every manager's motivational discourse circulating around it, Carlyle's work ethic emphasizes commitment by owners, managers, and workers alike.

Notwithstanding Pahl on the mythological content of a golden age, Thompson argues that 'it is sometimes forgotten how rapid the abrogation of paternalist legislation was ... in the space of ten years, almost the entire paternalist code was swept away' (*Making* 595). Pahl and Thompson would not necessarily disagree: paternal relations do not ipso facto amount to a golden age. Undoubtedly sensing a movement away from social organicism in the contemporary present, Carlyle paints a picture of cohesion and molecular harmony in the past. The Abbot's order is not mechanically controlled from the outside, but emotionally driven from within. He has a 'thoughtful sternness, a sorrowful pity: but there is a terrible flash of anger in him' (*Past* 96). The picture is framed by a patriarchal and feudalistic nostalgia for paternalistic work relations. Elsewhere in *Past and Present* he speaks of the lost bonds of guardianship that 'Gurth born thrall of Cedric' (244) had enjoyed, and in 'Signs of the Time' (1829) Carlyle demands that governments operate as a 'father' (233). The Abbot's demeanour and energy, meanwhile, imply a critique of the aloof, passive, and unproductive habits endemic to aristocratic property owners. Antonio Gramsci also speaks of a 'European tradition' of aristocracies 'with no essential function' and thus 'purely parasitic': 'pensioners of economic history' (281). He notes that in the United States even the richest millionaire maintains the pioneering, active spirit despite having no financial need (305). In some ways this is a different spirit than the one Carlyle wants to rekindle in the European aristocracy, the universally sanctioned paternal spirit. But the subtext behind Carlyle's criticisms of a 'Phantom Aristocracy ... not in the least conscious that it has any work longer to do' (*Past* 142) juxtaposes the spirit of active capital to passive property and it is not accidental. By attempting to synthesize divine fiats, organic and hierarchical communities, and economic projects, Carlyle reflects, but also contributes to, the rise of a competition-oriented, nationalistic consciousness.

The story of the Abbot, however, is far from being a manifesto on the virtues of capitalist England. Under political economy the idle aristocracy elude criticism. If work is associated only with economic incentives, with disutility and no intrinsic or social benefit, then wealth excuses idleness. Under the theory of political economy only the poor and unemployed are charged with the opprobrium of idleness. Moreover, the cooperation in the Abbot's workplace is a criticism of laissez-faire just as the representation of authority and obedience is a calling and model for active managements and peaceful workers. The monastery also contradicts the hedonistic underpinnings of utilitarianism by demonstrating that a society functions best when it refuses to treat work merely as a means to secure pleasure. In the abbey, 'work' and 'life' are not confined activities. But the most significant criticism of all political economy is the correlation of spiritual and economic order. Before the Abbot arrives, the abbey is in spiritual and economic turmoil. The success ensuing from the blurring of theology, good economy, morality, productivity, diligence, spirituality, bookkeeping, ritual, efficiency, and faith is a snub against the strict demarcation (and privileging) of *homo economicus* by political economy from the plurality of what constitutes humankind in any of its activities. Eternal laws, for the economically astute and triumphant Abbot, are always 'interpenetrating the whole of Life' (*Past* 72). Economic savvy can go hand in hand with Work, but only when it is made not to contradict the concept of Work.

However, in light of the asceticism and obedience pressed upon the monks, the workers, their 'whole of life' is somewhat limited. The monks reproduce working-class culture or, more exactly, are used to reproduce a normative working-class culture when they reduce economic life to ritual life. Ritual here regulates and orders daily life, eliminating even the need to feel the pressures of economic life. That which seems to be or is represented as a diligent work ethic, a self-effacing absorption in a task, can always be the product of a worker's fear of employer tyranny – a line that neither the Abbot nor Carlyle has problems crossing. In 'Chartism' Carlyle represents not only the violence of the working-class movement, but also the awakening of their class-consciousness as a crisis. He shares the trans-historical, traditional, tragic sensibility often accompanying a belief in Work. To be human, *homo faber*, is to Work, to struggle, to face self-defining challenges and not to negotiate the details of labour. For *homo faber*, struggle is a moral and not an economic issue. But the idea that 'All men submit to toil, to disappointment, to unhappiness; it is their lot here' ('Chartism' 188) can easily be shaped into a defence of worker self-denial or of the indefensible wages and working conditions that produce unhappiness. Again, Carlyle does not seem to hesitate from transgressing the line between inevitable toil and domination. The working class might agree that the world is tragic, but the idea is never detached from an economic point of view, from the point of view of being dominated. The emergence of a rationalist economic theory, the rise of the bourgeois, and the proliferation of religious scepticism had made for the *theoretical* possibility of the end to controlled systems of authority. But the institutionalized religious revival was immediate, powerful, and saturated with appeals to authority and duty. Carlyle's noninstitutionalized religious zeal contributed to the evangelical spirit. He witnessed the factory becoming a place of order, discipline, regularity, and authority that could act to substitute any understood absence of transcendental law. His doctrine of Work allows for that substitution by insisting on Work's wholesale domination of social relationships so that the hierarchies in the workplace would be reproduced outside of it. At the same time, his Gospel of Work counteracts political economy by guaranteeing stability in accordance with universal truth, an order sufficiently authoritative, though moral as well. Both approaches amount to validating liberalist notions of progress through free (but autocratic) industry.

Positive change, as the example of the Abbot is meant to demonstrate, comes from above. Carlyle approves of the Abbot's stubborn unruliness but insists that the subordinates, even as they themselves become artisanal, remain obedient. The entire notion that human beings are social beings is predicated on a directive to obey 'God-made superiors' (*Past* 283). Carlyle assigns mental functions to owners and managers, those who '*can* articulate,' whereas 'almost stupid' workers must labour (*Past* 23). That is, definitive character ratifies the functional division of labour rather than being determined by the conditions and fact of that division. Carlyle insists on work that is appropriate and specific to the preordained function of the worker primarily because he seeks to reinforce or reestablish hierarchical relations. The economic basis of those relations is concealed through the representation of moral relations. If we accept Pierre Bourdieu's theory that within working-class culture an 'economic rationality of conduct' (*Logic* 120) prevails even if it is not governed by purely moneyed transactions and motivations, it stands to be doubly true that those insisting on the predominance of non-economic relations in working-class work from outside of the class but with material interests in working-class work would emphasize honour, obligation, trust, loyalty, and so on. Bourdieu argues that 'the only way that relations of domination can be set up within [the pre-capitalist economy], maintained or restored, is through strategies which, if they are not to destroy themselves by revealing their true nature, must be disguised, transfigured, in a word, euphemized' (*Logic* 126). Converting honour into economic capital (after it had been converted from economic to 'symbolic' capital) is the simplest step.

Carlyle's working class has only the most rudimentary economic knowledge. In his construction of working-class culture, both theory and resistance are as alien to the best of the working class as Work is central to it. To describe the working class as 'thick' or simple-minded, oblivious to itself as a group with mutual interests, content and best off when following orders from 'above,' even worshipping those 'above' it and defending hierarchy; and to castigate Chartism, working-class assemblies, and any other variation of working-class consciousness, is to prescribe a petrifaction at the very moment it appears to be slipping away. Thompson's *The Making of the English Working Class* (1963), which shows that the union movement in England began with artisans and not 'the proletariat' (289, 291, 326), brings out a major contradiction in Carlyle's attitude towards work. Carlyle would re-create labourers into Workers, artisans. But he would restrict their obstinacy and trade-union-mindedness that would follow such a transformation. In other words, he desires workers to counteract political economy but needs labourers to get on with the business of production at hand. He delivers two distinct Gospels of Work. He instructs the middle-class Captains of Industry to Work and be obstinate; he instructs the workers to Work and be submissive. Such hierarchy not only replicates the tradition of Englishness as seen by Carlyle but also stays in step with 'natural law.'

The apportioning of historical relations to intuited eternal law is in accordance with the always-present temptation to withdraw that Carlyle inherits from the Romantics. But instead of granting poetry or art the authority to confirm that intuition or to express the spirit that industrialism was threatening as the Romantics do, Raymond Williams's 'culture,' Carlyle invests in a transcendental idea of Work: 'a small Poet every Worker is' (*Past* 205). Work becomes the validation of that which was, as Chris Vanden Bossche says, 'absent from or even destroyed by newly dominant discourses like political economy' (vii). But work, to pick up Williams's argument in *Culture and Society* (1958), becomes independent; it gets separated from everyday political life, just as the Romantics treat art (or 'culture') as if in a 'superior reality,' a different realm than the organization of 'society.' In that way, Work and political economy, or Work and labour, become unrelated items – the Benthamite nods in approval, and political economy reaches its privileged position of the 'real' and 'rational.' Williams is surely not wrong when he says that the 'idea of culture as the whole way of living of a people receives in Carlyle a marked new emphasis.' But the emphasis is on a spiritualized idea of work, which in a much more immediate way than 'culture' or art is interfused with 'society.' Work (Williams says 'culture') is 'the ground of his attack on Industrialism: that a society, properly so called, is composed of very much more than economic relationships' (*Culture* 83). The Worker (Williams says 'the artist') becomes a 'special kind of person' (*Culture* 43), divorced from the problems of labour or 'society.' Ironically, by attempting to make Work/culture a 'whole way of life,' Carlyle routinely dislodges it from the discourses of economic and social theory. That is, he dehistoricizes, withdraws into, and finalizes Work.

For Williams, Carlyle represents an early example of the writer detaching himself or herself (though in Williams's book it is mostly 'himself') via 'culture' from society and its daily business. But Carlyle, as I will attempt to demonstrate, gets very involved in the economic details of the state, only not when he is representing the working class. Moreover, for Carlyle the act of writing was the means to link himself to the worker, to elide the distance between writer and subject. Ford Madox Brown's painting entitled *Work* (1852–65) attempts to illustrate that Carlyle and F.D. Maurice, standing among strapping, sweaty navvies, were 'participating' in Work life, doing the Work of the intellect. Carlyle and later Ruskin consistently verify this vertical division of labour – while vilifying horizontal divisions of labour – and by this means claim the authority to speak for England's Doers. Carlyle, in so doing, also claims direct knowledge of and access to the life of his working class, albeit from above. To write is to participate in working-class activity (in his own version of working-class life) and to leave economics to the scientific approach of the detached observer. He could thereby express the supposed affinity that the working class has to anti-rationalist instincts in his writing. Carlyle's style simulates good Work; it is the language of action and creation as opposed to rule-governed, mechanical production. As John Holloway argued in 1953, he does not so much use language as he makes or remoulds language (41–2). His language in this way acts to entrench his critique of the utilitarian ethic. His prose, in other words, dramatizes an attack on political economy and its language of instrumental rationality and utility (methodical, systematic, impersonal, exact, non-emotional, and 'functional' diction). In order to antagonize the language of use he combines the topoi, tropes, and conventions of the sermon, the romance, and the epic. When he speaks against 'jargon' he is pointing to technical and business language and when he speaks against 'ornamental' prose he is pointing to commercialism and the discourses of advertising.

It is not unusual for critics to refer to Carlyle's style as dense, 'grotesquely inflated' (Levine 47), deliberately unconventional, circuitous, or 'tantrum prose' (Frye 328): it is all that and more. Both Carlyle and Orwell call for 'earnest' speech and both find political significance in the use of language. Carlyle says, self-consciously of course, the 'kind of Speech in a man betokens the kind of Action you will get from him' (*Past* 153). As historians, Orwell and Carlyle are conspicuously anti-scientific, but rather moralistic, prophetic, and opinionated. The comparison between the two writers, however, ought not to be taken too far. In speaking on work, Carlyle's language also picks up all the corollaries of Carlylean Work, creating authoritative, violent, religious, and universal tones that can be perceived in Orwell but are mitigated by his demotic idiom and his deferment to specificity and variability, the struggle with the absolute declaration.

Carlyle's language and the attitude it conveys remain fairly consistent as he shifts from lambasting concrete labour to glorifying abstract Work, though a more substantial change in tone occurs when he moves from that heightened discourse to one that accommodates labour. Still, the change even then is hardly dramatic or unmistakable. Orwell's style heavily favours a nitty-gritty discussion of labour: he very rarely adopts an elevated, intransitive Work discourse even when he speaks as a participant and generalizes about the Work and culture of the working class. The exact inverse situation holds true in Carlyle's case. Carlyle is somewhat incapable of writing guarded, even-keeled, detached, and non-universalizing prose. He rarely adopts the subjunctive mood or conditional tense even when discussing economic policy. (For example, he does not say 'emigration would resolve the problem of a labour surplus.') Rather he sticks to the imperative and descriptive: 'Canadian Forests stand unfelled, boundless Plains and Prairies unbroken with the plough' ('Chartism' 237). The exaggerated use of capitalization (exaggerated in a time when the upper case was used frequently), italicized words, superlatives, ('feeblest, trivialest' [*Past* 159]), inculcation, accusation, and the compounded biblical references keep his rhetoric at an exhaustingly intense pitch. His performative utterances, verbal nouns, exclamatory phrases, alliterative diction, and repetitious rhythms – 'Dalai-Lamaism, even Dalai-Lamaism, one rejoices to discover, may be worth its victuals' ('Chartism' 205) – underline his defence of action (or motion) and his belief that writing itself, his job, is Work. His distrust of statistics and logic, when it is not explicit, emerges in his use of coinage, narrative, and chaotic syntax. The convoluted sentence construction acts as if to continuously interrupt and redirect cause-and-effect sequences and reasoning. Later we will see that Carlyle contradicts these appeals to the language of Work by referencing a 'rational giant' and the 'practical apex' of hero-worshiping – 'This is not theology, this is Arithmetic' (*Past* 171, 39, 229). But even when he borrows the antiseptic or scientific terminology of calm consideration he does not become coolly analytical. Rather, he maintains the unabashedly dogmatic, pigheaded, passionate, explosive, original-for-its-own-sake, and meticulous (but never mechanical) craftsmanship of the artisan.

Some of the more characteristic examples of Carlylese include constant hypostatizing, personifying, and labelling. As with Orwell, Carlyle favours things over words. If Orwell tries to achieve the status of a tangible thing in his prose – through precision, clarity, and directness – Carlyle does the same through the density of his prose, as if in its entanglements his prose collects weight and becomes material. Personified – and it's fair to assume that Carlyle would think of his writing as a kind of character who has mass and achieves action – *Past and Present*, for example, would be a bully:

> How one loves to see the burly figure of him, this thick-skinned, seemingly opaque, perhaps sulky, almost stupid Man of Practice, pitted against some light adroit Man of Theory ... The cloudy-browed, thick-soled, opaque Practicality, with no logic-utterance, in silence mainly, with here and there a low grunt or growl, has in him what transcends all logic-utterance: a Congruity with the Unuttered. (160–1)

Carlyle's bully, his 'Mr. Bull,' might be illiterate and silent, whereas *Past and Present* personified would be articulate to the point of splitting eardrums, but Carlyle flirts self-consciously with stupidity in the bald, bulldozing directness and aplomb of his discourse. Such a pose is not self-deprecating when one's 'stupidity is wiser than their [politicians', reformers' et al.] wisdom' (162). At the same time, Carlyle without doubt praises the absolute moron, as will both Conrad and Orwell: the 'ox' who never complains about working conditions and the 'slow,' naturally conservative man are a prerequisite for a return to feudalistic hierarchies and elites. One of the consequences of bringing the serf – the man 'insensible to logic' (163) – back to life is that the serf, and by extension the working class, does not negotiate his, or its, labour. Carlyle writes archaically in order to downplay the need for economic negotiation: *Past and Present*, then, lords above the mute English workingman. Carlyle and the English workingman are represented as having the same values and essentially doing the same thing: producing despite their nonrational approach. But as the 'grim inarticulate veracity of the English People, unable to speak its meaning in words, has turned itself silently on things' (169), Carlyle, like a feudal Baron, thinks and speaks for those Working in his care.

The authority in Carlyle's voice might act as a reminder that his discourse is not so much playful as it is 'Workful.' Today we tend to associate play with spontaneity, creativity, freedom, and innovation while we associate work with routine and circumscribed activity. But for Carlyle, Work represents what we today call 'play,' with the added emphasis on the rules involved. In fact, Work for him is 'playful,' and his style is fittingly playful, in Johan Huizinga's sense of the word: spontaneous but disciplined, creative but heavily structured, and, moreover, indicative of a kind of contest or a challenge. Carlylean Work corresponds to Huizinga's 'play' insofar as it accommodates rules and subordination on the one hand and (artisanal) autonomy, stubbornness, independence, and a challenge to utilitarian order on the other.

Carlyle's rejection of the utilitarian fetish for mechanical structures may have led him to Gospelize work, but it is nonetheless remarkable that he writes about Work in such an abstract manner. Carlyle's preference for concrete things does not extend into his representation of actual work. Statistics may lack 'soul,' but work is never an intransitive experience: one always works at something. Carlyle ignores the context, content, and effects of work – 'Work, and therein have wellbeing' – as he glorifies it; that is, when directly appealing to the working classes to keep on working and to deny the injustice they suffer. When he addresses the middle class, Utilitarians, and Unworking Aristocracy, the intransitive mood hardens into vivid descriptions of what work had in fact become (what I call 'labour'). At that point Carlyle explodes upon those same injustices. Elaine Scarry argues that language expressing the abstract comes easily, that the abstract accommodates language, whereas language expressing the concrete and immediate 'can seem inappropriately quick and cavalier' (3). It is possible, I would think, for the exact opposite to be true. A contract between an employer and an employee, suffused in legalese, is hardly 'quick.' However, language expressing the abstract does come easier to at least Carlyle, who needed to add metaphysical ideals to material ideas in order to introduce an economic materialism that would accommodate the unshakable hierarchy and order of feudalism. He could not have argued for a return to feudalistic systems by referring to pragmatism or the finer points of economic history.

Even so, Carlyle conspicuously minimizes the language of labour, the specific and almost pedantic language of the pragmatist. He adopts the rhetoric of Work when addressing the working class. He shifts that discourse to one that berates the upper and middle classes when speaking on what they have done to Work – but the language of Work is still active at these points. When discussing economics – emigration and education policies, wages, Corn laws – he does not shift to the language of economics as might be expected. It is possible to detect a slight decrease in the impulsiveness of his diction, but he certainly does not resort to numbers, hard facts, or the political tones we hear in Orwell when he discusses everyday life from an observer's perspective. Carlyle, the Writer/Worker, is permanently a participant. This is not to say that a shift in attitude or subject matter is in any way less dramatic than in Orwell, but only that Carlyle, to a much greater extent than Orwell, does not struggle with his absolutism, that he does not see it as being at odds with his economic and social mandate. He was more at home in the language of Work than the language of labour because the everyday life he envisioned includes the systems of absolutism (absolute authority, order, and so forth) that were amenable to his language of Work.

Carlyle's language of Work periodically extends into a clear rejection of political reform. Not only does eternal law obviate political action, but any systematic school of interpretation or etiological solution dislocates the concept of reform, of reforming the conditions of production. Carlyle judges society against 'Eternal Facts,' a heuristic 'reality' that transcends change and reveals the inadequacies change brings to the contemporary world. To say that the narrative of *Past and Present* is a longitudinal material history would be to concede that Carlyle's solutions to contemporary problems are anachronistic. History at best is the pejorative details of essential law. Solutions to its waywardness from the predestined course lie in the unfettering of that law rather than in 'bursts of Parliamentary eloquence' (*Past* 19).

Carlyle was also a moralist, as was Orwell, and as such thought that one had to change oneself before one reformed the world. Believing that a moral and not a structural problem haunted England, he derides reform as 'Morrison's Pills.' Paradoxically, all measures for reform are equally untenable because they are partial. Carlyle may call for massive change, but without falsifiable reforms the only means to implement change would be through revolution, a course he specifically censures. Orwell is right to challenge Carlyle as an 'intellectual' (*CEJL* 3: 100). A social critic's refusal to specify social policy discloses intellectual detachment. However, offering overarching, noncontingent criticisms and few practical, if incomplete or temporary, ideas that would necessitate political action – deferring to absolute law – is nonetheless political. In Bourdieu's words, 'the ethic of honour' that is integral to the pre-capitalist operation and fundamental to Carlyle's politics, 'presents itself as the most economical mode of domination because it best corresponds to the economy of the system' (*Logic* 127). The domination Bourdieu refers to comes from within the group itself, whereas Carlyle posits an external domination by 'born leaders.' With this shift in place, Carlyle would ratify the Bourdieusian *habitus*: 'Social formations in which relations of domination are made ... in and through personal interactions [and] contrast with those in which such relations are mediated by objective, institutionalized mechanisms such as the "self-regulating market," the education system or the legal apparatus' (*Logic* 130).

Carlyle dismisses political activity but is unmistakably political in a different way when he argues that the wages 'of every noble Work do yet lie in Heaven or else Nowhere,' and certainly not in 'Owen's Labourbank' (*Past* 203, 204). He does not believe that toil under Mammonism provides its own rewards, but because he attempts to satisfy a Victorian epistemological desire for closure by appealing to final knowledge, he holds in abeyance the historical contexts that at other times receive his unmitigated wrath. Strategy or otherwise, the result is political. The idea that 'money alone is *not* the representative either of man's success in the world, or of man's duties to man' (*Past* 179) strikes out against political economy and supports the cause of labour by integrating it with the case for Work, notwithstanding the suspicion it may justifiably arouse from the point of view of labourers. But 'the brave man has to give his Life away'; 'Blessed is he who has found his work; let him ask no other blessedness'; and 'Who art thou that complainest of thy life of toil? Complain not' (*Past* 204, 197, 202) are absurd and dangerous sentiments that surreptitiously transform 'final knowledge' into silence.

Yet Carlyle writes on the borderline between entelechy and conditionality, universal wisdom and social fact, or 'cultural' disinterest and pragmatic investments. There is a second side to Carlyle, a side that is transitive, concrete, historical, and modern. Critics often find that Carlyle 'combines attitudes generally held to be antithetical' (Rosenberg, *Carlyle* 116) and oscillates between dealing in generalities and constructive politics. The second side of Carlyle admits knowledge cannot be enclosed and is integrated with day-to-day political life. It is consistent with a kind of gritty, bread-and-butter perspective and the economic status quo.

Faced with an England on the brink of widespread violence, Carlyle calls for specific types of action. As Corn Laws drove up the price of bread, Poor Laws and workhouses made for more corruption than what they replaced, angry Chartists gathered, parasitic aristocracies withdrew, and the industrial sector found Mammon, England's future was quite clearly either in reform or violence. In *Past and Present* Carlyle proposes government legislation to regulate and inspect factories, mines, wages, and bureaucracies; in addition, he proposes controls over sanitation, emigration, pollution, education, and housing. These are, by his own standards, Morrison's Pills. Still, he stands against the Corn Laws (laws which the Tory Party continued to defend) and for some of the more moderate objectives of Chartism. He cautiously suggests that workers could become part owners with 'permanent interests' in their manufacturing companies. Though they would be without real, comparative agency in relation to the Captains of Industry, the idea is to allow for labour's bargaining power even in periods of a surplus labour force. Carlyle advocates for governments to enforce feudalistic systems of management in order to remove workers from the uncertainty of the market. In 'Chartism' he outlines a plan for 'Universal Education' and 'general Emigration' (228–38). He would also introduce recreational parks for the working-class family and frequently repeats a 'Fair day's-wages for a fair day's-work,' a very political stance indeed as it was also the slogan of the craft-unions (Perkin 232). These are significant arguments to make in the 1840s, when it was increasingly understood that humanitarian projects could be left to volunteers and were not the responsibility of government (Brantlinger 2). Addressing the middle class, speaking on behalf of but not to the working class, he considers issues surrounding labour, issues that preclude trumpeting Work.

Carlyle bids government to address 'that question of work and wages,' not the 'Wealth of Nations, Supply-and-demand and such' (*Past* 26). Yet he also gets his own hands dirty in the macroeconomic mud by advising British manufacturers to '*equal*-sell' rather than undersell their goods (*Past* 184). The idea is that if the textile industry were to 'satisfy,' not maximize profits, it might stabilize the market and thus wages as well. This is a far cry from an intransitive entreaty to Work and for industrial decency. Again in 'Chartism' he attacks 'Paralytic Radicalism,' or those who assume 'nothing whatever can be done in it by man, who has simply to sit still, and look wistfully to "time and general laws"' (227). Finally, as Williams points out, Carlyle's disparagement of democracy was 'a most relevant criticism' of the influence or 'political arrangement' of laissez-faire (*Culture* 80).

Unlike Arendt, Carlyle does not distinguish between action and work. Both entail that the subject transcends himself or herself by interacting with an environment. This is one of the meanings behind his appeal to 'Think it not thy business, this of knowing thyself ... know what thou canst work at' (*Past* 196). Though he mystifies and depoliticizes action by conflating it with Work (work as a social activity but also as an interaction with the cosmos), his emphasis is on a lack of self-interest and thus is a direct attack on the utilitarian ethic. Though involvement in contemporary social debate, besides jarring against the Gospel of Work, is only 'in partial conflict with bourgeois hegemony,' as Terry Eagleton argues, because it 'seeks to accommodate itself within it,' objections to such involvement also demand scrutiny – especially as an all-or-nothing approach has proven itself to be quite accommodating to the ruling class. Eagleton makes it next to impossible for the members of the 'Culture and Society tradition,' shy of revolutionary action as they are and intermittently addressing specific historical contexts as they do, to engage in any social criticism whatsoever. If their 'labourist ideologies' capitulate to 'bourgeois state-power,' their 'Romantic' ideologies preserve it 'by displacing political analysis to a moralist and idealist critique of its worst "human" effects' (*Criticism* 25).

By and large, however, Eagleton is right: Carlyle backs reform because it promises wealth for England. The emigration he favours means a developed commonwealth and thus increased trade. The Captains of Industry would revitalize the economy and challenge foreign competitors. England 'shall be well' if it works 'better than all people' (*Past* 185). The manorial principles Carlyle wishes industry to adopt would fraternize the factory floor but they would also enforce the ideology which holds that the interests of labour and capital are the same, thereby precluding unrest and ensuring production, 'Practical Material Work' (*Past* 169). Building parks for labouring families is an 'excellent investment' because it would discourage 'mutiny' (*Past* 276). Here Carlyle blends into the school of manufactures, voicing the ideas of Ure, who only eight years before *Past and Present* argued that it takes 'a Napoleon nerve and ambition, to subdue the refractory tempers of work-people accustomed to irregular paroxysms of diligence' (16). Once when Carlyle suggests that a fair day's wage is necessary, he notes that it keeps 'your worker alive that he may work more' (*Past* 203). Even G.K. Chesterton, a conservative like Carlyle, finds fault with Carlyle for coming to terms with industrialism, because he 'never contradicted the whole trend of the age as Cobbett did' (23).

Carlyle also fails, for the most part, to document the details of his activist 'program' and, in general, obfuscates his reformist proposals by yoking them to inevitability. Any 'philosophy of praxis' posits historically determined relations because they are the only ones changeable (Gramsci 133). Williams understands that 'Carlyle is for practical beginnings,' but that he retracts from pragmatism because he considers it essentially inadequate (*Culture* 81–2). In order for work to be an effective therapy it must be meaningful, the type of Work which brings self-objectification, not alienation. Carlyle never suggests, as did Morris, how factory work could be changed in order to foster that necessary sense of creation which occasions salutary effects. His attitude towards Work implies revolutionary change, but his attitude towards labour explicitly rejects and undermines the radicalization of the context in which work takes place.

Carlyle has two very different attitudes toward work. To the working class he urges the need to work for work's sake and to all other classes he validates the logic and practice of the economic in its own terms. The tendency to alter one's attitude towards work depending on one's proximity to the working class or one's consideration of it organizes the dichotomization of Work and labour. Carlyle, when reaching out to or taking account of the working class – 'Awake, ye noble Workers ... It is to you I call' (*Past* 271) – or more specifically when proselytizing to his middle-class readers the best way to consider, speak to, or treat the working class, speaks intransitively, unconditionally about the virtues of Work. When directly appealing to the majority audience of *Past and Present*, the middle class, he raises issues surrounding labour, often finding a way to endorse the industrial structure of the age. When he does preach Work to the middle and upper classes he advocates artisanal obstinacy, pride, and independence; to the working class he recommends subservience and self-deprecation. The two discourses of Work and labour never confront each other because they are addressed in different directions.

Sometimes Carlyle attempts to include both modernity and transcendence, to lend the world the authority of corresponding to a moral universe. In 'Signs of the Time,' discussing the Ideal and the Real, he argues:

> To define the limits of these two departments of man's activity, which work into one another, and by means of one another, so intricately and inseparably, were by its nature an impossible attempt. Their relative importance, even to the wisest mind, will vary in different times, according to the special wants and dispositions of those times. Meanwhile, it seems clear enough that only the right co-ordination of the two, and the vigorous forwarding of *both*, does our true line of action lie. Undue cultivation of the inward or Dynamical province leads to idle, visionary, impracticable courses, and especially in rude eras, to Superstition and Fanaticism ... Undue cultivation of the outward, again, though less immediately prejudicial, and even for the time productive of many palpable benefits, must, in the long-run, by destroying Moral Force, which is the parent of all other Force, prove not less certainly, and perhaps still more hopelessly, pernicious. This, we take it, is the grand characteristic of our age. (237–8)

But Carlyle, as with Matthew Arnold here pre-echoed, would only conflate the Ideal and the Real within middle-class circles. In fact, seeing a non-contest between the Ideal and the Real assumes identical class interests or uniform ideals and 'reals.' The resolution and union he imagines, or the injection of Moral Force he prescribes, are premised on disregarding what is real for the working class, and what might be ideal for them, and on bypassing the most salient and *real* conflict that divides Work from labour – bypassing the conflict between Work and labour. Occasionally, as in *Past and Present*, he interrupts his political discourse on, for example, the need for permanent labour contracts by appealing to 'higher values' – 'I am for permanence in all things' (277) – but so much transcendental rhetoric suffuses *Past and Present* and is generally kept so far apart from the details of labour, that critics such as Himmelfarb can 'wonder how Carlyle proposed to operate an industrial system without some cash-payment mechanism' (206) even though he is quite straightforward when discussing the minute intricacies of wages.

Carlyle's pragmatism is ultimately vague. Philip Rosenberg argues that readers are drawn towards doing, not withdrawal (21). But doing what? – Carlylean Work is predominantly intransitive and in any case, unaffected by the dominant character of work in that period. An anonymous reviewer in 1843 criticized Carlyle for reducing social problems to that which can be 'attributed solely to the want of a right spirit in the breasts of the capitalists' (which is also Orwell's criticism of Dickens and George Woodcock's criticism of Orwell), but concludes by softening that criticism in light of the *fact* that the 'object' of *Past and Present* is 'a well-conducted scheme of emigration' (Trela and Tarr 144). It is arguably not. The critic was closer to the mark with his first observation. *Past and Present* conveys the idea of practical activity; it is just not clear of what kind it ought to be. Carlyle is not disingenuous when he says that the 'Ideal always has to grow in the Real' (*Past* 63). Only he represents the Ideal and the Real without forcing them into a dialectical confrontation: a confrontation that would undermine the Gospel of Work and the business at hand.

Industrialism is outside of the culture/society dichotomy insofar as it was part of Victorian culture. Though Carlyle condemns uncontrolled mechanization and the 'proposition of utility as the source of value' (Williams, *Culture* 63), and even though his almost Manichaean worldview divides phenomena into the consummate blessed and the pragmatically shaped, he does not assume a permanent rift between 'cultivation and civilization.' But he never mixes spiritual, Ideal values together with an industrialist, entrepreneurial idea of society in such a way as to dialectically oppose them, which is in fact to segregate them. Carlyle reads points of continuity between creativity and industrial expansion and even between *homo faber* and *homo economicus*. Society had only to restore the proper balance between the spiritual and the material, to ordain hieratic leaders, and to channel individual interests into the interests of the nation. The role of government was to ensure the practice of individual morality. At the bottom of Carlyle's thought is the idea that complete human beings change institutions and not vice versa. With only an improvement of the 'moral-sense,' Plugson of Undershot can fulfill his destined role in the 'Ultimate genuine Aristocracy' (*Past* 193–4). The anti-capitalism of Carlyle and most of early nineteenth-century social consciousness is marked and profound, but it is in response to particular crises thought repairable through an awakened moral sense; it is not a condemnation of industrialization but of the fetishization of industry into an isolated activity independent of all 'cultural' activity and, in turn, into a business mentality. Still, Georg Lukács is right to argue that there are two Carlyles: one who denies it is 'possible to be human in bourgeois society,' who maintains that 'what morality we have takes the shape of Ambition' ('Signs' 243), and the other who asserts that 'man as he exists is opposed without mediation ... to this non-existence of the human' (*History* 190), who claims that people have never been guided by 'Profit and loss, for any visible, finite, object; but always feel some invisible and infinite one' ('Signs' 235).

Contrasting it to Dilettantism, Carlyle welcomes Mammonism, Plugson, '*any*thing we are in earnest about ... were it even work at making money' (*Past* 148). His attitude towards Mammonism explains why he could become so popular a figure in bourgeois England. Mammonism is attuned to nature insofar as it embraces work, needing only to augment its instincts with selflessness or a national consciousness in order to fall into 'the inflexible Course of Things' (*Past* 290). Because he argues that industry is compatible with universal law, Carlyle presses himself into thinking that it would not need to be regulated by human law. It is 'above all by their own shrewd sense [that the Captains of Industry will be] kept in perpetual communion with the fact of things, [and] will assuredly reform themselves' (*Past* 179). Still, at the same time that Carlyle would allow industry the freedom to balance morality and profit, he would introduce a 'law-precept' because it had failed to do just that (*Past* 208). But by making the Captains of Industry the heroes of *Past and Present*, 'virtually the Captains of the World' (*Past* 268), and relegating blame for the condition of England to a temporary moral failure, Carlyle ultimately confirms liberal free enterprise. In the long run, that is, those who control the industrial development of England will enroll themselves into the 'Course of Things.'

Labourers must also participate in this course but would be 'forced to find out the right path, and to walk thereon' (*Past* 211–12). Carlyle is modernizing and totalizing Calvinism: taking it out of a denominational context, resituating it on class lines, and rebuilding it as to vehemently shepherd a national flock. Labourers only lack the technology unique to the new 'greater Elect,' the Captains of Industry, to find their 'task set by God' and a 'definite field in which to work,' Weber's summation of the 'calling' (*Protestant* 79). Commentators from Froude onward have outlined Carlyle's lingering Calvinism, but the ideas of a predestined social function and a vanguard of industrial captains proceed from it, St Simonism, German Idealism, and, less abstractly, nationalism and the desire to defend the industrial grade.

It would be unfair to connect Carlyle to the political attitude of a Harriet Martineau, though she was a good friend of the Carlyles. Her *Illustrations of Political Economy* (1834) judges all social events from an economic viewpoint; Carlyle distorts the liberalist message to the working class. Martineau didactically tells the working class to resign itself to the economic laws of supply and demand, wages, rent, scarcity, and hardship. According to Malthusian logic, governmental or philanthropic interference in the market produces only additional suffering for all. She has what Karl Polanyi calls a 'mystical readiness to accept the social consequences of economic improvement, whatever they might be' (33). She thinks in terms of a visual rationality that considers productivity to be a real value in itself, sure to absolve any injudicious side effect. Her vantage point is not Carlyle's, but characterizing unions as parasites and emphasizing the benefits of working-class obedience to employers, or telling the working class to Work while telling the middle class to produce, are common features to both of their writings, as they are to the 'industrial novel' on the whole.

Carlyle's acceptance of industry entrains a capitulation to the central arguments of political economy, though he treats the yoking of industry to utilitarianism as accidental. The validation of their present-day industry and denigration of the business that surrounds it is a basic contradiction, rarely approached dialectically, that vitiates the thought of many nineteenth-century socially conscious writers. For Carlyle, utilitarianism, an economically centred, rationalized mode of social functioning, supplants the normative mode of society, albeit industrial. A proper society refuses to treat economic laws in isolation from value-giving imperatives. This means for Carlyle that the relations of production, economically centred relations, are necessarily reified by a value-giving society (or cosmos). His argument with economic reasoning is that it erases all paternalistic, feudalistic, and moralistic relations within inevitable social and economic hierarchies.

The first priority for Carlyle is always to refer to absolute laws, inevitable hierarchies, because the contest in the nineteenth century between capitalism and 'culture' was being waged in terms of final truths. 'Freedom,' as Kenneth Burke confirms, was appropriated by early capitalists as 'the "God" term' (God being wholly free) and used synonymously with humanism, free markets, industrialism, and capitalism (350–4). Carlyle is so adamant to banish laissez-faire that he correlates all principles of freedom to 'Atheism' and economic individualism. Thus, utilitarianism replaces an inflexible moral authority that sets universal interests as its goal with an egotistical 'freedom': the '"Liberty to die by starvation"' (*Past* 211). Political economy in any form circumscribes or rewrites relationships outside of any absolute standard and into (theoretically) variable relationships based on the relativity of exchange value, but it does not override the idea of 'final knowledge.' It claims that all relationships, all phenomena, have a functional basis or at least can be explained in terms of instrumentality (or a lack thereof). The unknown, the difficult, and the unsystematic become problems to be resolved through rationality, science, and the finalizability of knowledge. As political economy proceeds, vitalistic concepts of a superadded life force are explained away in 'positive' terms (positivism), and spiritual values, art, and the humanities are relegated (notwithstanding that they relegate themselves, at least in public declarations) to the useless, superficial end of a bourgeoisie–artist split.

Political economy asserts that the 'rational impulses' of *homo economicus* are the final laws governing human behaviour. A society ruled by the precepts of political economy is no less based on absolutism than Carlyle's ideal society, but it 'alters the base of domination by gradually replacing personal dependence ... with dependence on the "objective order of things"' (Marcuse, *One* 144) as established by the 'rational' economic laws of a free market. I quote Herbert Marcuse because his work shows how industrial rationality and social theory merge into a fixed and final 'instrumentalist horizon of thought.' It immediately follows that 'rationality is a political process' (*One* 165, 168). Carlyle might agree and add that sceptical rationalism also fosters solipsism, self-centredness, materialism, secularism, liberalism, the 'din of triumphant Law-logic' (*Past* 15), and contractionalist thought (or the 'rationalistic tendency to hypostatize society' [Rosenberg, *Seventh* 55]). Rationalism emphasizes a clear division between reason and intuition, the objective and subjective, thought and feeling, utility and art, economics and specializations, work and leisure, and so forth. Carlyle understands political economy as the discourse creating the division; that until its widespread acceptance practicality and imagination, facticity and intuition, and so on, were not oppositional terms but free to intertwine. The juxtaposition of rational and intuited (or traditional) knowledge is doubly a false opposition because rational knowledge is never purely objective (nor subjective); that is, it has its tradition (or ideology).

Rationalism is also at the root of liberalism, insofar as individuals are said to reach conclusions through independent inquiry (and no one using rationalism will vary in his or her conclusions). It rejects empiricism and the reliance on nature for knowledge: it assumes reason is an independent source of knowledge and the very substance of reality. Its activity is deliberately directed towards a premeditated end and governed only by that purpose. The rationalist-liberalist therefore rejects authority that is not its own, tradition, systems of faith, or any other potential impedimenta. It is easy to see why Carlyle would reject it wholesale.

But he does not. Carlyle adopts a discourse of rationality, even as he attempts noncontingent or final knowledge. In his pragmatic 'mode,' the concession to modern rationalism, to technical advances, and the vindication of economic logic is somewhat expected. But Carlyle also appeals to rationality as a property of the metaphysical. He does not rely on an argument of faith, insisting rather that eternal laws are knowable, if not to the empiricist then to the rationalist. Besides affirming the link between asceticism and rationalism (the irrationality of creatureliness, and so on), Carlyle attempts to wrest and rescue the language of rationality from the official dogma of political economy because it was the lingua franca of Enlightened Victorian epistemology. Even though rationality as the pursuit of ends is antithetical to his morality, all evaluations being equally nonrational, he adopts its logic, its language, and demands to see its evidence. That is, in order to show that rationality is not fixed forever by a stipulated convention as political economy would have it, Carlyle points to the 'Facts' of eternal law, the 'practical apex' of hero worship, the 'rational giant' embedded in the Gospel of Work, the 'irrational' aspects of Mammonism and the 'rational soul of it not yet awakened,' and the 'Book-Keeping' of the 'Mother-Destinies'; he claims that his philosophy 'is not Theology, [it] is Arithmetic' (*Past* 39, 171, 207, 190, 229). The examples are so numerous that it is highly unlikely he is merely or always using sarcasm to deflate the pretensions of utilitarianism.

Carlyle does not here use 'reason' in the Platonic sense of seeking truth for its own sake. Rather, he takes part in the industrialist's adoption of rationality, insisting that the 'immethodic,' 'waste' and 'Disorder,' be transformed into the 'methodic, regulated ... obedient and productive' (*Past* 201). That he surrenders the term 'freedom' but subverts political economy's presumption of a privileged affiliation to 'rationality' captures a distinct allegiance to industrial production. He also assumes the universe and its eternal laws are rational. His conquering heroes, national leaders (industrial captains and inventors), governing World-Urge, and vitalistic universal laws assert the rationality of history (despite his belief in its meshed thickness). Hegel's historiography also challenges the possibility of linear development while simultaneously maintaining 'the rational necessary course of the World-Spirit' (10). Both Hegel and Carlyle are trying to dissociate 'Progress through Process' or crude optimization from 'Becoming.' Yet in terms of later twentieth-century thought, Carlyle often seems to be plugging into the irrational. To argue 'might is right' because only a rational universe would give the 'right' strength enough to succeed, however, is not entirely different from a neoliberalist doctrine that merely substitutes 'market' for 'universe.' For Carlyle, political economy and laissez-faire are temporary glitches in industrial and universal rationality. He saw that modern rationality under utilitarianism meant the marginalization of ethics, irrationality, chaos: that what is is not right. But he does not dialectically confront industrialism and rationalism, despite the work rationalization that dominates industry.

Utilitarians, Benthamites, and Political Economists claim a special connection to rationality and its language. Carlyle refuses to surrender that discourse, resisting the rise of the economic and the assumption that *homo economicus rationale* could be the standard measure of human character. The word 'economy' originally described the management of households. As working relations became rationalized with the shift from feudal to contractional systems, 'economy' came to designate public, nonpersonal exchange systems. At that time, 'economy emerged as a distinct discourse that could become the foundation for other discourses' (Vanden Bossche 5) and, in turn, other non-economic practices (moral, social, and even psychological: capitalism creates its own distinct psychosis). Though Carlyle endorses Captains of Industry, he never accepts the prioritization and proliferation of the economic in its own terms, even if his organicist vision is ultimately based on economic domination. Adam Smith was the first in Britain to adopt and unfold the concept of laissez-faire from French Physiocrats. In *The Wealth of Nations* (1776), Smith represents the division of labour as a principle of social cooperation, whether it occurs on the factory floor or in the marketplace. Though Smith was a moralist, his economic theory posits a self-sufficient system: labour competes to sell itself and merchants compete to sell goods in a self-regulating system. Smith was not envisioning social or moral law. Liberals would later object to any external, social or political, interference in the realm of the economic. It was thought that such a self-enclosed, self-adjusting system would develop its own ethics and values (no one promoting laissez-faire economics ever argued that it was value-free) according to the laws of supply and demand, private property, and market rationality.

Yet shortly after the new economic science proposed that the market was best left isolated, utilitarian and Benthamite rationalism treated it as having greater moral and social reach. Political economy maintained its ethical laws need only be generated and organized from within. But there can be no ethical law with 'market rationality,' the idea that minimizing the influence of nonmarket factors in exchange systems will ensure the system operates with maximum rationality (efficiency in the pursuit of ends). Utilitarianism inferred this and then stepped in to say that if society wished to be rational, economic law must govern social and moral law. Carlyle also saw the thinness of the line between economic and social theory; his own social theory, after all, is based upon work relations. But Carlyle understood that utilitarianism was an *economized* moral theory. Every action is judged by its consequence and no action is ever right or wrong in itself. Consequences are judged by their ability to bring about the greatest happiness to the greatest number, a principle adopted from political economy's 'market rationality.' He understands that the 'counting-up and estimating [of] men's motives [as] ... adjustments of Profit and Loss, to guide them to their true advantage' is untenable because 'those same "motives" are so innumerable, and so variable in every individual, that no really useful conclusion can ever be drawn from their enumeration' ('Signs' 234).

The introduction of economics as a behavioural model meant more than freedom of contract, minimum taxation and tariff, and a rationale for individualism, competition, and acquisitiveness: more than the policies of the Manchester School. Economism is the idiom of maximizing.

In terms of production, industry is further rationalized into a linear, accountable process of cost and profit, input and output. The purely economic organization of manufacturing fragments the work process, reduces workers' control over it, and alters the meaning of work from being a dynamic process tied to non-economic factors (loyalties, intrinsic satisfactions) to revolving around the calculation of quantifiable, static objects (the workers, their output, and their pay). Economism reaches politics as a liberalism shored up by the paradoxically twin values of science and freedom. John Locke's marriage of protected property (land) and individuality is overwhelmingly confirmed. In the juridical realm, it means laws to protect economic action and property. But the deepest effect of economism occurs by way of a template for society, restricting consciousness, at the very least, to the contours of rationalist values. The cultural work of rationalism cannot be overestimated, though it is not as easily quantifiable as paid labour. Public character is expected to conform to the logic of an instrumentalist practice, the systematic pursuit of self-advantage that respects others only in competition or function. Instead of acting the same way economically as in normative relations, the assumption and expectation of pre-capitalist economics, *homo economicus* is presumed to rationalize as a matter of course. By way of its extension beyond economics, 'rationalism' (maximizing efficiency in the pursuit of maximized ends) formed Victorian 'reason' (common sense). In the still brilliant *Keywords* (1976), Williams shows that the Victorians carved out a new use for *rationality* to distinguish it completely and forever from *emotion* and *feeling* (252–6). Benthamism or utilitarianism was only the most pronounced arrangement of economics circulating as a widespread social philosophy.

The advocates of an economic culture did not assume, however, that all society was rational. Economics was a first-order principle, but not all activity was categorized under purposeful logic and maximized utility. Instead, economic thought reinforced a system of oppositions under a rubric of rationalisms and nonrationalisms. Under the aegis of economism, divisions were hardened between:

cognition/feeling	business/friendship	public/private
objective/subjective	logic/spirit	active/passive
things/words	science/art	hard/soft
numbers/words	Science/Humanities	male/female
labour/Work	applied science/ideas	fact/opinion
paid time/free time	inventions/abstractions	model/story

The immediate consequence of dividing the world into disjunctive, either/or indices is that it restricts any interaction between the concepts (such as friendly business). Limiting the imagination to strict alternatives also hypostatizes both ends of the opposition. The result is the strict division of 'sides' – a masculine side and a feminine side – which only ratifies nonvariable, nondialectical constructions of thought. Society emerges as being composed of static types, even if the individual subject performs more than one role. To make final the separation between rationalist and nonrationalist constructs is also to place a premium on the former. This is evidenced in part by the emotional clampdown for which the Victorian period is uniquely famed. Carlyle was not guided by economism (except in reaction to it), and though affected by a binary ideology he disturbs the dominant discourse of rationality. Victorian novelists after him primarily expressed their anti-rationalism by introducing the ideology of organic unity, of *only connect*, into their narratives, as if intuiting the divided sides of Carlyle's frame of mind. However, as with Carlyle's treatment of the ideal and the real, that representation of connection only undermines inherently dialectical conflicts. Efforts to mediate the industrialist's idea of rational economic relations, to connect business and *caritas*, are vitiated, sentimentalized, or deliberately withdrawn as the place of emotion is represented as perfecting the economic-as-is, not countering it.

Speaking on the 'rational actor' theory and its loudest defenders, Bourdieu argues that

> they are able to give the appearance of accounting for rational conduct ... but in fact, by refusing to recognize any other way of founding it in reason than by giving reason as its foundation, they simply introduce a being of reason, an ought-to-be, as a *vis dormativa*, in the form of an agent all of whose practices have reason as their principle. This is because, by definition, by the simple fact of accepting the idea of an economic subject who is economically unconditioned – especially in his preferences – they exclude inquiry into the economic and social conditions of economic dispositions that the sanctions of a particular state of a particular economy designate as more or less reasonable (rather than rational) depending on their degree of adjustment to its objective demands. (*Logic* 47)

The construction of *homo economicus*, man as maximalist, as M.H. Dobb pointed out in 1937, is a 'description of how the system worked *ipso facto* [which] became a presumption as to how it should be allowed to work'

(49). By evolving *homo economicus* into dominance and marginalizing nonrationalized behaviour, nineteenth-century economism restricted the imaginative order. It is that restriction which, by and large, Victorian writers conversant with Carlyle challenge. But not all writers who disagree with the description of how the system works (the definition of man as a self-interested maximalist) disagree that the system should be allowed to work that way, at least intermittently. The fine, untrodden line between the denial of rationalism's content and effects and the defence of its form and activities is a permutation of the Carlylean separation of Work and labour that locates a transcendental order in work.

The anti-utilitarian literature of the Victorian period also continues to assign a special knowledge of Work to the working class and reserve the world of labour and economic negotiation for itself, the middle class. Following Carlyle, it observes two Gospels of Work: a middle-class Gospel of ascendancy through thrift, perseverance, and effort (Carlyle's obstinacy) and a working-class Gospel of endurance (Carlyle's subordination). But it also separates representations of middle-class moral Work, and its attending values, from the certification of that same class' own unique access to economic acumen and its business or industrial imperatives. Though purely economic acts are forcedly converted into social acts, take place 'off-stage,' or are rendered unrecognizable by the refusal to acknowledge their underlying properties, such strategies of concealment are always accompanied by the 'understanding' that economic practices are being effectively managed. Not only is the middle-class Gospel of Work sheltered from assumptions that were shaped by the concrete indices of the economic, but Work is also kept removed from a set of aspirations that directly sanction and enforce the economic.

Still, when evaluating Victorian approaches to work it is important to historicize the challenge faced by advocates of the non-economic imperatives of Work in an age of utility and economism. The critique of economism based on the assumption that Work provides intrinsic and social benefits was itself critiqued. The procrustean Ure argued on the behalf of industrialists that the 'most perfect manufacture is that which dispenses entirely with manual labour' (1). Though the nature of job satisfaction is dynamic and conditional, the strategy from Carlyle to Orwell when facing economism is to locate a work ethic beyond self-interested, paid labour: to rework it as psychologically and socially meaningful – not the same reaction they have when facing economics. Even if the most important question of who owned the profits of work was not always properly raised until Morris, the intransitive imperative to Work emerged from the anti-utilitarian tradition in order to prevent energy and self-interest from becoming synonymous. In the representation of Work as a therapy for introspective anxiety or neurasthenia (though the question of what is worth doing would cause its own anxiety) is a refusal to reduce work to its disfigured meaning in political economy. Understandably, the working classes who need to work hardest in order to make ends meet never embraced this abstraction (Burnett 19), even if – according to Carlyle and the ensuing, mostly liberal, faction – they are the last to bow down to the habits of economic reasoning.

Reviewing Carlyle in 1855, George Eliot noted that there had scarcely been a book written in a generation that he had not influenced in one way or another (213–14). After Carlyle – that is, after *Past and Present* and in step with *Past and Present* – the reaction to economism, to a definition of the world as a place of commodification and competition, was either 'generally reactionary and conservative,' as Lukács shows, or acquiescing to economic individualism, as Ian Watt shows – or perhaps both. Lukács and Watt emphasize class interests. Lukács looks at the historical novel in order to identify the reaction against moneyed relations. The awakened consciousness of capitalism as a 'historical era,' as a framework for society, was answered by an 'ideology of immobility' (*Historical* 24). Thus, for example, Carlyle's and Ruskin's fascination with the Middle Ages and rejection of democracy. Watt looks at the realist novel as a literary form developed for and by the bourgeoisie to consolidate their interests by favourably representing hard work, thrift, and 'the idea of every individual's intrinsic independence' (*Rise* 60). Gone are the larger-than-life heroes with larger-than-life inheritances; in are the adventures of autonomous development (financial, social, familial, total). *Robinson Crusoe* (1719) is the classic example, but the sheer literary output in the nineteenth century implies that success can be gained through individual effort and has something to do with bulk, with production. The Triple Decker novel suggests that production in itself was highly valued. Though the size of the most thoughtful novels may imply a rejection of utility, of 'getting to the point,' the reader was not to waste time reading them, but to learn the lessons of effort, perseverance, and Work. Williams, whose argument in *Culture and Society* has affinities to Lukács, and Walter Houghton, whose *The Victorian Frame of Mind* (1957) is closer to Watt, would agree that the responses to the new economic world are entangled, though neither suggest that the faraway moralism implicit in the reactionary position or the concrete economic logic surfacing in the bourgeoisie approach are dialectically opposed to each other. Both

Williams and Houghton emphasize the 'contradictory elements' (Williams, *Culture* 20) of the era. Houghton shows conflicting attitudes by drawing up conflicting categories of thought, for example, 'optimism' and 'anxiety.' Carlyle bounces between an aristocratic desire to freeze social relations in rigid hierarchies and the typically middle-class position that self-made wealth signifies goodness. Dickens first ends *Dombey and Son* (1848) by making a fine statement against ambition. Then, in a sort of coda, the industrious Walter Gay quickly rises into Mr Dombey's world of finance. Conservative and liberal values constantly intersect in the Victorian period – an intersection that Carlyle and later Orwell epitomize.

Charles Dickens

Dickens's *The Chimes* (1844) directly responds to economism, specifically a June 1844 review of *A Christmas Carol* (1843) in *The Westminster Review*. The critic asked, 'Who went without turkey and punch in order that Bob Cratchit might get them – for, unless there were turkeys and punch in surplus, someone must go without' (quoted in Russell, *Novelist* 13–14). In *The Chimes*, Mr Filer reprimands Trotty Veck for eating tripe, 'the least economical ... article of consumption,' by saying, 'You snatch your tripe ... out of the mouths of widows and orphans' (100, 101). In concert, the Benthamite Filer, the unnamed conservative (who repeats that the 'good old times' were vastly superior to anything 'now-a-days'), and Alderman Cute (who would jail the suicidal and dispossessed) pessimistically allot every action to a value and seek a predictable regularity in behaviour. Filer's Gradgrindery, his facts and Malthusian logic, most obviously exemplifies the genre of hard, utilitarian rationalism. But nearly every righteous, rigid, all-knowing would-be-disciplinarian in Dickens's worlds borrows something from the rationalism of the age.

In contrast to characters claiming systematic knowledge are self-effacing doers such as Little Dorrit and Esther Summerson. Will Fern and Stephen Blackpool are Carlylean workers trying to realize themselves against, respectively, Do-Nothingism and Mammonism: ultimately against societies built upon utilitarian rationalism. But by juxtaposing Joseph Bowley's false Carlylese, his call to 'feel the Dignity of Labour' and 'exercise your self-denial' (*Chimes* 111), with Will Fern's readiness and gratitude for genuine paternalism, Dickens gestures that it is only the lack of sincerity in work relations that precludes worker 'realization' and warrants scrutiny. He parodies what at other times he promotes (the Dignity of Labour and exercising of self-denial) because his invective is almost uniformly directed at self-absorbed and delusional manipulations of evidently fine systems. Dickens's insistence on 'a change of spirit rather than a change of structure' (Orwell, *CEJL* 1: 427), what Orwell and so many others find objectionable, expresses a liberal nostalgia for a 'moral economy,' albeit now capitalist. The line between liberalism and conservatism is here quite thin. Shaw points out that Dickens 'adopts the idealized Toryism of Carlyle and Ruskin, in which the aristocracy are the masters and superiors of the people' ('Introduction' 338). In its treatment of the working classes and the long-established function they are to have in the new order of things, the anti-utilitarian tradition is as conservative and reactionary as it is liberal and bourgeois.

Dickens, in other words, does not turn a blind eye to the propagation of Economic Man, but his ideal role for the working class, to Work, is not the same role that reformers/leaders are to have, which is to control the conditions of labour. Shaw continues to observe that 'Nowhere does he appeal to the working classes to take their fate into their own hands and try the democratic plan' ('Hard' 338). His poor and working class are only saddened by the abrogation of paternalist economics, not angered by the loss of artisanal independence. In *Hard Times* (1854), a novel dedicated to Thomas Carlyle, it is a variation of the working class, the circus folk unaffected by the world of labour, who know about, who live, who have mastered, and who can impart the value of nonrationalism. The circus members are not represented as 'working class' by the standards of labour. They are not seen to earn wages or do not make a living in industrial conditions, but they are working class insofar as they belong to a class. Sharing the carnivalesque camaraderie that we will see in Orwell's bistro workers, and the simple, unassuming, idiosyncratic, carefree attitude of all Orwell's workers, they have special insights into the world of nonrational Work. Again, that knowledge of Work, that working-class endowment of an anti-utilitarian consciousness, acts as if to preclude an economic consciousness. When the middle class demonstrates its anti-utilitarianism, it does not forgo economic knowledge or activity – it just compartmentalizes them.

From within the circus tent, economism, the view that 'the whole social system is a question of self-interest' (218), appears as completely unnatural, an insufficient summary of human vitality, and an attempt to dull the moral imagination. Igor Webb, Himmelfarb, and many, many others criticize Dickens for making the circus literally and figuratively peripheral to the factory, making play and work or fancy and fact unrelated items (Webb 96; Himmelfarb 477). The structure and central metaphor of the book, however, is somewhat misleading. If the failing of Coketown is an all-intrusive utilitarianism, Dickens is probably not suggesting that spontaneity has its time and place. Rather, he represents play as a de-homogenizing supplement to rationalist organizations and thought. In any case, Sleary's circus shows up on 'the neutral ground upon the outskirts of town, which was neither town nor country' (8), and it is Coketown's rationalists who insist on severing it from their turf. Gradgrind tells Sissy that if she comes with him, 'it is understood that you communicate no more with any of your friends who are here present' (29). Dickens's comment that Mr Gradgrind only 'over-does' 'reason,' that 'by dint of his going his way and my going mine, we shall meet at last at some halfway house' (*Letters* 354), is not backsliding. As in *Wuthering Heights* (1847) before it and *Howards End* (1910) after it, there is a sense in *Hard Times* that the circus and the Utilitarians need *only connect* in order to facilitate real social restructuring. As it is overrun with rationalist thought, Coketown needs to join with circus thought.

The connection between the 'wisdom of the Heart' and the 'wisdom of the Head,' however, which Gradgrind comes to see as the source of true value (170), is never written in the terms of a potential conflict. Though *caritas* and efficiency are set up as hard alternatives to each other – 'the Good Samaritan was a Bad Economist' – the conflation of moral decency and pragmatic expediency would apparently proceed without difficulty. Moral and pragmatic activities are effectively compartmentalized. The values associated with Sissy Jupe are not in the end in conflict with or antithetical to Gradgrindery, but rather amenable to it and vice versa. The easy unity of an oppositional set of values that do not fully cohere, as with the nonconflict between Work and labour, gives way to or is symptomatic of a self-sufficient moralism, the individual breaking free of the all-encompassing system written as if to fully construct the individual. Even in *Hard Times*, a novel that perhaps more than any other in Dickens's canon demonstrates the effects of systems and isms on subjectivity, the galvanizing of the final morality of man is simply a matter of awakening to instinct and holding the once-ubiquitous systems, systemization itself, in abeyance. Ultimately, this is what *Hard Times* does.

Dickens also entreats for compromise when regarding political economy, finding it to be 'a mere skeleton unless it has a little human covering and filling out' ('On Strike' 381). In *Dombey and Son*, a story treating finance as *Hard Times* treats industry, Mr Dombey is to be forgiven for his monomania because 'vices are sometimes only virtues carried to excess' (914). Industry is not censured in *Hard Times,* only the seepage of work rationalization into social relations (what Lukács calls reification) and the repulsive aesthetic residue of production. Stephen's problems arise from his wife and his union, not his job. By ignoring the process of industrial production in his most industrial novel, Dickens, very much in step with Carlyle, argues the nonrelationship between industrial (rationalized) work and the widespread instrumentalizing or rationalizing of human relations that he despises. Having fallen into the pit, when Stephen does address working conditions, not his own but mining conditions, he downplays any potential conflict between morality and economy that would arise by pointing his finger at rationalist industry. He had read

> as onny one might read, fro' the men that works in pits, in which they ha' pray'n and pray'n the lawmakers for Christ's sake not to let their work be murder to 'em, but to spare 'em for th' wives and children that they loves as well as gentlefolk loves theirs. When it were in work, it killed wi'out need; when 'tis let alone, it kills wi'out need. See how we die an' no need, one way an' another – in a muddle – every day. (207)

Amazingly, for someone like Bounderby is responsible for and rich because of the mine, he says his piece 'without any anger against any one. Merely as the truth' (207). Even Dickens's 'pragmatism' tends to or attempts to devoid itself of political content.

In *Bleak House* (1852–3), it seems as if Dickens acknowledges that by changing the social, political, and economic relations in which work is embedded, the meanings surrounding it also change. Esther's self-prescribed palliative of becoming 'so dreadfully industrious that [she] would leave [herself] not a moment's leisure to be low-spirited,' loses its universal application if Mr Vholes is also to be found, as he says, always with a 'shoulder to the wheel' (288, 611). In fact, Uriah Heep, Mr Dombey, and Mr Veneering are as industrious as David Copperfield, Walter Gay, and Lizzie Hexam. Dickens endorses the need to work for work's sake but also shows a growing doubt about its universal application (though never because the call to work is redundant for the working class or because it mobilizes that class to work for the interests of the capitalist class). At other points, in fact most of the time, Dickens simply divides Work from any problematical context. In *Bleak House,* Dickens can only 'resolve' the conflict between self-serving and self-denying work ethics by removing Esther and Allan from competitive London and insisting on the importance of moral, individual change. The newlyweds move to pastoral Yorkshire, where there is the prospect of nothing but a 'great amount of work and a small amount of pay' (873), an integrated community, a 'family romance,' and contentment (certainly not social mobility). For Esther and Allan to fully engage themselves in a community and gain non-economic, psychologically stabilizing benefits from Work, they must disengage themselves from the greater part of society and go where there will be little need for psychological stabilizers. Luckily for them, they apparently do not need to worry about earning a living.

In counteracting utilitarian thought, the tendency of Victorian literature is to subordinate determinism to character, setting the dynamics and idiosyncrasies of the underdog protagonist and his or her allies against the utilitarian image of a guiding self-interest. Character, the moral individual, remains largely impervious to circumstance, to external determinations. Introducing *Dombey and Son*, Williams speaks of Dickens's awakening to the agency a general condition, society, can have over character, even if vice is sometimes reducible to 'faults of the soul' ('Introduction' 16). But in *Dombey and Son*, as in *Mary Barton* (1848) or *Sybil* (1845), where class position creates vice (mostly lower class for Gaskell, lower and middle for Disraeli, and upper for Dickens), vice *is* the susceptibility to socialization. Succumbing to the material base of society is a sign of weakness, a misplaced work ethic, or a manifestation of a 'natural' correspondence between inner character and outer environment. This is certainly not always the case. In *Bleak House*, the sympathetic Phil Squod has been physically deformed by capitalism, by a life of labour. But even in this example, if labour creates an identity, the apparatus to identify character (physiognomy) is nonetheless upheld. Dickens, for one, does not think in terms of definitive external determinations.

Both Williams and Himmelfarb accuse Orwell of misreading Dickens because in 'Charles Dickens' (1939) he finds that individual moral deficiency is *always* Dickens's root of conflict (Williams, *English Novel* 49; Himmelfarb 487). But Orwell is not far off the mark, especially as he acknowledges Dickens's developing consciousness of the 'helplessness of well-meaning individuals in a corrupt society' (*CEJL* 1: 418). The peculiarity of Orwell's essay is that Orwell wrote it. Orwell, as I will later show, defensively represents idiosyncratic, moral individuals, that is, when absorbed in a discourse of Work. Woodcock famously critiques Orwell as Orwell critiques Dickens in his essay on him:

> In one of his essays there is a portrait of Dickens which might not inappropriately be applied to Orwell himself. 'He is laughing, with a touch of anger

in his laughter, but no triumph, no malignity. It is the face of a man who is always fighting against something, but who fights in the open and is not frightened, the face of a man who is *generously angry* – in other words, of a nineteenth-century liberal, a free intelligence – a type hated with equal hatred by all the smelly little orthodoxies which are now contending for our soul.' The open fighting, the generous anger, the freedom of intelligence, are all characteristics of Orwell's own writing. And that very failure to penetrate to the fundamental causes of social evils, to present a consistent moral and social criticism of the society in which they lived, which characterized the nineteenth-century liberals, has become Orwell's own main limitation. ('Liberal' 246)

Orwell himself, at a moment when he is distanced from a Work discourse, makes these very same standard criticisms of liberalism, of Dickens the liberal.

The main fault in Orwell's essay lies in the claim that Dickens 'has no idea of *work*' (*CEJL* 1: 445). In *Hard Times* Dickens says the English people are as 'hard-worked' as any in the world (48). Saying that they are the 'hardest working' would be defining the English people from the bourgeoisie point of view, repeating its central line of defence (interestingly, this is how Carlyle defines the English people [*Past* 159–66]). Though there may be few industrial proletarians in Dickens's novels, paid and unpaid work never stops. The Mayhewian peculiarity of the work, from doll-making to recovering dead bodies, shows a rare cognizance of urban diversity. Shaw said it better than Orwell in his introduction to *Hard Times*:

> Dickens knew certain classes of working folk very well: domestic servants, village artisans, and employees of petty tradesmen, for example. But of the segregated factory populations of our purely industrial towns he knew no more than an observant professional man can pick up on a flying visit to Manchester. (338)

Orwell also says that Dickens's characters dream of and are rewarded with idleness. Idleness in Dickens (as with Carlyle), say for Richard Carstone, is an aberration, a sickness. Orwell, however, is clearing ground to indict bourgeois culture of concealing proletariat labour. A culture excelling in a free market economy would use any means at its disposal to obscure the labour that provides for modern comforts and opportunities but does not secure proportional benefits for the workers. But

Orwell cannot find *any* 'work' whatsoever in Dickens, not even in the busyness of the heroes. When keeping with pragmatic definitions, when observing rather than attempting to participate in working-class culture, work for Orwell involves making money and answering necessity. In any case, only physical or materially based work can be work; only the proletariat works. For Dickens, work reflects character and is justifiable only if it is attuned to a moral completeness. Those who do not work solely for financial and social ascendancy are awarded with ascendancy. That kind of disinterested work is easier put off-stage. In *David Copperfield* (1849–50), David and Uriah pursue similar ends, but David's story is of personal growth whereas Uriah's is of the explicit and reckless pursuit of self-interested gain. Orwell is basically right, just as Dickens does not criticize society 'as a system,' the value of work (though Dickens has a prejudice against certain occupations – lawyers, bureaucrats) depends upon the individual's approach to it.

Despite his belief that isolated acts of goodness adequately compensate for the world capitalism creates, Dickens's art works through demonstrating symbiotic social interconnections. *Bleak House* especially shows the need to recognize common human bonds between disparate social groups; connections impose themselves between characters at any rate through disease and plot entanglements. The idea of 'only connect' reaches back to Carlyle's description of the Irish widow in *Past and Present* and ultimately to a version of his organicism. Carlyle recalls William Alison describing a Scottish widow, 'her husband having died in one of the Lanes of Edinburgh.' (Carlyle himself had to pass through similar lanes as a university student.) She is ignored and unaided by society. But catching typhus fever, she infects and leads to the death of seventeen others. Carlyle uses the story to demonstrate not only a common humanity and its relentless bonds but also, from a rather sardonically pitched economic perspective, that it would have been more cost-effective to have assisted the woman before she infected others. But he is mainly interested in explicating the consequences when 'all government of the Poor by the Rich has long ago been given over to Supply-and-demand, Laissez-faire and such like' (151). The notion of the social whole, of the advantaged individual's responsibility for the poor, of the implacable nature of business left strictly to its own interests, of 'only connect,' whether in Dickens or Gaskell, continues not only Carlyle's profound compassion for the dispossessed but also his conservative faith that benevolent individuals billow out of benevolent class structures.

Dickens writes to deliver the woven social fabric. But he also writes for the individual underdog and against unionism, equating unionism and utilitarianism as equally dangerous to human relationships. He correlates rationalist economics and amorality but also confirms that industrial interests are collected, national interests: that the 'interests' of masters, men, and the entire nation 'must be understood as identical' ('On Strike' 381). He treats industry, commerce, and ambition ambiguously, as either vulgar or noble depending on the motivation, the degree of self-interest or goodwill behind the activity. He fashions a social ethic which discourages egotism so that it is compatible with work ethics, career ethics, and progress ethics, all of which quietly elevate individuals into prosperity. Myopic rational*ism* and industrial*ism* are censured but the alternative validation of traditional morality stays clear of the imperative to produce. ('Produce! Produce! Were it but the pitifullest infinitesimal fraction of a Product, produce it in God's name!' says Professor Teufelsdröckh [*Sartor* 149].) Discourses of Work (or anti-utilitarianism) and labour are altered in order to keep moral issues removed from the world of industry, the world that enabled the ascendancy of the middle class. Without a hard division between economic and 'human' values, labour and the imaginative (decontextualized) realm of Work, the ensuing dialectics would topple the appeal to both pragmatic and moral action.

Elizabeth Gaskell

The readiness to see a nonaffinity between business, the rationalization of human relations, and industrial production, the rationalization of work, testifies not only to a Carlylean crack between moral and pragmatic investigation, a cleavage in responses to alternate pressures of morality and money, but also to a delight in modern inventions. Alternately, the treatment of work as Work, as something other than the basis of the economic, something removed from business, whether it be representations of the middle-class 'Protestant work ethic' or a supposed working-class Gospel, seeks to render invisible the economic practices that increase the wealth and monetary ability of the nonworking class. The classic formula for the Victorian novel that involved itself with the 'Condition of England question' recognizes business as an anti-social activity per se, but accepts that the social effects of industry depend upon the state of the individual factory. Industry itself was exonerated and removed from the reproduction of human relationships and character. It is not the industrial mode or the subsequent relations of production that lead to John Barton's 'monsterish' brutality, for example, but ultimately a cognitive 'misunderstanding.' In Gaskell's *Mary Barton*, the refusal of unions to accept and a 'want of inclination' of capitalists (Mr Carson) to demonstrate the parallel interests between the classes, or the law of supply and demand, suffice to explain the antagonism between employee and employer, notwithstanding the understood correlation between vice and sedition thought to be surrounding the lower classes. The failure lies in not teaching the laws of political economy (which is precisely Gaskell's project, despite her claim in the 'Preface' not to know those laws). The failure to communicate circles back to a lack of understanding and brotherliness. It is also important to note that John Barton has a first-rate attitude towards Work but becomes disoriented and violent when he attempts to approach issues surrounding his own labour. When Carlyle praised the book in 1848, initiating a friendship between Gaskell and the Carlyles, he took care to emphasize that writers need to work on their novels with the same singleness of intention as the best Workers they represent work at their tasks (*Letters* 154–5). Everyone has a job to do and a role to play.

But from dislocating class issues it does not follow that Gaskell was insensitive to the problems of industry. In *North and South* (1855), Thornton awakes to the need for employers to transcend the cash nexus, but also concedes that strikes are an inherent feature of industrialism. In *Cranford* (1853), Gaskell is entirely against political economy, striking out at its principles of maximization and self-interest. Economic relations in the community of females, or of 'female principles,' run on mutual respect, moderate ambition, and the pursuit of *modest* happiness ('satisficing'). Financial exchanges defy the laws of political economy, undermining Smith's famous definition of society. Smith wrote: 'It is not from the benevolence of the butcher, the brewer, or the baker that we expect our dinner, but from their regard to their own interest. We address ourselves, not to their humanity but to their self-love' (*Wealth* 26–7). Miss Matty's teashop provides subsistence and satisfaction, despite the fact that she gives away goods and refuses to compete with Mr Johnson (who then sends her clients). In light of the trust she shows the coal men by not weighing their deliveries, they give her excess amounts. (Mary's constantly suspicious father is skimmed of a thousand pounds per year.) Men, but specifically political economists, have been removed from Gaskell's utopia. Still, it is a utopia, and the practical problems surrounding the rationalization of work that Gaskell tackles in *North and South* remain as unrepresentable as the business that undoubtedly surrounds Sleary's circus. The finality of the moral act is not represented as if in conflict with the logic of pragmatism, or with the economic society in general, but beside it, removed from it, or beyond it.

Gaskell's place in the history of cultural reactions to economism, her use of the 'only connect' theme in *North and South*, is as close to Carlyle as it is to J.S. Mill. Gaskell's plea to marry emotional to industrial (and business) values in some ways dramatizes Mill's critique of Bentham, which would marry Coleridge to Bentham. Eagleton reads Mill 'mechanistically harnessing Coleridge to Bentham' as one of the 'palpable instances' of the 'Culture and Society tradition,' containing a Romantic, humanist, and 'idealist critique of bourgeois social relations, coupled with a consecration of the rights of capital' (*Criticism* 103, 102). Eagleton is largely right, though Mill's desire to introduce some nonrationalism into Benthamism is much more emotionally wrenching than mechanistic. Mill's tempering of his family's entire legacy was – though not simply – a rebellion against his own childhood education. It is interesting that he called Bentham 'essentially a boy,' as if intersecting with the values surrounding nonrationalism, such as play, made Mill a grown-up ('Bentham' 125).

But Mill primarily apologizes for utilitarianism, whereas Gaskell, like Carlyle, primarily backs industry, even though such defences turn out to be nearly identical. In *North and South*, industrialists 'defy the old limits of possibility.' The text, subsequently, attempts to squeeze out some excitement for those 'anticipated triumphs over all inanimate matter,' though these are not its most memorable moments (163–4). But Gaskell, however, wanted to inject some pre-industrial values into the organization of society as a site for driving, instrumentalizing individualism. Margaret's values, essentially rural and feminine, temper and humanize Thornton's business values: the connection leads him to shed his maximizing psyche. A shot of old-world *caritas* disencumbers rationalized work from its counterpart, political economy. In *Mary Barton*, the connection Gaskell sets out to affirm is between master and worker, between classes. It is not successful, ending less in reconciliation or a viable social network than in a massive exodus. Though one must recognize that industrialists such as W.D. Greg, spokesman for mill owners in Manchester and family friend of the Gaskells, criticized Gaskell for misrepresenting his class as inhuman and that Gaskell's criticisms of industrialism were not run-of-the-mill, arguments about the separation of the classes are raised only to be denied. The gap between 'master and man' turns out to be 'not really the case ... [but only] what the workman feels and thinks' (24). Connection, in other words, is any display of brotherliness precluding working-class unrest.

In *North and South*, the 'only connect' theme takes the form of uniting not only people (classes), but also values. Oxford men are to interact with practical men, age is to meet youth, duty is to moderate defiance, industry to coincide with agriculture, labour to work with capital, and the old to convene with the new. In its most Carlylean moment, *North and South* also maintains that the values of the past can mesh with 'the next day's duty' (335). But Gaskell moves beyond Carlyle insofar as the servants she represents are to have agency in the family model of nationhood. Carlyle's monks and in fact all his workers are defined by their readiness to submit to authority. The ending of Gaskell's novel even goes so far as to suggest that the members of the English family might challenge roles preset for them. If Thornton is to have a place in a kitchen then either he has an awakened maternal instinct or, more radically, the text is arguing that someone like Margaret might have a place in management. Moreover, the marriage of Margaret and Thornton is ultimately an uneasy one, suggesting that continued dialectical tension between opposites is necessary for both social and personal growth. But the union of 'opposites' and the new family model for Englishness always depend upon the initial goodness and combinability of the subjects. Extremes are categorically undermined. The past needs an injection of the present to escape superstitious and lethargic backwardness; the industrial present needs men who, like Thornton, are predisposed to 'cultural' values. The novel, accordingly, is also exceedingly fastidious about the limits of defiance: though we may celebrate Margaret's rebelliousness, we are not to accept defiance as an idea (Frederick's mutiny, for example). Finally, political economy may be understood to prevent Masters and men from ever eliminating their conflicts of interest, but the *social* conflict is written as a failure to 'explain our reasons' (117), a repairable glitch in the paternalist (and maternal) order. Again and again, connection can take place only if and when an initial process of moderation takes place, if and when conflict is already worked out.

The ideology of 'only connect' in Gaskell as in Dickens includes a denial that conflict need exist between classes or between values (morality and money). It denies the basis for conflict between classes and between values. It reenacts the separation of Work and labour by denying, concealing, and simply bypassing the inherent tension between antirationalisms (the past, play, etc.) and the rationalist order (industry, political economy, etc.). The 'only connect' theme also substitutes for

Carlylean paternalism by insisting on the potential for social harmony given the absence of an inherent conflict. Benjamin Disraeli, a conservative, also represents fundamental divisions, especially class divisions, only to deny them. Moderate reform, good will, and identifying the few irresponsible agitators of collective action obviate structural questions about the ownership of industry. In *Sybil*, Disraeli attempts to show that the use of a phrase such as 'the two nations' is indicative of the kind of inflated and dangerous rhetoric that adolescent malcontents such as Dandy Mick or Devilsdust, or dangerous radicals, Chartists, and Owenists such as Stephen Morley, misuse. Even though Egremont recognizes the aristocracy's responsibility to the lower classes, Disraeli ultimately reveals a lack of commitment to the idea of class connection. In a Fieldingesque, providential discovery of birth, the marriage between the rich Egremont and poor Sybil, of course, turns out to be between two nobles. The main difference between their union and that between Thornton and Margaret promised at the end of *North and South* is that Gaskell implies that a marriage of contraries will not ease the ideological or financial (and sexual) tension between the couple, just as she recognizes that labour unions are part of industry and by nature at odds with employers. But as Margaret is practical from the novel's opening and Thornton is already 'cultural' (disinterestedly interested in being tutored in the Classics by Mr Hale), their state of opposition is as nondialectical as Egremont and Sybil's.

Though some are dandies who have forgotten their obligations to the workers, Disraeli's patricians are historically alive to the responsibilities attending their privileges (which, as Marx said, pace Gaskell, the middle class are not). Trafford, a displaced aristocrat with 'gentle blood in his veins,' knows his social duties, keeping 'other ties than the payment and receipt of wages' (*Sybil* 179). For the most part, however, in the Victorian period, it is the liberal middle class, the Gaskells and Geraldine Jewsburys, who utilize the Carlylean image of the good industrialist, making the case for its social ascent. The claim of a triumphant morality in the midst of institutionalized exploitation (and invocations to Work hard, obey the law, and respect private property in the name of common interests) led Marx, a very moral philosopher, to dismiss all 'morality' (Norman 146).

Jewsbury, a good friend of the Carlyles and especially intimate with Jane Carlyle, resembles Gaskell in being a liberal quick to narrativize Carlyle's Captains of Industry. As with Carlyle and Gaskell, the beneficent industrialist, the capitalist as social reformer, however, is often juxtaposed with malevolent employers, suggesting the way employers might be and not the way they always are. In *Marian Withers* (1851), John Withers's and Mr Wilcox's model factories contrast with Higgenbottom's unsafe workplace. Still, readers do not see the bad factory: only the benign ones are described. Emphasis is placed on the harmony between worker and machine, on individual morality, and on the treachery of unions and aristocracies. Jewsbury's novel is amazing for its sanitized representation of Manchester, 1825. The central conflict, outside of the romance, involves the morality of the parvenu – if adopting upper-class taste is the only way to have the middle class understand 'anti-utilitarianism,' that possessing wealth is not an end in itself. Jewsbury is here providing a model for Gaskell's Thornton. John Withers does not have any aspirations toward gentility, but neither is he a counterfeit Captain of Industry interested in get-rich-quick speculation. He spends his capital on perfecting machinery, on pursuing economic development, not on displaying his personal wealth. Like Thornton he is unaccountably predestined to be 'Cultured' in a world bereft of predestination and Culture.

Withers is a self-made man whose Smilesian 'spirit of self-help' is 'at the bottom of all success' (2: 23). He refuses to beg even when homeless and starving. The test of personal value, a labour theory of value, is passed or failed in terms of action, not inheritance. Instead of birth, economic activity defines the social spectrum, defines society. But in the Victorian period of anti-utilitarianism, the case of the autonomously developed selfhood – overcoming circumstance to achieve success through hard work, self-control, ambition, and persistence – is accompanied by non-economic developments that balance (not dialectically confront) a conscious rationalism with a sense of communal and familial duty, in effect isolating them from each other.

When profit, money, and mobility are blended with decency as the rationalizing grounds for action, when character is the centre of meaning, and when moral praise is earned in accordance with success, poverty itself becomes suspect. Such is clearly not the intention of Jewsbury, Dickens, or Gaskell when they depict self-made men (Withers, Rouncewell, or Thornton). Nor is poor-bashing a deliberate part of the *bildungsroman* or novels in which underdog orphans without inherited resources rise to successfully restart a family. But the implication of individual economic responsibility is unavoidable. Failure becomes the great taboo – a sign of idleness, carelessness, or profligacy. In *North and South*, Thornton succeeds by following 'the habits of life which taught [him] to despise indulgences.' Those who do not succeed must answer to 'the natural punishment of dishonestly-enjoyed pleasure' (85).

Apart from the profligate, the working-class poor appear as either passive victims, suggesting the need for political reform, or dangerous free agents (Devilsdust, Barton) if they fight for those reforms themselves or simply adopt a discourse of labour. The self-made man, on the other hand, is active and sensible; he has his middle-class attributes, such as perseverance and honesty, before he ascends. Thornton is as if born into the wrong class, made before he made himself. The image of the good, self-made man with a higher purpose validates the utilitarian principle of happiness by showing that in pursuing self-interest, happiness and goodness accrues. In other words, the convention of the self-made man does little to separate the anti-utilitarian tradition from rationalist habits, despite an egregious Nicholas Bounderby here and there.

Malthusian political economy argued that labourers could only help themselves by reducing the supply of labour. In more ways than just expenditure, large families made the poor responsible for their own condition. Thomas Malthus maintained that the population would always increase up to the limit permitted by the means of subsistence, that the population is held in check by the food supply. Charity then is either futile or increases the number of the poor, thus lowering the demand for work (lowering wages). David Ricardo turned the subsistence theory of wages into an Iron Law of Wages, a supposedly equilibrium price of labour also designed to impede market interference. The anti-utilitarian tradition desired to rekindle nonrationalist values in order to divorce itself from the violence directed towards the poor. But they attempted to do so without interfering with the idea that freedom, individual prosperity, social progress, and personal development were healthy quadruplets; that industry itself was blameless; and that initiative allows all self-relying Robinson Crusoes a fair chance – thus the altering Work (moral) and labour (pragmatic) discourses.

Thomas Cooper

Middle-class liberals such as Dickens, Mill, Gaskell, Martineau, and Jewsbury were often on friendlier terms with Carlyle's ideas, and with the Carlyles themselves, than many conservatives, such as Disraeli. The ideological lines separating liberals and conservatives could be very thin, especially in the representation of working-class culture. The overwhelming tendency is to imply that the best of the working class has a special relationship with Work and is especially ignorant or disinterested when it comes to its own economic power. The middle and upper classes may enter the arena of economics on behalf of the lower classes, but for the lower classes themselves to enter this restricted space signifies the worst kind of greed, perniciousness, and disorder. In any case, the working class is not represented as having the skills necessary to negotiate its own place. Working-class tolerance and working-class Work turn out to be one and the same thing: the rejection of and even the refusal to comprehend its own economic strength.

Between working- and nonworking-class cultural productions of the working class there are undeniable points of similarity. In both versions the working class is somewhat constructed in opposition to others more than others are referential to it (the history of the novel is, after all, genetically tied to the history of the middle class). In both versions the working class are submerged in backwater virtues, emphasizing community but with loners for heroes. And in both versions the working class desire Work but are confronted with its rationalization. The major difference between working- and nonworking-class representations of working-class culture is that the working class generally placed Work and labour in dialectical opposition to each other: Work cannot be actualized under the existing conditions of labour. In the hands of the working class, there is a clash between the full realization of its being and dull practicality. As a result, Work and socialism or Work and unionism are no longer opposing forces, and the best labour organizers work towards bringing about the conditions for Work.

If the old guard had the historical novel and the bourgeoisie had the *bildungsroman*, then the working class had the dialectical novel: a unique conflation of romance and didacticism; melodrama and gritty, journalistic realism; determinism and the *deus ex machina*. Ian Haywood reads 'most working-class writing' as illustrating that 'pleasure is an insecure and transitory escape from the brutal cycles of economic life (sunshine and shadows, to recall [Thomas Martin] Wheeler's trope)' (32). Yet pleasure, sunshine – and Work – exist, but exist demonstrably in opposition to and interrupted by hardship and the realm of labour. The working class tends to represent itself in a way that challenges the image of Carlyle's picturesque working class at Work (or his image of a threatening mob) by demonstrating the collapse of Work in the face of economic subjection and impotence. Though the working class represents itself as having a unique relationship to the dialectic of Work and labour, it also represents itself as having very little agency in the structuring of the space where a contest could take place.

In the working-class fiction of the Chartist period, from the 1830s to about 1850, economic and political consciousness is commonplace. I am focusing on Thomas Cooper; one will find similar ideas to his in the works of Wheeler or Ernest Jones. Cooper was the son of a dyer in the textile industry, became a leader in the Chartist movement, and was arrested and charged with sedition, spending two years in Stafford Gaol. He was also a political writer. In one scene of '"Merrie England" – No More' (1845) a working man declares that 'our eyes are getting opened ... they may be able to kill us off by starvation, at home; but I hope young and old will have too much sense, in future, to give or sell their bodies to be shot at, for tyrants' (55). The narrator then reports that 'These, and similar observations, were uttered aloud, in the open street, at broad day, by hundreds of starved, oppressed, and insulted framework-knitters, who thus gave vent to their despair. Such conversations were customary sounds in John's ears' (56). Working-class apathy is not denied, even before 1850, but the working classes often emphasize the political, economic, or social impediments to autonomy and 'consciousness.' They show the economic conditions that led workers to become preadjusted to the objective conditions of labour. The following conversation by two unnamed workers in Cooper's 'Seth Thompson, the Stockinger' (1845) is not unusual:

> I'll neither smoke nor drink any more ... the tyrants can do what they like with us, as long as we feed their vices by paying taxes. If all men would be o'my mind there would soon be an end of their extravagance, – for they would have nothing to support it.
> ... You'll never persuade all working-men to give up a sup of ale or a pipe, if they can get hold of either; but, not to talk of that, what's to hinder the great rascals from inventing other taxes if these fail? (49)

Such conversations are far from the discourse of volition and autonomy in *North and South*. In fact, the popularity of the *deus ex machina* among working-class writers can in some ways be attributed to a deliberate inversion of the middle-class ideology of self-help and the self-made man. From the perspective of the working class, the only way to be upwardly mobile is through some miraculous inheritance. In 'Seth Thompson,' Seth inherits his fortune from a rich uncle. Only then can he become a small master in the artisanal tradition and a 'well-informed, and deep-thinking man' (49). Martha Vicinus reports that Cooper 'was an important exponent of self-help and gradualism. Inordinately proud of his own learning, gained under difficult circumstances, he veers between advocating education as a panacea for working-class ills and appealing to the better-off to recognize their obligations to the respectable poor' (13). But in 'Seth,' self-help, a diligent work ethic, attention to the craft, honesty, loyalty, and so on have no way of translating into economic success and do not do so. After all is said and done, Seth loses his shop and is ostensibly defeated by economic circumstances he cannot control.

As a general rule in early working-class fiction, economic reality confronts and frustrates inspired beliefs in the value of Work. As Cooper says, 'Merrie England, No More!' The working class is typically portrayed as informed, intelligent, and autonomous: cognizant of that which impedes access to Work. The consensus in 'Seth Thompson' is that economic and political injustice will never 'be redressed till we redress 'em ourselves' (50). In 'Merrie England' religious zealots and tract missionaries try to convince the working classes not to mind about politics. The workers realize it is 'humbug' 'to keep us down.' The story ends with a direct message to the nonworking classes – middle-class philanthropists and Tory Radicals – to 'let it be understood that ... whoever enters Leicester, or any other of the populous starving hives of England, must expect to find the deepest subjects of theology, and government, and political economy, taken up with a subtlety that would often puzzle a graduate of Oxford or Cambridge' (58).

Yet another typical feature of the early working-class story is its emphasis on Work as a source of identity, well-being, or intrinsic value. It is also understood to be a source of income: without extrinsic, economic satisfaction there is no intrinsic, supereconomic satisfaction. The main conflict involves the desire to work on the one hand and economic hardship on the other. In 'Merrie England' an anonymous worker says, 'each of us here, though we are willing to work, should have to starve' (54). The main difference between the Carlylean complaint about the lack or dehumanization of work and the working-class complaint on the very same subject is that for the working class issues surrounding the rationalization of work or unemployment raise the idea of a radical restructuring of *economic* practices. In this way the internal and external rewards of work are always interconnected, and the possibility of the intrinsic value given the extrinsic framework is denied.

John Ruskin

In some ways, Ruskin belongs to as radical a wing of the anti-utilitarian tradition organized around Work in contradistinction to industry as

Cooper. His near machine-breaking attitude protests the reduction of 'value' to wages, of aesthetics to utility, and of craft to mechanics. In a pre-Marxian theory of alienation, Ruskin argues a direct correspondence between seamless production and the enslavement of the producer, the worker. In the *Philosophical Manuscripts* (1844) Marx says that 'the more refined his product the more crude and misshapen the worker' (*Early* 123). Both writers contrast *homo faber* to the emergent *homo industrialis* in order to target the economic base behind and within the mode of production. Ruskin especially saw industrialism – rationalized, mass production – and market culture as turning workers into the working dead and eliminating the intrinsic values occasioned by Work. Arguing that labourers 'have no pleasure in the work by which they make their bread, and therefore look to wealth as the only means of pleasure' (*Works* 10: 194), he pinpoints the defence of degrading work central to political economy and its theory of disutility. Work and identity for Ruskin (as well as for Marx and Carlyle) are directly linked: Work effects a process of endless self-conversion, of reworked subjectivity. Not only does each and every worker produce and express difference, but the individual worker also avoids personal homogeneity, stagnation, over time. Industrial work, producing sameness, destroys the opportunity for self-development and autonomy, control and skill. For Ruskin, industrialism also makes the world ugly, which he equates to banishing Truth or God. Art is work that expresses pleasure or freedom in the work process, and a universal sublime. Insofar as art can only be as good as the society in which it is created, Ruskin's aesthetic theory, he allows Metaphysics and materialism and culture and infrastructure to meet, an enormously important direction for British socialism (Williams, *Culture* 135–9).

But as with Carlyle before him, Ruskin treats Work as a refuge to withdraw into, eliding at those points the reformism and recognition of class struggle that appear elsewhere in his writing. Instead of seeing a confrontation at the intersection of Work and labour, he posits, as Carlyle does, that 'with brave people the work is first and the fee second' (*Works* 18: 413). The working classes are always those brave people. Vilifying labour, he treats efficiency as a moral concept: efficiency becomes a matter of 'organic' hierarchies, elites, and nobility. His conservatism, explicit in his attitudes towards leaders and an inflexible, class- and gender-based organization of society, essentially confirms a societal division of labour as opposed to a manufacturing division of labour. If *The Stones of Venice* (1851–3), which in some ways is the Victorian social climber's textbook to art and architecture, guides the middle classes toward admiring the recalcitrance and manly or savage independence of the worker, Ruskin reserves an entirely different discourse for the working class. The first lecture in *The Crown of Wild Olive* (1866), 'Work,' was initially a speech addressed to factory workers in Camberwell (who, of course, did not have the benefit of working under paternal guidance). In it Ruskin recounts for them the virtues of Work and of paternal worker–master relations: he does not report on the degradation of work. His jeremiad against the cheap, dishonourable, and unjust character of capitalist organizations, or simply of bourgeois capitalists, is cut off from his direct appeals to the working class to Work. He tells the workers to develop the 'character of right childhood,' which is to be 'Modest ... Faithful ... Loving ... and Cheerful' (*Works* 18: 429–30). Ruskin, prescribing as much as he is describing working-class culture, demands fair wages, but his noble workers are to '[trust] somebody else to take care of to-morrow' (*Works* 18: 430). He resounds Carlyle's brand of organicism again and again in his insistence that workers 'trust their Captains' and accept a leader (*Works* 18: 429). His concern for the working class often boils down to ratifying *existing* structures of authority, a consequence of preaching Work in the conditions of labour – itself a consequence of dividing Work and labour and separating the message he delivers to the working class from the one he reserves for the rest of society.

As with Orwell, Ruskin values the environment, handwork, and working-class culture. In such uncorrupted simplicity both writers find the last vestige of a resistance to the dominant ethos of capitalism. They both also invest Work with a very male libidinal component. Defining himself as a 'socialist of the most stern sort but also a Tory of the sternest sort' (quoted in Mendilow 181), in any case anti-capitalist and conservative, Ruskin is a natural forerunner to Orwell, especially if seen against rationalist politics. Whereas Ruskin and Orwell favour decentralized community organizations, Bentham's centralizing mind offers the panopticon for prisons, industry, workhouses, schools, and hospitals. Ruskin and Orwell would agree that wages ought to be fixed by something akin to custom rather than supply and demand. For Bentham, less centralizing when thinking in terms of economics, the government's role was to remove obstacles to market freedom.

Points of connection between the two, as between Carlyle and Orwell, nonetheless need to be qualified. Ruskin's aristocratic longing for an immobile chain of authority gives way to an exaggerated and problematic paternalism that would erase working-class autonomy and the freedom to challenge authority. Orwell thought the attempt to reintroduce feudalistic hierarchies was a back door to fascism. Though not a very powerful criticism to make of an unsuccessful movement circa National Socialism and the Second World War, he was right to be suspicious of the hypostatization of social roles – 'rough men must do rough work, gentlemen must do brainwork' – which Ruskin confirms in nearly all of his major works. Ruskin undoes much of his own speechifying about the value of Work by arguing that

> it is of no use to try to conceal this sorrowful fact [the 'division' of labour between rough work/rough men and brainwork/gentlemen] by fine words, and to talk to the workman about the honourableness of manual labour, and the dignity of humanity ... Rough work, honourable or not, takes the life out of us; and the man who has been heaving clay out of a ditch all day, or driving an express train against the north wind all night, or holding a collier's helm in a gale on a lee shore, or whirling white-hot iron at a furnace mouth, that man is not the same at the end of his day, or night, as one who has been sitting in a quiet room, with everything comfortable around him, reading books, or classing butterflies, or painting pictures. (*Works* 18: 417–18)

Ruskin, however, is not arguing his deep-seated belief in hierarchy at the expense of Work. He is, in fact, reminding workers of the inevitably 'tragic,' hard life in store for them. The myth of the hard life corresponds to the specialized language of Work – a language reserved for the working class and cut off from the language of labour.

William Morris

Morris, working towards a reconciliation between Ruskin and Marx, shares a Ruskinian appreciation for the Work of art, the art of Work, and the decline of Work into labour, but would effect change by empowering workers, not by reempowering a newfangled aristocracy. The most important point of divergence from Morris to Ruskin, Carlyle, and the nonworking-class Victorians in general, is that he, more often than not, brings together Work and labour in such a way as to underscore a dialectic. In this way, he is the voice of dissent in a tradition he eagerly adopted. As Lawrence Lutchmansingh observes,

> Carlyle's positive acknowledgement of the worker's contribution to human progress and Ruskin's celebration of work's redemptive moral power were

valuable to Morris only up to a point. For their Tory utopianism, complete with worker obedience until the grave and submission to 'the law of heaven,' still harbored an element of condescension, which would, in the end, render a genuine and revolutionary politics impossible. (12)

The titles of Morris's essays – 'Labour and Pleasure versus Labour and Sorrow,' 'Work as It Is and as It Might Be,' 'Useful Work versus Useless Toil,' 'How We Live and How We Might Live,' or 'A Factory as It Might Be' – speak of his vehemently dialectical approach. He cuts through his own eulogizing on Work and production to focus on the ownership of labour and production. He recognizes that 'it has become an article of the creed of modern morality that all labour is good in itself – a convenient belief to those who live on the labour of others' ('Useful Work' 287).

Just as Morris desired the objects of Work to have equal parts aesthetic appeal and use-value, he brought together an intrinsically oriented approach to work with an understanding of its context and effects. Carlyle and Ruskin express the Gospel of Work to the working class as an imperative to work but deliver it to the middle and upper classes as a critique of their role in allowing work to become mechanical and dehumanizing. Under Morris, the relative value of work is a sign of its preconditions or the environment it takes place in regardless of which class he addresses. Discussing the need to 'beautify our labour' in 'The Lesser Arts' (1877), a lecture originally written for workers, Morris only tells them of 'the blessing of labour' as it is 'wrapped up ... with changes political and social' (236). Later on in the same essay, again discussing Work, he tells his audience:

> I believe that as we have even now partly achieved LIBERTY, so we shall one day achieve EQUALITY, which, and which only, means FRATERNITY, and so have leisure from poverty, and all its griping, sordid cares ... for surely then we shall be happy in [work], each in his place, no man grudging at another, no one bidden to be any man's *servant*, every one scorning to be any man's *master*. men will then assuredly be happy in their work, and that happiness will assuredly bring forth decorative, noble, *popular* art. (253–4)

This is decidedly not scarcely more than an echo of Ruskin's words (235), as Morris humbly declares his essay to be at the beginning of the lecture. Unlike Ruskin, Morris understood that intrinsically valuable work must involve more than just the craftsmanship of a 'free' worker.

The worker, simply put, in order to take pleasure in the work and thus make a work of art, also has to decide for himself or herself what it is that he or she is going to make and then have full social and intellectual access to it.

Morris conflates Art and Work; his idea of Art pre-echoes Arendt's definition of work. Artistry for Morris is activity that produces goods that remain beyond the immediately consumable products of labour, 'leaving to future ages living witness of the existence of deft hands and eager minds' ('Art' 383–4). He thought a socialist future would heal the class-oriented division between art and daily life. In his survey of work and literature, David Meakin distinguishes between two ethics of work: a 'protestant ethic,' which assumes work is a good in itself or treats it as a moral duty regardless of its form or function – thus reinforcing or upholding the status quo – and another ethic, which entails 'a different kind of society' (174). Morris, he argues, belongs to the latter category, whereas Carlyle and Ruskin belong to the first. Though I cannot agree that Carlyle and Ruskin were subsumed into a neat Protestant ideology or that they did not desire a 'different kind of society,' he is right to point out the difference between the three. Morris, always explicitly reverent towards his 'forefathers,' seems to blatantly challenge them in 'The Revival of Handicraft' (1888): 'the worst tyrants of the days of violence were but feeble tormentors compared with those Captains of Industry who have taken the pleasure of work away from the workmen' (338).

One of the best expressions of Morris's fundamental grasp of the opposition or contest between Work and labour might be in his long poem 'The Pilgrims of Hope' (1886). It is the only one of Morris's narratives to have a working-class, poverty-stricken hero (Boos 147). In the tale a skilled joiner, radical in his views on socialism, the value of Work, and the changes needed to arrive at a fair distribution of those values, commands the respect of his boss and co-workers but only because he has a private income. When his lawyer dies and his inheritance curiously vanishes – 'So I who have worked for my pleasure now work for utter need' (140) – his boss recognizes his views as subversive and he is fired. Reduced to a commodity looking for work, he is no longer able to idealize it. His financial situation (a matter of privilege, of inheritance, of class) allowed him to interpret and experience Work.

Orwell for one did not see Morris's appreciation of Work, which is as pronounced as Carlyle's or Ruskin's, as dependent upon a consideration of labour. He dismissed Morris because Morris's name was so closely associated with medievalism and rural utopianism. Orwell did not think that Morris had come to terms with the rationalized world. But Morris knew that the idea of moving backwards to outdated modes of production was 'preposterously futile' ('Hopes' 325). Even in *News from Nowhere* (1890) a small number of machines exist. Morris wrote his utopia as an alternative to Edward Bellamy's *Looking Backward* (1887). He was especially offended by Bellamy's idea of a 'workers army' and the implication that work is not a pleasure in itself but necessarily burdensome and mechanistic. The function of machinery in *News from Nowhere* is to perform duller tasks so people could dedicate themselves to a *variety* of creative crafts and 'practical aesthetics' (58). He undoubtedly idealized and de-historicized medieval work. Margaret Grennan points out that Morris 'arrived at his conception of the medieval workman not primarily from the study of surviving records of conditions of labour and real wages but from the study of the surviving product – the art of the Middle Ages ... his conclusion [being] that only under satisfactory conditions of labour and in relative freedom could such results be effected' (70–1). But he was mindful of the improvements to the overall standard of living in the modern world. In fact, he created his utopian society, the society of *News From Nowhere* – as is common to science fiction and fantasy literature, whether utopian or dystopian (Orwell should have known better) – as a critique of the contemporary world and as a model for the direction of immediate (in this case socialist) politics. Though he understands that Work must be premised by an unanxious life, he also understood that people would be comfortable with about a quarter of the goods that were available to them, the rest being merely quantity or waste. In this way he was more pragmatic than Marx, who very much worked according to an assumption of high productivity. Morris also knew that undesirable work would always exist; he only maintains that it ought not to be done by one class only. He sought 'practical Socialism' to conflate the principles of Work with an understanding of necessity. His concept of art, complete in its own way, was also, as said, a metaphor for Work, but not in the way that art or 'culture' was used as an alternative to 'society.' He understood that the mutually exclusive discourses of Work and labour betrayed deaf ears towards class issues, towards context, and insisted that the only manner in which to introduce the union of beauty and usefulness, to reintroduce Work, was through a total restructuring of class, the elimination of exclusive levels.

Despite Morris's explicit call to combine Work with a steady acknowledgment of the needs, conditions, and immediate context of labour, it must be said that he was less pragmatic in practice. Thompson is right to argue against debating where Morris falls on the line between Romanticism and Marxism (*William* 892–9); but Marxism does not imply or lead to practical reform. In *News from Nowhere* there are no politics, as the elimination of private property makes the need for laws and so forth unnecessary. The whole of the people are the government. Morris was an anti-parliamentarian, arguing a Policy of Abstention and calling not only parliament but also unionism a 'palliation.' He violently rejected Fabianism, state socialism, and the idea of tinkling with wages and working hours. He saw piecemeal reform as negligible to the *whole* system of labour, which he did contrast to the holistic implementation of Work. His concept of labour was shaped by Marx and Marxism, and he was thus antagonistic towards the state. Because of this, because he viewed labour, pragmatism, and reform as a matter that outreached specific issues, he again placed himself outside of the group herein described and their brass tacks of action. Morris thought it was his role not to concede anything, to take the high road, and that there would be others to negotiate and plead with government – that part of his thought was immensely practical. But as Thompson confirms, such an attitude limited his influence among the working class, especially among working-class reformers (*William* 455–64). It is one thing to censure 'the hypocritical praise of all labour' as 'there is some labour which is so far from being a blessing that it is a curse,' and another thing to extend from that 'that it would be better ... [to] refuse to work, and either die or let us pack him [the recalcitrant worker] off to the workhouse or prison' ('Useful Work' 287). The postulate that 'compromise is of no use' is not one familiar either to reformism or to those who would have to do the dying.

Morris can also betray the habit of Work enthusiasts who compartmentalize business or pragmatic matters. In his own commercial affairs, with Morris, Marshall, Faulkner & Co., Morris & Co., and finally the Kelmscott Press, he pursued competitive business strategies. In *Art, Enterprise and Ethics* (1996), Charles Harvey and Jon Press examine Morris's advertising campaigns, his 'shrewdness' in challenging competitors, and the financial pressures he was under which necessitated trading at a profit. Even though Morris himself was disgusted by commercialism and profit-mongering, and was motivated mostly by creative impulses, he recognized that abandoning all 'financial aspirations' would quickly translate into compromising his artistic and cultural aspirations. Harvey and Press argue that he 'formed compartments in his mind. His idealism, his revolutionary socialism, his zeal for the past, live in one compartment;

his commitment to the world of business lies in another' (64). Various permutations of compartmentalizing Work and labour underlie the Carlylean or Victorian elevation of Work. But with Morris, only direct engagement in a competitive trade divides Work from labour, inevitably, he might say, given the organization of labour.

If Morris's approach to labour (other than his own) was made impractically holistic by way of his adoption of Marxist tenets – that only revolution and a complete overturning of capitalism serves the *true* interests of 'labour,' anything and everything short of that being corporate, capitulating, colluding labourism – his approach to Work was nonetheless against the grain of the developing Marxist rhetoric. As Marx increasingly lost touch with the idea of Work, interpreting its Gospel as bourgeois or reactionary morality (or ideology), Marxists generally did the same. In 1907, for example, Paul Lafargue, Marx's son-in-law, wrote a treatise on the delusional working-class 'love of work,' urging 'the proletariat' to 'return to its natural instincts [and] proclaim the Right of Laziness' (9, 29). Morris, on the other hand, showing his ties to Ruskin, wrote about artisans and not the proletariat, or about the structural changes that needed to develop for the proletariat to once again become the artisan. Though this at points leads Morris to de-historicize, his utopianism, as I have tried to demonstrate, is always situated in a contemporary critique: his invocation to Work, in contrast to Carlyle or Ruskin, is designed to counter its real context and effects. Morris's refutation of labourism comes not only from an admiration of Work and its products, but also from the artisan's obstinate refusal to be regarded as a replaceable commodity on the labour market.

CHAPTER TWO

Joseph Conrad

In the last chapter I attempted to identify and contextualize an almost systemic *and* ritualized practice of oscillating between a moral idea of work and economic convention: a practice reared primarily by Carlyle against the background of work rationalization and an insomniac economization. On the one hand, we saw a reaction against constricting man – yes, man – into the role of a maximizing agent, *homo economicus*, his working-class brother into *homo laborans*, and public society into an organized, functionalized, yet unregulated *gesellschaft* association by appealing to a Gospel of Work. The censure of over-extended formal rationalisms in general unites with the censure of the rational organization of work and that formality; they become more than just metaphors for each other. In this 'mode,' Work has value in itself. On the other hand, we saw a sinking into rationalism, a cautious and conditional descent into work or social rationalization, sometimes to propose piecemeal change and sometimes merely to keep in step with economic law and industrial progress. At the economic level, the intrinsic value of Work is neglected, denied, or forced to heel beside the demands of the industrial order.

With Carlyle, the Victorians discussed in the previous chapter, and now Joseph Conrad, a unified ideology of Work and the historicized impossibility of that sanctification coexist only because they never directly and dialectically connect, meet, or clash. I am interested in the tendency to vacillate between the assumption of an unconditional, essentialist dignity of Work and the assumption of an inevitable economy that can only be tinkered with, between the needs of 'culture' and 'society' in Raymond Williams's sense, between 'work' and 'labour' in Hannah Arendt's, between the ideal and the real, final and contingent, visual and empirical; between assuming the realm of either freedom or necessity to the point where they get entirely cut off from each other. The slippages lay bare the imprint of synchronic habits of mind, in which two contradictory forms of social commitment that depend upon isolation for their survival sit side by side with equally unmitigated, unremitting finality. The political hybridization of conservatism, reactionaryism, organicism, liberalism, Romanticism, and reformism produces a chasm that intensifies and increases in relation to the degree to which the writer directly engages the rationalized world.

Contradiction and inconsistency here do not bear the intellectual opprobrium with which literary critics, formalist or anti-formalist, often measure success. Antinomies offend only theory and models, abstractions that the strong empirical side of Conrad, for example, rejects wholesale. For Orwell, consistency is the mark of orthodoxies and betrays the refusal to admit to or grapple with real tyranny. Inconsistency especially refutes utilitarian and liberal theory in which the individual is elevated into a predictably rational, self-interested agent: maximizing being his sum capacity. Inconsistency challenges the construction of this monological subjectivity and, it follows, the idea that maximizing self-interest maximizes society's interests. Inconsistency is also the keystone to work before or beyond rationalization. John Ruskin's individuated, inconstant Gothic architecture confers 'signs of the life and liberty of every workman who struck the stone; a freedom of thought' (*Works* 10: 193–4). Consistent production is measured only by quantity. When quantifiable production is the measure of success and the formal rationality of economic action prevails in the production of all values, including consumption values, then substantive ends tend be trivialized.

But a watermark inconsistency between moral and pragmatic work cannot be rescued from the deadlock of a subjective–objective split by appeals to a second order of deliberate contradiction. These competing ideas of work undermine and deny each other; the pragmatic parts never add up to the moral whole and the whole cannot be broken down into parts. Georg Lukács regarded this gulf as the 'dualism of economic fatalism and ethical utopianism' (*History* 196). The fatalism and contradictoriness are especially pronounced when the pragmatics are reviewed from the point of view of the 'utopianism,' the uncompromising moral idea of Work. But that is one reason why the moral and pragmatic ideas of work never meet. The real and immediate is not to determine or even have an impact on the possibilities of the ideal. Yet no level of isolation could prevent the two sides of the disjunction from working against each other.

The hiatuses, structural dislocations, displacements, fissures, impasses, or glitches between moral and pragmatic work signify the point where ideology surfaces (Eagleton, *Criticism* 117). In the specific case of the writers before us, the split signifies the point where ideology meets conviction, outruns it, and outlasts it. The hard split between moral and pragmatic work, more importantly, demonstrates a belief in the capacity of the individual to overcome the social formation, to resist determination. When a character can glean value from work which the author represents as objectively negative, can separate herself or himself from economic reality, she or he has the self-made resources that show where the author's individualism has become a challenge to her or his social awareness. 'Individuals' in these cases are those who work as if independently of an economic function. With their special insights into the world of Work, and their ignorance of and need for assistance in negotiating the world of labour, they often, though not always, belong to the working class. As a rule, the working class at least exemplifies Work. Still, regardless of what overdetermines the rift causing the Gospel of Work to sit undisturbed beside consistent labour, a belief in the armour of subjectivity dominates. The dualism of finding categorical value in Work as one conforms to the economic-as-is and as-seen-to-be is also typical of an age grasping for a totalizing moral compass in the felt departure of one. It is not only the indoctrinated automaton but also the struggling believer who will be wholly uncompromising in the outward projection of his or her belief. The uncompromising believer in a Gospel of Work might expose scepticism about its power in modernity, just as the religious fundamentalist might expose doubt about the strength of his or her faith by adamantly proselytizing it in inappropriate venues and then ignoring it in others. But the coin shining a manly worker swinging a hammer or a banner of unqualified hope on the one side and is flat dull on the other, the side listing interminable qualifications, was minted under an unwavering assumption that the individual can always choose heads.

In this chapter I am primarily investigating the way in which Conrad takes up the anti-rationalist tradition and splits a rhetoric of Work from a grammar of labour, responding as he does to alternating pressures of morality and money. Later in the chapter I focus on his contemporaries and the way in which they continue compartmentalizing Work and labour, even though the terms of labour mutate. Economics became more and more synonymous with enterprise and the marginalist focus on the consumer. Finance was now the opposite of work for work's sake, and though subject to the same kind of apprehension labour had undergone, it slides into the category of pragmatism just as 'labour' did before it. Though it continues to represent the formally calculated, rational maximization of a substantially irrational end, as pragmatic work, the logic of finance is kept entirely isolated from the attitude of moral Work. Here I look at H.G. Wells and the way in which his representation of Work and the economic fits with the model carried on by Conrad. With E.M. Forster, the schism between Work and finance begins to drift into more rarefied grounds where Culture supplants Work. These discrepancies, however, are subtle compared with the radically different point of view that emerges with Robert Tressell, a working-class writer and contemporary of Conrad, Wells, and Forster. Finally, as I am interested in the relation between economic theory and literary movements, I also touch on the way in which literary modernism came to terms with the economic and the subsequent disappearance of Work. Modernism in this context proves to be a movement antithetical to the Carlylean and Conradian idea of Work but sympathetic to the social philosophy that surrounds it.

Conrad's decidedly ambiguous attitude towards work places him firmly in good company with Carlyle and the Carlylean Victorians, not the moderns (or modernists). In *Criticism and Ideology* (1976), Terry Eagleton rightly finds that his 'need for value, and the recognition of its utter vacuity' is 'the deepest contradiction of Conrad's enterprise' (140). Eagleton reads Conrad as shuffling between organicist idealism and Romantic individualism, hope and disillusionment, activism and language whose spectral cloudiness would prohibit the *vita activa*. I am looking at the contradiction as it takes the form of an unresolved split between the Gospel of Work and economic orthodoxy. Conrad was a sailor immersed in nonrationalist Work. In *A Personal Record* (1912) he implores his audience to 'understand that there was no idea of any sort of "career" in my call ... that what I had in view was not a naval career, but the sea' (121). Zdzisław Najder, however, warns us not to heed Conrad's autobiographical comments naively, and that Thaddeus Bobrowski, for one, allowed the young Conrad to go to sea because it was a means toward economic security (37). In any case, if participating in the English merchant service 'fashioned the fundamental part of [Conrad's] character in [his] young days' ('Tradition' 196), it continued to shape at least the outward projection of his character long after that. But between arriving in England in 1878 and writing *Heart of Darkness* (1902) twenty-six years later, he shared a loss of earnest and energetic optimism with the late Victorians. The faith in Progress that flowed through the purer notions of imperialism and evolutionism would not survive the end of the century for most of the informed British. Still, as with many Edwardians or early moderns, Conrad also refused to concede the principle behind the thing, the idea of Imperialism or Progress (or Work) – even if that meant completely detaching the idea from the practice. Marlow's involvement with the Company he despises in *Heart of Darkness* is not resolved by a recourse to a saving illusion, the principle, the salvageable idea; his participation in the colonial enterprise is only *as if* removed from the idea, from work of value, by that illusion.

Despite the withdrawal that the saving illusion implies, Conrad never conclusively denies social reality (that people live among one another) or that life is lived in the realm of necessity and governed by an ascendant rationalist economic order. That is, after all, also implied by the need for a saving illusion. However, when reminding readers not to lose sight of the non-economic considerations surrounding Work – loyalties to group or ideas about nobility, honour, and emotional involvement – he isolates those values and shields them from reality. Though some of those values contain the residue of a very real reactionary economic and political agenda, by compartmentalizing them he forgoes social change for personal commitment. (Orwell's phrase, 'A humanitarian is always a hypocrite' [*CEJL* 2: 218] is again useful and appropriate.) The values associated with the sea-locked *Narcissus* render any non-Gospelized matter high and dry. They are raised to be untouchable values, more importantly, only because there is little reference made to the fact that the ship is also transporting goods, that there *are* economic factors surrounding work. Two very different systems of work take place in both *Heart of Darkness* and *The Nigger of the 'Narcissus'* (1897): moral Work and a subtextual order that would contradict every article in that morality if it were simultaneously addressed. Before looking at these two incompatible and segregated branches of work, I want to examine the explicit juxtaposition in *Heart of Darkness* between types of work: the search for intrinsically satisfying Work in the midst of perverted structures.

Conrad's philosophy of work, his pre-historicized idea of Work, differs little from Carlyle's. Both treat work with a trans-economic emphasis, confirming its ability to foster self-realization and solidify community. Both argue that social duty is *felt*, participation only impelling further consent. In 'Tradition' (1918) Conrad wrote,

> From the hard work of men are born the sympathetic consciousness of a common destiny, the fidelity to right practice which makes great craftsmen,

the sense of right conduct which we may call honour, the devotion to our calling and the idealism which is not a misty, winged angel without eyes, but a divine figure of terrestrial aspect with a clear glance and with its feet resting firmly on the earth on which it was born. (194)

Adventuring, the raison d'être of young Marlow in *Youth* (1902) or Jim in *Lord Jim* (1900), is not Work because it neglects or even negates the community, discipline, and clear sense of purpose that characterize Work. Unlike American transcendentalists, Conrad always roots the idea of 'idealism' in the 'terrestrial,' in something as tangible, physical, and practical as work. The subsequent split of Work from labour is fundamentally different than a split between metaphysics and history, especially when it involves a clear rejection of anything remotely mystical, because Work is – and is even thought to be – a real world activity. The history of this logic is one where spiritualism as the alternative to economic rationalism was centred in not only secular but corporeal activities, making the division between Work and economic activity all the more remarkable.

In *Heart of Darkness*, the abstract idea of work enables the subject 'the chance to find yourself' (59). Working, Marlow finds the opportunity to self-*au*thorize or be his own author in an existential affirmation, and to self-au*tho*rize or be his own authority in the absence of political, economic, or social rules. In *Heart of Darkness*, of course, no 'solid pavement,' public opinion, or law exists to regulate conduct. Only work allows Marlow to 'keep [his] hold on the redeeming facts of life' (52) by necessitating self-discipline. The Carlylean influence here is strong. In *Past and Present* Carlyle says, 'a man perfects himself by working. Foul jungles are cleared away, fair seedfields rise instead, and stately cities; and withal the man himself first ceases to be a jungle and foul unwholesome desert thereby' (196). In Conrad's articulation of Work, commitment is demanded in order that identity might be appropriated from the sheer effort. But contrary to this equation where Work entrains self-knowledge and self-control is the opposite one, where Work brings about self-subterfuge and *that* engenders self-control. Work provides the last defence against too much reality: the opportunity to immunize oneself against introspection and deny lurking frenetic impulses. Speaking on the effort involved in steering a ship, a metaphor for self-control, Marlow says, 'When you have to attend to things of that sort, to the mere incidents of the surface, the reality – the reality, I tell you – fades. The inner truth is hidden – luckily, luckily' (67). In *Chance* (1913), in a passage nearly as famous, Marlow says, 'to be busy with material affairs is the best preservative against reflection, fears, doubts – all these things which stand in the way of achievement. I suppose a fellow proposing to cut his throat would experience a sort of relief while occupied in stropping his razor carefully' (282).

The same dualism between fostering and denying self-knowledge is found in Carlyle's writings. In the last chapter I described the close resemblance between Carlyle's belief that work confirms identity by supplying the chance for the individual to see himself objectified in the product of his work (it is 'his') and Marx's early essentialist writings. But Carlyle also wrote, 'Think it not thy business, this of knowing thyself; thou art an unknowable individual: know what thou canst work at' (*Past* 196). In both Carlyle and Conrad, and in the general model(s) of work that I am discussing, Work functions alternatively to clarify identity and to conceal it, to establish it and to negate it.

The split between work as the means to either find oneself or hide from oneself is closely associated with the split between moral and pragmatic work. In each case, the individual is understood to be able to surmount undesired, repudiated conditions (and it is his or her moral duty to do so). The gap between the ethical and historical, between moral and pragmatic work, assumes that the individual has the power to wrest intrinsic (moral) value from Work despite its structural (historical/objective) organization for extrinsic purposes only; accordingly, the individual is represented as if outside of history. The disjunction between work that promotes self-definition in one breath and self-subterfuge in another also shows a belief that the individual can find or develop an identity that counters intermediaries lying outside of his or her will, in the case of *Heart of Darkness*, an irrational, primitive, or 'savage' identity deep within. But the inner identity is never conclusively defeated. The individual who finds himself through work lives cut off from the one who must hide from himself in Work. As that unchosen identity is confirmed and galvanized by modern relations of production, being able to muzzle it shows a self-engineered resistance to influence, whether it is external or internal.

The social confirmation and galvanization of the worker into a rapacious individualist under a laissez-faire structure is one of the basic themes of *Heart of Darkness* and ought not to be dismissively filed under 'reactionaryism.' Conrad brings to the surface the difficulty of accruing intrinsic benefits from work under alienating conditions in a way Carlyle never does. But contrary to what sympathetic critics such as Paul Gaston and Paul Bruss have been concluding for years, he does not qualify his

Gospel of Work or argue its indefensibility and impossibility in modernity. A generalized and universal creed of Work endures, given the imagined possibility of its seclusion. Undoubtedly and with vigour he explicates the vast discrepancy between the ideology informing colonialism, enlightenment, and Progress on the one hand and the barbaric practices that follow on the other. The representation of the pilgrims, for example, surfing the Empire's free market for profit and muttering 'Ivory' underlines the true nature of the colonial quest (the Company, of course, is 'run for profit' [39]). But Conrad shows no reservation when it comes to the solid canons of the Gospel, only frustration with what *would* impede or violate it.

Despite the power of the individual to work as if independent of his or her surroundings, grasping value from the presumption of isolation, the need to overcome circumstance embodies social – moral and structural – criticism. Maintaining a classic work ethic against the corrupted organization and economic base of work is the responsibility of the individual in conflict with an individualist society. Conrad vilifies nearly all specific acts of work being carried out in the Congo; Work is validated but not colonial work. The chief accountant devotes himself to his work as steadily as Marlow devotes himself to Work. Whereas Marlow repels impulses contrary to humanity by working, when the accountant works he ignores humanity. Marlow tends to resemble Carlyle, Orwell, and Conrad himself insofar as he idealizes Work as a participant and blasts labour as an observer of working conditions. Calculating, impersonal, and starched by routine, the accountant complains about the distracting noises of the suffering and dying when he has 'correct entries' to register (47). The formal rationality of the accountant increases the irrationality of the outcome, of substantive ends. There is nothing in *Heart of Darkness* to suggest that bureaucrats in inhumane institutions can be exculpated because they are merely 'cogs in the machine'; the individual is expected to bypass the machine, even if he continues to work for the Company. (Marlow, I am arguing, is not treated as a cog in the machine. Instead, with a Gospel of Work, it is as if he manages to slip out of it.) Despite the routinization and rationalization of work, all the colonists are competitive and ambitious. The papier-mâché Mephistopheles is 'upset' because Kurtz's success interferes with his plans 'to be assistant-manager' (56). Even the Roman conquerors were 'cheered' by a 'chance of promotion' (31).

When colonizers turn towards their work they add to their aggressive instincts and work's power to sublimate id and egoism gets turned on its head. Laissez-faire economics is not merely a device to generate a story about finding an interior Darkness after all systems of restraint are removed. The story is about the sanctioning of egoism, the rationalization and justification of the egoistic impulse, the shaping of it, and the liberation of it into everyday life. The manager prides himself on being a social-Darwinian beast, reaching ascendancy because he can stay healthy while others around him fall ill. With his uncle, he desires to be 'free from unfair competition,' meaning that 'anything can be done in this country' (64). The more work done, the greater the proliferation of savagery.

Kurtz also 'lacked restraint in the gratification of his various lusts' because 'there was nothing on earth to prevent him killing whom he jolly well pleased' (97, 95). At one time, Kurtz was an ideal worker; as a missionary and an ivory hunter he excelled, surpassing and causing envy in his fellow and rival colonizers. Before the 'jungle had found him out,' before his inner nature is elevated, Kurtz is a 'first-class agent' who 'sends in as much ivory as all the others put together,' and 'an exceptional man, of the greatest importance to the Company' supposed to go 'very far' 'in the Administration' (46, 51, 47). But devoting himself to his work only leads him to embody its principles. His work incites ambition; it involves negotiating and bypassing restraints, struggling with competition, acquiring excess, seeking promotion, and seeking ascendancy. Kurtz is a 'product of the new forces at work' (43), Empire and Capital, as much as he embodies freed primal lusts. He distinguishes himself from the profiteers by his plans to 'enlighten' and by being, as Ian Watt has observed, a Romantic individualist: bohemian, painter, poet, and political radical (*Conrad* 164). But that zeal has an individualist counterpart that seeks any form of gain. Even as a cultic, megalomaniacal leader he maintains the Company's work ethic and hoards ivory. When dying, he longingly recalls his 'immense plans' (107). Kurtz never ceases to show that 'all Europe contributed to [his] making' (86); that under the surface of civilized Europe is a savage will to ascendancy, aggravated by its economic institutions. Kurtz dedicates himself to work, but his work only arouses what Marlow's Work is meant to suppress.

Marlow attempts to bypass 'creepy thoughts' (70) by immersing himself in work. He counters the ugliness of Progress and his immediate surroundings by sticking to a traditional view of Work, apparently sufficient to divorce a moral imperative from the economic act. He finds solace in the meticulously crafted *An Inquiry into Some Points of Seamanship*. It articulates his belief in 'a singleness of intention, an honest concern for the right way of going to work' (71). For Marlow to Work, however, he needs rivets (in order to fix his boat). Riveting suggests a permeation of a phallic substance into hollowness. If Conrad insinuates or has unconsciously illustrated a libidinal transference through the act of riveting it is no doubt of less symbolic importance than Marlow's desire to fill meaning into nothingness and thus resist the morally sunken state of the Hollow men. But Marlow needs rivets; the lack of rivets brings him close to unrestrained, hysterical anger. Differentiating between Work and economic activity, Marlow realizes that 'rivets were what really Mr Kurtz wanted, if he had only known it' (59). Enraged, Marlow says that there were 'cases of them down at the coast – cases – piled up – burst – split!' (58). The coast caravan brings in 'trade goods' but not rivets; it brings 'ghastly glazed calico ... glass beads ... [and] confounded spotted cotton handkerchiefs' (58). Ruskin also associated mass-produced 'glass beads' with the proliferation of the 'utterly unnecessary' (*Works* 10: 197). Conrad and Ruskin, and indeed the 'culture' side of the 'Culture and Society tradition,' resist the emergence of the consumer age and are repelled by the shift from working as the origin of value, to production as value's flag, and finally to the fetishization of consumption, the satisfaction or frustration of desire.

In modernity Marlow is an anachronism. In the age of consumerism, steamships and mechanization, speculation (in *Lord Jim* the man with 'globular eyes' preaches the 'minimum of risk with the maximum of profit' [128]), and greed, where 'honour' is a charmingly antiquated curiosity, Marlow, Jim, and the crew of the *Narcissus* (excepting Donkin and Wait) do not fit in. Fredric Jameson complains that Conrad's 'feudal ideology of honour' has no place 'in the midst of capitalism' (*Political* 217). That honour and shame are out of step with capitalism is precisely the point. Marlow, when speaking about how Jim leaves one workplace after another, says that,

> They were all equally tinged by a high-minded absurdity of intention which made their futility profound and touching. To fling away your daily bread so as to get your hands free for a grapple with a ghost may be an act of prosaic heroism. We who have lived know full well that it is not the haunted soul but the hungry body that makes an outcast. (147)

Jim is an exception, obsolete: that is what the text says and that is what Jameson repeats. *Lord Jim* is both 'ethical' and 'historical' in the way that subjective ethics and objective reality clash. Jameson would be correct to point out the dualism between 'personal' values and social history because they regularly do *not* clash, a disjunction maintained by isolating 'personal' values from an otherwise pervasive history.

Against such history Conrad employs the saving illusion. The illusion is not in question because it is an illusion: as with all myths, it must be evaluated by its effect. In this case, it enables the practitioner to dig out value from what does not exist. But the willed illusion is also the device magically setting the individual apart from history, ever the more magical because the individual initiates the illusion when directly and actively participating in the very reality to be concealed. With volition, the individual converts the illusion into a separate, subjective reality.

A subjective reality, a functioning illusion, is nonetheless coincidental with objective history. The illusion does not mitigate objective reality nor does it reconcile 'personal' and economic values: it compartmentalizes them and protects them from each other. Marlow or the crew of the *Narcissus* work for the very companies or institutions that have perverted work. The idealization of work survives the corruption of modernity by insulating itself, becoming an entirely private value, but the actual work is unchanged by the innocence of the intention behind it. Kurtz, as an earnest 'emissary of light' *and* the best ivory-snatcher in the Congo, confirms what Conrad evades, that private intentions do not compensate for or in any way overturn corporate malevolence. Moreover, private intentions that enable salutary Work to thrive obviate political action. They challenge the post-Darwinian malaise about the lack of purpose in the universe by positing a local design. At least they assuage the hurt of being told about your existential emptiness. They disturb the slumber of efficiency that accompanies corrupt intentions and bureaucratic control. In *Heart of Darkness*, holes are dug for the sake of digging holes, cliffs are blasted indiscriminately for the sake of blasting cliffs, the brickmaker does not make bricks, the roadkeeper keeps no road, and the man with mustaches puts out a fire with a pail that has a 'hole in the bottom' (52). The bitterness of Marlow's sadly ironic remark that 'What saves us is efficiency – the devotion to efficiency' (31) is only augmented by the real efficiency of the accountant. Finally, private intentions provide an alternative to extreme and especially anarchistic social philosophies that lack positive mechanisms to effect change. But good private intentions that cooperate with the very rationalized work they would overthrow leave the political will to bring about change in the nonprivate structure of work looking pharisaically empty. That Marlow can maintain a belief in the intrinsic value of work even as he contributes to its rampant perversion, insofar as he works for the Company, points to a divisive and damaging fissure in the treatment of ideals and reality. The conviction to Work that lies behind the saving illusion is reduced to being the means by which moral Work gets separated from its economic and potentially political frame.

The same dualism makes for an ambiguity in Conrad's attitude towards imperialism. Just as work has been perverted in the Congo, imperialism, it would seem, has been perverted – it is not inherently or fundamentally wrong, but a fundamental good carried out in a perverted manner. In a letter to William Blackwood, Conrad wrote that *Heart of Darkness* would explore the 'criminality of inefficiency and pure selfishness when tackling the civilizing work in Africa' (*CL* 2: 139–40). Marlow serves colonialism under the moral safety net of private, personal values. Conrad's bottom line opens the way for a private colonialism. The disjunction between moral and economic work sees Conrad promote the social-economic status quo by representing personal psychic stability and maintain the social order by strengthening the personal one. Though Marlow recognizes that the ideology of Work will blindly be deployed to glorify the most brutal configuration of economic thinking, colonialism, he continues to will faith in that ideology. Before leaving for the Congo, Marlow parodies his aunt's blessing: 'I was also one of the Workers, with a capital – you know. Something like an emissary of light, something like a lower sort of apostle.' Despite acknowledging that his aunt is voicing the 'rot' of the popular press and even hinting to her that the Company is 'run for profit' (38–9), Marlow refuses to abandon what *Heart of Darkness* pleads with us to attempt, the spirit of making value or wresting purpose out of the void. Conrad knew his Carlyle.

In the structural conflict between work as an absolute moral principle and its specific applications in colonial chaos inheres Marlow's strength as an individual. Because he can rise above circumstance, the most effective weapon against modern work is his own industry, despite the fact that that industry contributes to the very organizations his traditional work ethic would abolish. Conrad distinguishes between effort and product, between process and item; he rejects the transition from a productivist to a consumerist ethic and the mentality that fetishizes accumulation. But he cannot help but confirm the ends along with the means, what is being worked for along with what is being worked on. In *Heart of Darkness*, the private value of work and the institutions worked for are treated as if entirely unconnected to each other, just as Carlyle keeps the moral and pragmatic ideas of work tightly compartmentalized or separates final from contingent knowledge. As with Carlyle and Orwell, Conrad also vacillates between positioning himself either inside or outside the whale, either treating the rationalization of work as an inevitable reality that must be coped with on its own terms or refuting it wholesale by returning to an independently reached moral idea of Work. Both Conrad and Orwell had given up relative economic comforts to pursue and explore vastly different manners of living where Work, not economic negotiating, was thought or could be represented to still dominate the job. With Carlyle they also treat writing, intellectual work, as the physical Work they extol. Intellectual work is one of the few types of work in which 'work' and 'life' are not easily and strictly separated, as in the rationalist design. As with Carlyle before him, Conrad assigns to the art of writing the value of Work and explicitly contrasts it to the language of science and facts. In *Lord Jim* Marlow reflects on Jim's situation by saying, 'They wanted facts! Facts! They demanded facts from him, as if facts could explain anything!' (27). He picks up from Carlyle and Dickens what Orwell would adopt in his turn: a distrust and disregard for the clean mechanics of scientism. In 'The Ascending Effort' (1921) Conrad writes that any attempt 'to league together ... science and the arts' is not only unforeseeable but also undesirable (73), confirming the antagonism between rationalism and nonrationalism that pervades his fiction. Conrad treats art and science as adversaries; science, including the human sciences, is an inadequate barometer for the unpredictability of humankind. In *The Secret Agent* (1907) he satirizes the public's overvaluation of science by imagining the outrage caused by blowing up time, the premier discourse of rationality. Throughout his career he took the stuffing out of a world that prided itself on scientific objectivity and incontrovertible 'facts' with style, the very inscrutability of his imagery and *brooding* of his prose.

Richard Ambrosini argues that Work in Conrad is a trope used to 'synthesize the aesthetic and moral implications of his artistic intention' (13). The union between artist and worker, in fact, brings us back to Arendt's definition of work. For Arendt and Conrad both art and Work demand an active life, service, and duty: to 'forget one's self' and to sacrifice one's self to the community (*Mirror of the Sea* 30). Both artist and worker enrich themselves with tradition and by embracing traditional forms are exacting, drawing out the best in the committed. Both art and Work last, creating a feeling of fellowship with all of creation over space and time. Labour goods are instantly consumed. Both art and Work also foster self-realization. And both create transcending beauty.

The 'Preface' to *The Nigger of the 'Narcissus'* includes an affirmation of the symbolist/impressionist manifesto 'art for art's sake,' but the context in which it appears entirely reverses the gesture towards amorality common to *fin de siècle* aesthetics. The emphasis in the essay, rather, is placed on process as opposed to product, effort as opposed to item. Conrad writes that the 'motive ... may be held to justify the matter of the work' (12). The parable of the 'labourer in a distant field' confirms an anti-rationalist position in its traditional imagery. The worker 'has tried' but failed at his given task. He is still worthy of praise because his aim was not 'the clear logic of a triumphant conclusion,' in maximizing the outcome (14). Such 'an avowal of endeavor' (12), along with the connection between writer and worker, transforms the doctrine of 'art for art's sake' from a self-indulgent, anti-utilitarian relativism to mean 'Work for Work's sake.' Art, as in the aesthetic creed, is not to be regarded 'for immediate profit, demands specifically to be edified, consoled, amused' (12–13). But unlike the aesthetic creed, art has value in the same way that Work has intrinsic value: it has moral value, that is, because it is not performed to maximize ends.

Even insofar as Conrad borrows from the avant-garde, from impressionism, his language is not, contrary to Jameson's argument in *The Political Unconscious* (1981), a strategic device employed to transform realities into pure style, to de-realize, to aestheticize and thus evade social reality. The Lukácsian dismissal of modernist style as categorically expressing decadence and displacing history is dogmatic enough to reveal the shortcomings of a legacy of asceticism and rationalism. To justify his assertion about impressionism's dissemblance, that the impressionistic text conceals real economic determinants, class stratification, and conflict, Jameson discusses the boiler room scene of *Lord Jim*. The scene runs as follows:

> short metallic clangs bursting out suddenly in the depths of the ship, the harsh scrape of the shovel, the violent slam of a furnace door, exploded brutally, as if the men handling the mysterious things below had their breasts full of fierce anger: while the slim high hull of the steamer went on evenly ahead. (20)

Instead of recognizing that this is a representation of labour, Jameson believes its presence is 'muffled ... easy to ignore (or to rewrite [for the reader] in terms of the aesthetic, of sense perception as here of the sounds and sonorous inscription of a reality you prefer not to conceptualize)' (215). The language may draw attention to its own aural qualities, but what is so airy about 'metallic,' 'clangs,' 'violent,' 'harsh,' 'scrape,' 'brutally,' or 'fierce'? Labour's sounds are also juxtaposed to the 'even' and calm language that describes life above the workplace. Still, even if the sounds draw attention to themselves as artistic and aesthetic, does it necessarily follow that the reader will be distracted from the content? Is it not as likely or even more likely that the content – the demands made on labour to ensure the ship's business – will be underscored through the attempt at descriptive atmosphere? Jameson discounts the amplification of meaning that aesthetic form confers to content in order to show the inward configuration or artificial boundaries of the 'ostensible' text. Only then can he reveal that *Lord Jim* has an unwritten subtext of class contradiction to which Conrad remained impervious.

The sentence that follows the description of the boiler room – the steamer 'cleaving continuously the great calm of waters under the inaccessible serenity of the sky' (20) – contains another juxtaposition, this time between hard 'c' and soft 's' sounds: between steamships (the *Patna*) and nature. The conflict is not really between man and nature, but between modern mechanization and traditional sailing. Steamships can 'cleave' the ocean under a 'serene' sky; a sailing ship cannot cleave water without cooperation from the sky (without wind). The sounds refer back to the unnaturalness of the technology and the rationalist system from which it developed. Impressionism can accommodate political form. When cleared of its hyper-subjectivity, and the example above is much too rudimentary to be thought of as self-involved, impressionism challenges rationalism, for if a process is to be rationalized it has to be systematically represented. Conrad, whether temporally Romantic, Naturalist, Realist, or Impressionist, or an amalgamation thereof, uses style to counter the systematic.

In 'The Novel as Art Form' (1993) Jim Reilly finds Conrad's 'yarns' 'disingenuously dubbed.' Citing Benjamin's *Illuminations* (1955), he argues that the proverbial wisdom implied by the oral narrative structures is 'transformed by all the relativizing, problematizing devices which are [Conrad's] decisive contribution to emergent modernism; hesitant and fractured telling, writing which writhes within the agonized intuition of its own lack of reference, evocation of the moral opacity of a world congealed into secret and deceptive forms, a radical indeterminacy of meaning' (59). Conrad may frustrate traditional orality, but the stylistic innovations primarily counter the clinical discourses of rationalism and scientific logic. Moreover, oral narratives ought to be more convoluted than written ones – most people talk in run-on sentences punctuated – at best – by dashes. Benjamin himself argues that the 'storytelling that thrives for a long time in the milieu of work – rural, the maritime, and the urban – is itself an artisan form of communication, as it were. It does not aim to convey the pure essence of the thing, like information or a report' (91). An oral structure enables Conrad to speak for tradition and against mechanical rationality.

Conrad's rejection of the language of rationalist science, of scientism and scientific management, of any attempt to define and thus limit the unwieldy, plural shape of humankind, was complete. He did, however, speak of science as Orwell spoke of technology; that is, with resignation. In 1897, he wrote:

> You cannot by any special lubrication make embroidery with a knitting machine. And the most withering thought is that the infamous thing has made itself; made itself without thought, without conscience, without foresight, without eyes, without heart. It is a tragic accident – and it has happened. You can't interfere with it. (*CL* 1: 425)

Conrad's style does interfere with it, but when Conrad wrote he played the role of a moral worker, the participant miles away from the shores of rationalism.

The major difference between Orwell and Conrad (or Carlyle) is that while tackling pragmatic work from an analytical, post-Work perspective, Orwell is inclined to insist on a politics of working-class issues, whereas Conrad (or Carlyle) is more likely to manifest his conservatism and a lack of sympathy for the working class. But they all have either a contemptuous attitude towards the political working class, reducing its struggles to laziness (as with Donkin in *The Nigger of the 'Narcissus'*), or at least denying its political consciousness – or the possibility of its political consciousness. Finally, all three reject extreme or revolutionary politics: rejecting the organized attempt to destroy exactly what a realization of a nonprivate, nonsegregated moral idea of Work needs to destroy.

Aside from but related to the attitudes towards work, perhaps the most distinct thread of connection between Conrad, Carlyle, and Orwell has to do with their conception of the individual. The entire Conradian concept of the individual is much different than in utilitarian or liberal theory. In *The Nigger of the 'Narcissus,'* the organic whole, the collective that works as one, *is* the individual, insofar as it acts as if independent of an economic function. The organic-conservative model insists on each person's responsibility for carrying out a certain prescribed function. Under the argument of time immemorial, and with presumably little mention of salaries and pay, workers consent to subordinate themselves to the community, effectively integrating themselves into a single body. As in Carlyle's political workshops, members of Conrad's organic group must fix their identity with a role and play it. Captains, who provide the mental, decision-making power, are to rule. The Captain in 'The Secret Sharer' (1912) incurs danger for all aboard his ship by allowing his crew rest from their duties. After Captain Allistoun quells the mutiny on the *Narcissus*, he tells his crew that 'If you knew your work as well as I do mine, there would be no trouble' (113). Solidarity in Conrad's organic model means that each man plays a part and develops a sense of identity under that part, though the parts are based on a hierarchical structure and not the movements of a rationalized, Tayloresque division of labour. The metaphor of society as a well-run ship parallels Carlyle's traditional Past, when workers 'were prepared to give their life for him [a Feudal Baron], if need came. It was beautiful; it was human' (*Past* 271). But the only way in which Conrad can wholly differentiate between the tenets of his organicism and utilitarian functionalism is to completely divorce the operations of organicism from its economic enterprise, trade. He then separates a discourse promoting Work and obedience from the one that vilifies the conditions of labour. The latter is reserved for the observing middle class, the reader – it is not the proper discourse for the ship's workers to utter. The individual members of the crew are located socially through their skill and rank, but not through an economic function, as what develops under classical political economy. As an individual, an organic whole, the crew acts outside of any economic, objective reality. But organicism does not act to erase, mitigate, or justify the material or commercial exploits ultimately driving the sails of the *Narcissus* (and which the values of organicism seemingly contradict), just as Marlow's devotion to Work does not undo his presence in the Congo. Organicism and materialism, or Work and imperialism, are rather treated synchronically, as discontinuous or different, so that moral and economic work *can* coexist.

For the whole to function in equilibrium Conrad divides it into hierarchized parts. A vertical division of labour guarantees that the collective operates in continuity and mutual dependence. Disruption occurs when individuals confuse or evade the functions set out for them or question the structure of the whole. When the crew of the *Narcissus* defend Wait or entertain Donkin they challenge the moral idea of Work.

Donkin and Wait are effective only when the crew has time to think about working conditions and economic matters, rather than about Purpose, which is a moral matter. When the crew focuses on the collective, on Work, Donkin and Wait are either absent or a declared nuisance. Pity, self-pity, personal resentment (Donkin's *ressentiment*), anti-authoritarianism, or worker solidarity that attempts to act independently of officer control jeopardizes the assurance that necessary roles will be performed. As with Orwell, Conrad shows little patience with would-be liberal sympathizers of workers' rights in the abstract. He insists that natural and inevitable crises demand an internalization of a disciplined organization of work: that without authoritative forces of constraint to keep people in check, primitive or chaotic impulses would govern. Yet one of the more important recurring motifs in Conrad's canon revolves around an existential test, and the preparation for that test. Apart from being a test of masculinity, the ability to 'take it' (as it certainly was for Orwell), the idea behind Conrad's existentialism is that one cannot know how one will respond to an object or a situation unless one faces it without the security of external scrutiny (without police, the opinions of others, God, etc.). Though existentialism abandons the apparatus to critically examine any deterministic force save the individual at the centre, Conrad's existential situation suggests a special circumstance, a special test of identity. But the crew of the *Narcissus* are never isolated in this way; they are only isolated from economic issues (except in special circumstances). The crew, never thinking of anything but their roles when functioning at their best, do not will their own moral attitudes towards work as Marlow does: it is willed for them for their own 'good.'

Conrad would agree with Orwell that 'liberty and efficiency must pull in opposite directions' (*CEJL* 4: 49). But Conrad attempts to treat efficiency as if it were a moral, not an economic issue. He is much more comfortable with the idea of deference and devotion to leaders, of honour, and of an authoritarian society than Orwell, even in Orwell's most conservative moments. Watt has pointed out that Conrad's hierarchies are 'not in general based on inherited, educational, or economic advantages' (*Conrad* 116). But the fixity of relations on the *Narcissus*, for example, suggests an antipathy for egalitarianism that I do not think Conrad would deny. His typical view of society simply bypasses the place of inheritance and holds economic matters in abeyance (education is another matter): it does not directly challenge them. Carlyle also juxtaposes liberty and efficiency, favours the latter, and would reactivate an aristocratic right to rule, though not the aristocracy. His feudal system of 'noble loyalty in return for noble guidance' would deter 'infidelity' with 'fire and faggot.' (He adds that that kind of punishment is 'difficult to manage in our times' [*Past* 272, 240].) The link between Carlyle and Conrad runs deep: Captain Allistoun runs his ship as Abbot Samson runs his monastery. In *Past and Present*, Carlyle pre-echoes Conrad by saying, 'they do not tolerate "freedom of debate" on board a Seventy-four!' (278).

For the generation tutored on Carlyle and Conrad what was almost conventionally accepted by the 1930s to be a contradiction between repressive managerial discipline and a defence of Work was quite easily 'resolved.' Both Carlyle and Conrad maintain that a worker who respects discipline and practises self-denial accrues psychological freedom and intrinsic satisfaction precisely from that discipline and self-denial. Only the more pervasive contradiction between the logic of modern economic relations and equally vehement sermons on the Gospel of Work remains entirely irrecoverable: nondialectical because neither side is qualified by or confronts its opposite. Carlyle and Conrad treat Work as if separate from its context and its effects, modern economics. The dislocation of Work and the traditional order it represents is also at the heart of the Orwellian inconsistency. Carlyle, Conrad, and Orwell do not deny that labour (and what it represents) exists, but behind the disjunction between Work and labour is an assumption of the individual's imperative to subordinate history, to treat it as that which can be surmounted by moral determination: to get Work from labour.

Conrad, Carlyle, and Orwell all find that tough and taxing physical work, albeit in a subordinated role, is inherently satisfying. They all validate a sense of independent, swaggering manhood that equates 'being able to take it' with honour. They share what is typically argued to be a labourer's approach to work and life. Conrad especially assumes that life is necessarily difficult, toilsome, and unpredictable – tragic or at least ironic. But if the working class expects life to be a struggle, that sensibility is born from economic, not metaphysical conditions; there are, in any case, economic conditions leading to that sensibility. Conrad's tragic sensibility belongs to his discourse of Work and confirms manliness in the ensuing struggle. (Economic consciousness, such as Donkin's, often goes hand in hand with physical weakness.) There is a difference between machismo promoted in order to put a shine on commitment, loyalty, comradeship, and trust, and the dissemblance of contemporary management firms who use a metaphor of sports or the team player to legitimize rules and encourage devotion to the company's profits. But

Conrad's, Carlyle's, or Orwell's hyper-masculine worker also labours for the owner of a ship, monastery, or mining firm; his labour serves others while his Work serves himself. The 'tragedy' of life simultaneously naturalizes and conceals service to the ruling economic class. The ideology that equates exacting labour with masculine affirmation only becomes tenable when the intrinsic value of Work is kept isolated from its economic counterpart. Pierre Bourdieu documents that 'accumulating the capital of honour and prestige' is good business for the disenfranchised (*Logic* 118); the point ought to be that it is very good business for the employer.

The toughness of the worker's gendered role is often matched by a lack of intelligence. However, it is not obviously true that Conrad, Orwell, and Carlyle celebrate the stupidity of manual workers: a lack of intelligence is often meant to signify Wisdom. Yes, Carlyle says that 'difficulty and work' make for an 'almost stupid' person, a person dependent upon those who '*can* articulate' (*Past* 23). Orwell, despite believing in working-class politics, agrees that workers need the guidance of the middle class. In Conrad's *The Nigger of the 'Narcissus,'* reflection leads to self-interest, irrational chaos, and the disintegration of the social fabric, whereas the body's activity leads to social integration. Singleton, the best of the crew at its best, is mute, 'unthinking,' 'easy to inspire' (31), and instinctually driven to duty. The positive, regulating properties of physical work are also sanctioned by a metaphysical mandate. Through 'the perfect wisdom' of the sea, the crew is 'not permitted to meditate at ease upon the complicated and acrid savour of existence.' Rather, 'eternal Pity' 'commands toil to be hard and unceasing' (80). Conrad and Carlyle especially imply the childishness of workers, represent sailors or factory workers as 'big children' (17), shelter the working class from valuable economic criticisms, and accordingly prescribe a severe paternalistic stance for the 'superiors.'

But stupidity is not the same thing as 'simplicity' or 'uneducated.' Engineering and navigational skills for Marlow are sufficient 'to save a wiser man' (*HD* 70) from being paralyzed by self-consciousness or mobilized by self-interest. Simplicity is not shameful if the results of studied and advanced intelligence are primitive urges systematically pursued. The consequence of fixing simplicity to Wisdom or Work, however, is that entrained in the coupling is a blind devotion to mind-numbing *labour*. It might be Work for Conrad, but it is bought labour power for Singleton's employers. Conrad can only validate the simplicity of workers by keeping them totally isolated from the economic structure. The place where Work occurs, the sea, is unreconciled with and entirely different, historically and symbolically, from the operation engaging that work, located on the land. Invocations to manhood and simplicity, to Work, occur as if they had no economic meaning, that capitalism had never reached the sea. Manly endurance and uncritical obedience may have been virtues in themselves, but only in themselves; otherwise, they were virtues contributing to the demise of the 'moral economy.'

But such is the advantage of representing a self-contained *gemeinschaft* community of nonrationalist Work, despite the outer presence of rationalist institutions and systems surrounding and setting up that community but never penetrating it. The sites of Work in Conrad's fiction have a protective coating of isolation and antiquation covering them – a hermetic seal that disallows any economic discourse. The work performed there is entirely nonrational, even anti-rational. In *Heart of Darkness*, Marlow and the foreman jig and 'behaved like lunatics' (60). As with Carlyle's language of Work, their actions match much of Johan Huizinga's definition of play. The dance is devoid of utilitarian purpose, 'bound by ties other than those of logic or causality.' It is 'outside the sphere of necessity or material utility' (Huizinga 119, 132). Marlow's personal project is *not* to bring everything under rational control: Kurtz's irrationality is very different from a nonrational jig. Conrad maintains a distinction between irrationalism and nonrationalism that is lost under the aegis of industrial and economic functionalism. The jig scene is also in direct opposition to the formally rational, the systematic: the charts of the Accountant. It shows that formal rationality confronts Marlow as something external to him, further away than his heart of darkness.

In *The Nigger of the 'Narcissus,'* Captain Allistoun's peccadillo, his 'secret ambition' to be 'mentioned in nautical papers' (36), is not a rationalist fault. Though it leads him to drive the ship with an overgrown sense of ambition (and maximize profits for his employers), he acts to satisfy his ego. Singleton alone might be faultless in his continuation of the old art and practices of seamanship that defy rationalist organization, modern technology, contracts, and so on. He is superstitious and unadapted to life on the land. Besides invoking feudal values, Conrad represents the sailors as children and the officers as paternal in order to contrast a metaphor of the family and the psychology of heredity to rationalist business. The fact that the ship operates best under chaotic, threatening situations overturns the liberal-rationalist idea that the organization of society is a scientific problem with an administrative answer. Liberal-rationalism insists that rational calculation, a planned society, eliminates disturbance: part of an assumption about the perfectibility of humankind. Conrad rejects the feasibility of the rationalist society because of an anti-Rousseauian, tragic sense of life that understands nature and human nature as uncooperatively unpredictable. His organicism, as Avrom Fleishman notes, challenges and rejects the idea of classic liberal theory that the individual is a 'rational being who could be depended upon to know his self-interest and to act on it in predictable ways' (52). Liberal theory, which also assumes that self-interest accrues benefits for the public good, is in every way antipathetic to Conrad's anti-rationalist organicism.

But his *Narcissus* operates in situations far removed from the threat of economic rationalism. Nonrationalist work provides an alternative to the rationalist, moneyed society associated with the land, but the community he depicts on the water works as if entirely oppositional or resistant to it. Conrad represents Work as a contest with nature, with the self; it is not an economic struggle, not a competition between persons, not a fight against the predominance of rationalist systems. The critique of rationalist economics (in super-economic terms) is never in doubt: it appears when the payclerk, a representation of the rationalist social order, calls Singleton a 'disgusting old brute' and Donkin an 'intelligent man' (140, 141); it appears as technology leaves tradition 'devoured and forgotten' (31); it appears when the 'invisible hand' that recalls the crew back to their 'duty' demands self-sacrifice and not self-interestedness (106). The criticism takes place on the land and implicitly whenever moral Work takes place, but it is not directed at economic institutions. Conrad's complaint is directed at the threat of economics penetrating the moral idea of Work. Finally, his critique of economization does not confront rationalist economics so as to recognize the economic function of the *Narcissus* itself.

Behind Conrad's criticism dwells an economic orthodoxy that never questions the organizations and institutions it serves. Economic issues never surface when moral Work is underway, as if moral Work precluded the idea of wages, profit, capital: as if the economic society ran only in the recesses of the moral one. But the economic society runs nonetheless. Conrad avoids the contradictions that become manifest when economics, the profits of shipowners for example, undermine the moral idea of Work. He may censure the quantitative values of a commercial, material, rational society, but his merchant marine vessels nonetheless carry cargo. The pragmatic Conrad knew that the 'British Empire rests on transportation' ('Confidence' 202). Along with Orwell, he would raise more than an eyebrow at any flighty protest for a friendly economy. But that pragmatic ethic or voice, preserved for the nonworking class, is pushed far into the background when the stage belongs to moral Work, the work demanded from the working class (sailors in this case), as it mostly does. Fleishman rightly observes that

> Conrad's nautical pieties: subordination to authority, devotion to the given task, fidelity to comrades, identification with the mariner's tradition of service, acceptance of the difficulty of life within destructive nature, and the manifestation of effort and courage ... have the effect of rationalizing the *status quo* by extending the relationship of a work situation to political life generally. (73)

Such an extension is made, though the extension between the work situation and economic life generally is not.

Though Conrad's nautical pieties act directly as political standards, they can only be claimed by removing the metaphor, Work, from the artificiality of contracts. If society/work is based on a contract, as the crew's or Marlow's work ultimately is, then there is little room left for organic spontaneity. Conrad may pursue the idea that the polis is the supreme end of Work, as does Arendt, but he arrives at the point by partitioning off and concealing the economic base and operations underlying it. Both Conrad and Arendt maintain that craftsmanship imparts continuity to humanity over time, a kind of historical organicism. Both of them lament the transformation of 'work' into 'labour' under modern production. They question and reject the 'rationality' of a utilitarian ideology that conceives of production as temporary, merely the means for further production (reducing it to 'labour'). And both of them regard work as finding full meaning in the polis; that the purpose of work, of the *vita activa*, is to develop and organize society. Though Conrad would not deny that that society would involve a good deal of pragmatic economics accompanying these more high-minded principles, his representation of a moral society, of Work, does.

Eagleton bases his criticism of Conrad on a perceived split between organicism and a 'sometimes solipsistic individualism – a metaphysical skepticism as to the objective nature of social values ... a view of human societies as essentially "criminal" organizations of selfish self-interests' (*Criticism* 134). But Eagleton assumes that the individual and the social whole, the polis, are at odds as a matter of course and refuses to admit that Conrad's rejection of the social whole is simply the rejection of a warped, rationalized social whole. Eagleton also refuses to admit Conrad's distinction between aloneness and individualism. If Conrad's letter to Cunninghame Graham were not so obviously sardonic, a criticism of what is as opposed to what might be, Eagleton would have very strong evidence for his assertion. Conrad writes,

> Man is a vicious animal. His viciousness must be organized. Crime is a necessary condition of organized existence. Society is fundamentally criminal – or it would not exist. Selfishness preserves everything – absolutely everything ... And everything holds together. That is why I respect the extreme anarchists. – 'I hope for general extermination' – Very Well. (*CL* 2: 160)

In a sense, Conrad's 'land' in *The Nigger of the 'Narcissus,'* and the Congo in *Heart of Darkness*, is based on organized malice and organized egoism.

The dominant disjunction in Conrad's work is not between the polis and the individual, but between ideal values and the ugly realities they support, or between moral Work and pragmatic economics. The gap is not furnished in the slightest by an appeal to the organic fellowship of the merchant marine service: organicism has nothing to do with the reason why the *Narcissus* is on the water in the first place and is not the only thing that keeps it afloat. The only way to ratify either moral Work or the material undercurrent is to treat them in mutual exclusion. Conrad was certainly attracted to the British 'practical bent of mind.' Pragmatism was so important to the particular set of English writers I am examining that their alternative to pragmatism is work, albeit 'moral' and not utilitarian. Conrad rejects economistic thinking; but he rejects the idea of rational agency *and* the idea that the individual is incapable of independent decisions, a mere cog of the commercial machine. His individual, the one who works to be 'one of us,' is decent, not self-interested, despite the indecency that surrounds him.

If one looks solely at Conrad's attitude towards work and society, it becomes clear that his closest contemporaries are Victorians, not moderns, and definitely not the avant-garde of high modernism, conservative in culture as it was. Most Edwardians, such as Rudyard Kipling, are generally Victorian or Conradian in their attitudes towards work. Kipling makes a point of glorifying Work *especially* in the conditions of labour. In 'The Glory of the Garden' (1911), he suggests that the sanctity of England, the Eden-like Garden of the poem, depends on working through laborious conditions:

> Then seek your job with thankfulness and work till further orders,
> If it's only netting strawberries or killing slugs on borders;
> And when your back stops aching and your hands begin to harden,
> You will find yourself a partner in the Glory of the Garden.

In 'A Truthful Song' (1910) he rather defensively sets his target on history itself. A brickmaker and a sailor, as if threatened by an encroaching modernity, insist that Work is impervious to the specificity of labour:

> We tell these tales, which are strictest true,
> Just by way of convincing you
> How very little, since things were made,
> Anything alters in any one's trade!

Though Conrad never goes so far as to neglect history, he does lament its movement, that the way things are made or are done have altered. His sarcasm is at its sharpest when he depicts the inflated confidence in the technological advances of his age, which he never thought could surpass the efficiency of seamen. At the same time, Conrad never would accept anything less than efficiency from seamen. Incidentally, Kipling, unlike Conrad, when musing on the connection between technology and the Empire, altered his attitude towards the changing nature of work. In 'McAndrew's Hymn' (1894) he writes,

> From coupler-flange to spindle-guide I see Thy hand, O God –
> Predestination in the stride o' yon connectin'-rod

H.G. Wells

In some ways the Conradian rupture between Work and labour is most notably reproduced in Wells's attempts to tackle modernity, though in other ways Wells marks a departure from the Conradian philosophy of Work and interpretation of the economic. Wells and Conrad were acquaintances; Conrad apparently had more appreciation for Wells than vice versa, judging by Wells's *Experiment in Autobiography* (1934). In Conrad Wells found 'something ... ridiculous in [his] *persona* of a Romantic adventurous un-mercenary intensely artistic European gentleman carrying an exquisite code of unblemished honour through a universe of baseness' (530). But Wells, in the vein of Kipling, had a dual admiration for rusticity and technology that led Orwell, who was never himself consistent in these matters, to suggest that 'vast contradictions' infuse *his* work (*Road* 177). The root of the contradictions may lie in the very place where Wells locates incongruity in Conrad's work. Orwell sees the split attitude in Wells as a struggle between science and romance:

> On the one side science, order, progress, internationalism, aeroplanes, steel, concrete, hygiene: on the other side war, nationalism, religion, monarchy, peasants, Greek professors, poets, horses. History as he sees it is a series of victories won by the scientific man over the romantic man. (*CEJL* 2: 169)

Orwell, typically not self-reflexive, is correct, except that the scientific man is not always crowned. In fact, Wells at times sees the dangers of science in Orwell's terms, representing a 'paradise of little fat men' (Orwell, *Road* 169) in *The Time Machine* (1895), the Eloi who had left all the physical work to the Morlocks. *The History of Mr. Polly* (1910) is a story of lower-middle-class frustration with its social role being severed from its natural inclination (working class at root) towards nature and authentic Work. Technology in the novel is implicitly admonished by Polly's position as a hands-on jack-of-all-trades at the Potwell Inn. The world's first slacker when in the city, the work that Mr Polly embarks upon in the country is 'News from Nowhere' work, potato digging and so forth. One of Polly's stranger jobs is that of 'recovering the bodies of drowned persons' (183), the most urban of jobs in Dickens's *Our Mutual Friend* (1864–5). For Wells to associate it with romantic Work suggests that what was in Dickens's day cruelly urban had become pastoral nostalgia forty-five years later. Polly's Work is in fact validated precisely because it is the opposite of technological labour, rationalist learning, utilitarian goals, and a scientific epistemology. His duties span two pages of text as if to emphasize that a jack-of-all-trades is a position that is the complete opposite of the division of labour. He is also intuitively skilled at the work he embraces. He grows strong in the country and is able to fight Jim with a manliness not available to him in the city. In other words, Work, along with chivalry, questing, and combat, is part of the Romance genre missing from the prose of his everyday life. However, in *Tono-Bungay* (1909) and in his nonfiction, Wells is a self-appointed spokesperson for machines, for the 'adventures of mechanism' (*Bungay* 254). Wells moves quickly and absolutely between endorsing rational science and romanticizing the imagination, between technological optimism and social pessimism. The two sides of Wells, rationalist and anti-rationalist, pragmatist and sentimentalist, scientist and moralist, are in constant opposition in his writings. That dualism remains undialectical because Wells finds an escape hatch in what I call moral individualism: 'Romantic adventurous un-mercenary' Workers 'carrying an exquisite code of unblemished honour through a universe of baseness' (*Experiment* 530).

Tono-Bungay and *Mr. Polly*, more than any other of Wells's novels, slip out of the contradiction between validating distinctly opposing values by withdrawing to the nonrationalist (nonmaximizing), moral (self-changing) mindscape of the doer. *Mr. Polly* confirms this brand of individualism in contradistinction to the individualism of the businessman. The conflict in the book is simple: 'modern business conditions,' the ideology of 'getting on,' and the 'hard old economic world' versus the imagination, Work, and a 'healthy, human life': bookkeeping against books. Even Polly's departure from shopkeeping to the non-economic world is not a calculated, rationally chosen act, but a carefree leap into the unknown with little concern over whether or not something will turn up. Unlike Jim's failure to deal with reality in *Lord Jim*, an over-inflated romantic sensibility and idealistic expectations are not in any way to blame for Polly's disenchantment with the real. Wells's own sense of the determining power of the environment, and in fact the whole materialist movement in post-Victorian fiction, is undercut by Polly's declaration that 'If the world does not please you, *you can change it*' (172). The statement perfectly expresses the attitude of moral individualism. The individual is presented as capable of cutting himself off from an economic reality and material circumstances that were previously represented as ubiquitous, unremitting, and unforgiving. The history of Mr Polly, before his escape, is an economic history. Polly's leap from a world where 'things happened to me' into a happy, comfortable trampdom and peaceful, rustic living is generated by a moral commitment to break free from circumstance and necessity. The nonrationalist split from pragmatism and economics, the Conradian split that assumes that the individual can get beyond the rationalized world, voids itself of political content. Polly's escape from the economic world can only confirm the power of volition by creating a chasm between the two worlds of romance and economics. Polly becomes a 'Visitant from Another World' when he returns to see Miriam (223). The discrepancy between his private utopia, where he lives life on his own terms, and the powerful economic and social determinism of his life as a lower-middle-class shopkeeper reflects the same split between Work and labour, Work and economics, Work and pragmatism, or Work and necessity found in Carlyle and Conrad. The split remains nondialectical in all three writers as they avoid having the opposites cancel each other out by withdrawing into a disinterested individualism.

The dualism between Work and economics or Romance and rationality continues in *Tono-Bungay*, even though, because of Wells's faith in rationalist science, the terms get mixed up. Work, George's flight of fancy, is written as a rational, technological, engineering enterprise: 'the fine realities of steel' (9). In *Tono-Bungay*, sceptical science, aeronautics, and the dream of Progress replace 'Culture,' 'Art,' and 'Work.' With Woolfian overtones George admits that he regards science as the 'enduring thing,' as others see art (353). Edward, furthermore, is a romantic, a dreamer; in fact, George rationalizes Edward's business by insisting on increasing efficiency and reducing production costs (119–20). The tension in *Tono-Bungay* is nonetheless familiar. On the one hand it explores economic activity and financial corruption and on the other hand it withdraws to romantic, imaginative, passionate, questing, moral Work. The disjunction between moral and economic work does not collapse in Edward and George Ponderevo; rather the dreamer and the economist in both George and Edward are not forced to confront each other. Though the reader is never allowed to forget that George's romanticized science is bankrolled by Edward's commercial success, his work is an escape, not affected by that money or by the need to market inventions, by pragmatic economics. In a similar way, Edward's economic scheming does not arrest the basically moral side of his character. At one time he is the petty egotist/capitalist selling waste and at another, the harmless comic hero. Edward is an attractive character, committing what are ultimately represented as the peccadilloes of a 'Child' (330). Whereas he is supposed to incite reader sympathy, the society that allowed him to become a fraud is held responsible for the wrongdoings. Just as the city is at one time 'cancerous' and 'sinister' and then 'illimitable' and full of extraordinary life (90, 94), or the flux and aimlessness of trade is countered by the exhilarating prospect of change, Wells has an ambiguous attitude towards Edward. A part of him manages to remain isolated from the economic realm that otherwise determines his entire character. Wells ultimately gets swept up by Edward's energy and the 'Romance of Commerce' (62), not unlike Defoe's enthusiasm for his naughty Moll Flanders.

The incoherence and inconsistencies of *Tono-Bungay* stem from the same dualistic tendency found in Carlyle and Conrad. The main difference has to do with the shift, sparked by economic analysis or reflected in it, from an emphasis on the producer to an emphasis on the consumer. When Carlyle complains against advertising, the rise of Public Relations or planned obsolescence, it is from the point of view of someone who understands commercialism as an adjunct to the product. Wells understands value, at least when it comes to determining price, as determined by the subjective or ideological desire for the product, not by the labour invested in the product. Instead of Work being contrasted to labour, then, Work is contrasted to marketing, business, capitalism, profiteering, finance, and consumption. Faced with the loss of the institutions that were thought to stabilize history – Work but also the church and marriage – Wells places faith in science and not in the return to the fixity of a rural aristocracy. But the division between Work (science and industry) and economics (finance and commercialism) resembles the more 'traditional' split between Work and pragmatics in that the worker, George, avoids pragmatism and the pragmatist, Edward, rises above it.

Wells's belief in the redemptive value of a rationalist technocracy and a scientific elite, socialistic but politically authoritarian, places him awkwardly in a line of disjunctive pragmatists/romantics. He was likely whom Orwell had in mind when the latter said that 'the Socialist is always in favour of mechanization, rationalization, modernization – or at least thinks that he ought to be in favour of them' (*Road* 176–7). That Wells was a radical balancing an anti-democratic platform with a program for a version of economic socialism is not altogether a departure from the company in which I have placed him. Expressing faith in rationalism, however, is very alien to the group. The pragmatic/socialistic Fabian movement, which Wells criticized as much as he contributed to, marks the rebirth of a utilitarian and positivist schema that was the catalyst for much of the anti-rationalist writing I have discussed from Carlyle to Conrad. Fabianism is a child of Benthamism insofar as it is super-rational in its approach to gradual social reform, but a wayward child insofar as it contested laissez-faire policy. Contemporary socialism, in many ways, has been reduced to a Fabian idea of governmental involvement, and the meaning of 'liberalism' has been transformed, in part through Fabian ideas, from signifying governmental silence to meaning social nets and the welfare state. Still, the prominent feature of Fabian socialism is its adulation of the fact and its application of the scientific method to social, economic, and political arrangements. It emphasizes practical, unvisionary efficiency rather than a moral imperative, experts and elites rather than popular opinions, and numbers above all. Beatrice Webb in particular has received criticism for her exaggerated appreciation of the scientific method, partly because she called herself a 'Gradgrind' and asked that remarkably queer question about literature, 'what have the whole lot of them, from the work of a genius to a penny-a-liner, accomplished for the advancement of society on the one and only basis that can bring with it virtue and happiness – the scientific method?' (385), but also because her rationalism did not fit the feminine stereotype. But as Williams points out, Bernard Shaw's association with Fabianism 'marks the confluence of two traditions which had been formerly separate and even opposed.' Utilitarianism, in other words, was redefined by 'the direct successor of the spirit of Carlyle and of Ruskin,' Shaw, who was 'telling Carlyle and Ruskin to go to school with Bentham, telling Arnold to get together with Mill' (*Culture* 181–2). The question, however, is if anyone in the Fabian school listened, including Wells. The Fabians, despite Shaw, had an amazing capacity to think solely in terms of economic man, re-creating society as an economic enterprise. Art and culture or Work could only be incidental, not a factor to influence the serious planning and organization of society. The Fabians were not moral morons or philistines, but the movement speaks amazingly well to the enormous methodological split between moralism and pragmatism in the English attitude towards reform.

E.M. Forster

With Forster and 'low modernism,' basically the modernism that did not aspire to obscurantism and the avant-garde, the structural conflict between moral vision and an ideology of an inevitable economics began to take on, in a widespread manner, the specifically Arnoldian terms of culture (knowing) and anarchy (doing), not Work and society. Perhaps Matthew Arnold's frame of reference gains precedence during this period in proportion to Fabian utilitarianism, but be it high or low, modernism turned to Arnold and not Carlyle or Conrad, Culture and not Work. Arnold's rejection of utilitarianism included work as part of all that is *vulgar*. Because Work no longer represented anti-rationalism, the working class and its culture or activity was identified as part of the anarchy otherwise reserved for the philistine, rationalist bourgeoisie. Consequently, modernism not only sequesters (or ignores) all economic or political discourses within 'Hebraism,' but it refuses to extend its ideas about itself to the political and economic systems from which it is based. Arnold was an inspector of schools, politically active in his day-to-day life, but he suffers from the tendency to strictly demarcate the cultural and social and to treat them as polar opposites – all the more so as he deletes Work from culture.

Forster's return to Arnold in this period, however, is complicated by a fascination with individual consciousness and unconsciousness. Consumerist/marginal theory and psychoanalytic theory arrive at roughly the same time, and to ascertain which came first or which was more influential on the other and in determining the course of modernism is beyond the scope of this study. Nonetheless, the two theories are remarkably similar. Sigmund Freud may have based his conception of consciousness on the irrational whereas consumerist theory sees only rationality, but even Freud attempts to explain in scientific terms the predictability of mechanisms that determine behaviour. Both theories placed emphasis on desire and the subdivisions of consciousness. Both consumerist theory and psychoanalysis are also interested in the social valuation of work, in the psychological dimension of economic activity (in prestige and the display of wealth or social contribution). Most important, both theories are organized around a pleasure principle. In fact, not only consumerist, but economic theory in general assumes work is undesirable and that people must be provided with external rewards in order to work. In contrast to Marx, work for Freud could not itself be a source of satisfaction. He speaks of a 'natural human aversion to work,' 'that men are not spontaneously fond of work' (*Civilization* 30n; *Illusion* 9), and that work is a device used for necessary social coercion. 'Civilization' for Freud means a submission to the reality principle, to the undesired, to labour. Freud does not differentiate between Work and labour, revealing the same ahistorical gap in thinking that vitiates both classical and neoclassical economics.

In its traditional or Carlylean form, Work obviates psychoanalysis. Carlyle and Conrad both make the point that one of the advantages of Work is that it replaces introspection, cutting short neurasthenia or any neurosis. For all of Freud's writing and his admission that work is the primary technique in sublimation or attaching 'the individual so firmly to reality' (*Civilization* 30n), he rarely, with the exception of a footnote in *Civilization and Its Discontents* (1930) and a paragraph in *The Future of an Illusion* (1927), speaks about work in detail. For Freud, the process of Analysis is in itself worthwhile, just as for Carlyle or Conrad the process of Work is in itself worthwhile.

D.H. Lawrence's obsession with instinct on the one hand and his censure of industrialism on the other suggests that he has links to Freud *and* Arnold (his criticism of the sterile bourgeoisie lies somewhere in between), the former link being much stronger than the latter. The balance of the relationship is inverted in Forster. Lawrence was originally from the working class and had sympathies for their supposed earthiness and affiliation with hard, physical work. In *Lady Chatterley's Lover* (1928), Mellors, the gamekeeper, is juxtaposed to the soulless, effete, rationalist, Fabian intellectual Clifford Chatterley. Still, Lawrence's connection to Freud, not his understanding of labour, disrupts his attitude towards Work and the working class. It disrupts his Carlylean anti-industrialism; it disrupts his pseudo-Marxian focus on class; it disrupts his Hardyean argument that an immediate contact with the earth imparts a sense of community, identity, and a special moral knowledge to the 'aristocrats of the spirit,' manual workers; and it disrupts his Orwellian argument about the importance of moral criticism, that we read to be morally affected, not to observe the finer points of style. As has been frequently said about *Sons and Lovers* (1913) (see Christopher Harvie's *Political Fiction in Britain* [1991] or Graham Holderness's *D.H. Lawrence: History, Ideology, and Fiction* [1982]), the class conflict between Mr and Mrs Morel is depoliticized and displaced onto the ahistorical, ephemeral terms of psychological turmoil. Similarly, Clara's political frustration is reduced to a frustrated sexuality. The spirit of Work that informs the text's early pages, the children getting 'united with [Mr Morel] in the work, in the actual doing of something' (63), is replaced by a narrative of sexual desire, Lawrence's locus for the nonrational. The conflict between Mrs Morel's bourgeois dream for her son to 'get on' and Mr Morel's working-class roots is quickly overshadowed by a more decisive Oedipal conflict. In the initial conflict, Work and economics are contrasted, not split; in the substitution of Work and pragmatism for sexual psychology or instinct, the conflict between Work and economics is neglected – Work *and* economics are neglected.

If Lawrence absorbed a Freudian or psychological model that dislocates Work, Forster absorbed an Arnoldian, liberal model that ended in a similar result. Forster was burdened by a world dominated by business and sought to achieve an Arnoldian balance between Hellenism and Hebraism. Only connect – culture and economics, moral and pragmatic values, or simply with others – is the liberal plea, along with democracy, reason, and tolerance. Like Lawrence, Forster responds to the rank philistinism of bourgeois society but questions the alternative to that philistinism if held in isolation, in his case culture (in Lawrence's sex), as Lawrence never did. First, he recognizes that culture exists because of money made without 'cultured' values and he faces the awkward questions regarding social justice that follow. In *Howards End* (1910), the Miss Schlegels acknowledge that the eight hundred pounds a year they receive makes their culture possible. Second, he admits that on its own culture becomes effete, as with Tibby, or impotent, as with Helen. But in *Howards End*, culture and economics are never reconciled: before Margaret, Henry was married to the original Mrs Culture (Mrs Wilcox) and was nonetheless able to operate as if divorced from her influence. There is nothing in *Howards End* to suggest that the connection between Margaret and Henry will curb or influence his economic behaviour. The only way the reader knows that the Wilcoxes are sympathetic is through Margaret's assertions. Forster cannot seem to represent the pragmatists as anything but calculating philistines. The symbolic, personal relationship between Margaret and Henry acts in the place of a confrontation that would mitigate Henry's economic fanaticism, just as Lawrence withdraws to sex and instinct when faced with the opposition of Work and economics.

Forster's message in *Howards End* is the same as Gaskell's in *North and South* (1855); that both heroines who initiate the connection between compassion and practicality are named Margaret suggests that Forster was resituating the 'only connect' story from an industrial context to a financial one. That connection seeks to unite male and female principles, materialism and spiritualism, age and youth, prose and passion, the world of contracts and love, economics and culture. Just as in the earlier novel, the connection is sought above the social level where a connection might empower those who would benefit from a little morality in the economic sphere. Gaskell and Forster are aware of the contradiction in a world dominated by economic man who claims to carry Christian sentiment everywhere except into business, where it might be most effective. But Leonard Bast, the new version of the working-class man, has no place in Forster's blueprint to reshape England: Bast is an infringement on and an inconvenience to both culture and money. He is not to connect with anybody, but rather to be superseded. He adds little more to the necessity of connection than being the unwitting occasion for liberal humanism and an indifferent capitalism to connect, exactly the role of industrial workers in Gaskell's novel. In *North and South* the character named Leonards is a despicable and disposable mercenary who threatens to expose Margaret's brother Frederick, forces her to lie, and by doing so ultimately brings about Margaret's union with Thornton. Mary Eagleton and David Pierce argue that 'the alliance of the Wilcoxes and the Schlegels suggests a rearguard action, a last attempt to sustain the class against internal decay and the advance of the Basts of the world' (*Attitudes* 100). It is a convincing argument, implying that Helen and Leonard's child is merely a purification of the world's Basts. Forster was a humanitarian, but he evidently knew little about the lower classes except that they do not fit into his idea of culture or economics. He does not think that the lower-middle class would be first interested in getting money. Though Bast does come to realize the value of the pragmatic, his instinct is to gain cultural experience. Bast reads Ruskin to improve his cultural sensitivity (which Forster represents as comically absurd), but could read him for Work or economics. It is only absurd that Bast is blind to those sides of Ruskin. A meaningful connection between thinking steadily and thinking whole could only take place at the level of the world's Basts, where those who labour (Henry puts others to labour) could affect their own material conditions, whether it is what they do or what they do it for.

The dismissal of the 'very poor,' the 'unthinkable,' those 'only to be approached by the statistician or the poet,' is more likely the narrator's (the narrator has a definite personality) flip concentration of subject matter than Forster's snobbery (58). It is, however, indicative of the elitist level at which the connection between the moral and pragmatic is to take place. This elitism, the nervous reaction to the 'crassness' of working-class-turned-consumer-class culture, the expression of disgust at advertisements for 'antibilious pills,' bridges low to high modernism. In the novel's defence of rural permanence, the diatribe against cars and the encroaching city, elements of radical anti-industrialism and social criticism connect with a reactionary nostalgia for conservative principles in the same way that reactionary values infuse the anti-rationalist high ground of modernism. Even Forster's reaction to cars is problematic: he is obviously saddened that they, the harbingers of nature's declining status in modernity, have 'come to stay' (198). In this sadness is the idea that, as with the city, cars mark the emergence of a classless society, insofar as all drivers have to follow the same rules. Again, Forster was a humanitarian, but he betrays an anti-democratic desire to shelter Culture from becoming a marketable item and thus open to the driving influence of the new consumer.

Howards End appears to make the argument that Carlyle, for example, ought to connect his two disparate directions of thought, moral and pragmatic. In fact, Forster wants the world of morality to accept Wilcoxian economics. He endorses a brand of rationalist, utilitarian, imperialist (the source of Henry's wealth), free market economics. The Wilcoxes have *grit*: 'This outer life, though obviously horrid, often seems the real one – there's grit in it' (41); 'they had grit as well as grittiness, and [Margaret] valued grit enormously' (112). Margaret's defence of Wilcoxian pragmatism means that she and the sympathetic reader must abandon criticizing the specific type of economics Henry follows, which is nonetheless obscure to begin with. Those are the economics that 'have formed our civilization' (112). In other words, a socially responsible economics, and specifically socialism, is not to be considered as *pragmatic*, whereas rationalist capitalism and an unregulated market are. Helen, who prepares to make a (presumably left-wing) speech on political economy when Margaret speaks to Tibby about the value of work (not Ruskinian Work, but bourgeois, utilitarian, Wilcoxian work), is entirely unconnected to the pragmatism of Wilcoxian economics – only Henry's economics are pragmatic. By having culture accept the Wilcoxes, Forster proposes that their economics are the only viable economics. The discourse of economics is once again isolated from culture (which had earlier been represented by the working class and its supposed affiliation to Work). The impact on economics culture is to have (by Forster's own definition – culture sees things wholly) does not include specific changes. *Howards End* does not propose to connect moral and pragmatic values, but to accept each in its time and place. By no means are moral and pragmatic values asked to *confront* each other, not even symbolically. Towards the end of the novel, Margaret asserts, 'It certainly is a funny world, but so long as men like my husband and his sons govern it, I think it'll never be a bad one – never really bad' (269). Just as Wilcox pragmatism remains on its own, Schlegel culture gains nothing from its opposite. At the end of the novel, Mr Wilcox is absent. He has nothing to do with culture, is still allergic to it, and is not needed. In other words, the moral flourishes without the pragmatic and the pragmatic operates best independently of the moral. The locus for change in *Howards End* takes place only at the level of personal relations: it is never a dialectical change and it never insists on a need for social change.

Robert Tressell

Though Forster shied away from representing work, gospelized or rationalized, at least one of his contemporaries did not. Robert Tressell, unlike Conrad, also represents gospelized and rationalized work at odds with each other. Tressell was an unsuccessful Hastings signwriter who fell to pneumonia and was buried in a pauper's grave in Liverpool at the age of forty. His *The Ragged Trousered Philanthropists* (1914) brings the dialectic form of Thomas Cooper and the pre-1850 working-class writer to the twentieth century, while continuing to politicize working-class apathy. *The Ragged Trousered Philanthropists* includes working-class characters who can be sympathetic or villainous, brave or lazy, intelligent or willfully stupid, and 'very poor.' Ian Haywood suggests that *The Ragged Trousered Philanthropists* is 'a salutary exercise in deromanticizing and deheroicizing the working class' (25). It is, but it is also a deromanticizing and deheroicizing of a nonworking-class version of the working class in which economic ignorance leads to the pleasures of Work.

Tressell, however, does not imagine a working class that actively juxtaposes Work and labour or that is ready to overturn the characterization of working-class disinterestedness that usually follows the Carlylean or Conradian dichotomy. In fact, in *The Ragged Trousered Philanthropists* he represents an active resistance to working-class consciousness, not simply the fatalistic attitude that economic knowledge or power is 'not for the likes of us,' but a working class against itself. After Easton's near accident, 'most of [the workers] said that it would have served him bloody well right if he *had* fallen and broken his neck' (402). The attitude enrages both Frank Owen, the central character, and Tressell himself. Deliberating on the working classes, the provocatively named Owen thinks that

> *They were the enemy.* Those who not only quietly submitted like so many cattle to the existing state of things, but defended it, and opposed and ridiculed any suggestion to alter it.
>
> *They were the real oppressors* – the men who spoke of themselves as 'The likes of us,' who, having lived in poverty and degradation all their lives considered that what had been good enough for them was good enough for the children they had been the cause of bringing into existence. (45–6)

Later he argues that 'they not only refused to help to bring about a better state of things for their children, but they ridiculed and opposed and cursed and abused those who were trying to do it for them.' Socialists, according to the working class, are thus 'fellows who were too bloody lazy to work for a living, and who wanted the working classes to keep them' (395). But Tressell explains the self-defeating attitude of passively condescending to one's oppressors and defiantly resisting one's own political interests in terms of active historical forces. Either the church is in collusion with business and the status quo (the pastor 'tells them that

God made the poor for the use of the rich'; that 'they mustn't grumble, or be discontented' [81]) or the working class suffers from being indoctrinated into thinking as children: 'From their infancy they had been trained to distrust their intelligence' (204). At one point, when Owen is attempting to distribute socialist pamphlets, Tressell apologizes for the workers who reject them by suggesting that 'the argument was generally too obscure to be grasped by men whose minds were addled by the stories told them by their Liberal and Tory masters' (368). The workers are represented as either forced into dumb submission by the ideology that says things 'can't never be haltered ... There's always been rich and poor in the world and there always will be' (28) or because 'They were usually so tired when they got home at night that they never had any inclination for study or any kind of self-improvement' (394).

Tressell also argues that the new, popular working-class culture, especially of sport, precludes a political consciousness and plays into the hands of capitalism. Owen is outside the new working class because he takes no interest in smutty stories, football, or royalty watching. He desires a socialistic revolution because it would evidently usher in 'the benefits of civilization; the necessaries, comforts, pleasures and refinements of life, leisure, books, theatres, pictures, music, holidays, travel, good and beautiful homes, good clothes, good and pleasant food' – 'a full share of the things that are made by work' (29, 30). The scene where the workers take to the countryside for their annual pastoral excursion and banquet is meant to contrast the old leisure traditions with the new emphasis on cheap consumption. Though Tressell attempts to make allowances for the workers, taught from infancy to regard themselves as 'lower animals' (546) and almost forced to drink – 'so long as men have to live and work under such heartbreaking, uninteresting conditions ... the only remedy for this evil is to remove the cause' (427) – he cannot help but *show* disgust and anger at the lack of working-class agency. Owen is a teetotaller and Crass loves his drink. In fact, Tressell is somewhat Forsterian in his antipathy towards working-class culture, an antagonism that extends itself towards the working-class itself: 'When we get Socialism there won't be any people like us. Everybody will be civilized' (497). The best of the working class are alienated from it, like Owen, or alien to it, like Barrington. Still, Tressell's point is that the working-class culture of sport, drink, and so on is ultimately external to the working class, that it has been internalized. He gives an account of working-class apathy that references a presupposition to specific historical realities, not abstract 'character.' Finally, he makes it clear that working-class conformity to the dominant ideology of its intellectual inferiority (leading to political fatalism and from there an economic weakness that almost guarantees further economic weakness) may be widespread but it is not universal.

Though only a minority of workers attempt political consciousness and agency, nearly all of them to the man engage in silent warfare against their bosses, 'stealing back time' and so forth. 'This is where we get some of our own back' could be the novel's refrain (38; see also 207). Owen and Tressell ultimately judge such acts of defiance as ineffective because they don't address the social, economic, or political roots of the problem. Sounding a bit like William Morris, Owen claims that 'There's so much the matter with the present system that it's no good tinkering at it' (147). The workers, however, get the endorsement of Tressell/Owen when they desire to do quality work. The novel constantly opposes those who want to do real work, artisanal work, and managers who will not let them because it reduces profit. The higher the rank, the lower the level of skill. The more heroic the character, the better skilled he is: Owen is an 'exceptionally good workman' (18), the best at what he does. He had been apprenticed by a 'Master decorator,' 'not merely an employer but a craftsman of high order' (65). (Part of the censure of rationalism includes condemning the demise of the apprenticeship system.) Managers have an unhidden hatred for quality craftsmanship. For Hunter,

> scamping the work was with this man a kind of mania. It grieved him to see anything done properly. Even when it was more economical to do a thing well, he insisted from force of habit on having it scamped. Then he was almost happy, because he felt that he was doing someone down. (33)

Tressell seems personally offended by sloppy work, by the idea of work discipline being reduced to rationalization, and by the system that demands it. But he also illustrates the fact that by doing quality work, by living up to the Conradian ideal, the workers do economic damage to themselves. Newman, one of the workers,

> knew quite well that Hunter objected to any but very large holes or cracks being stopped, and yet somehow or the other he could not scamp the work to the extent that he was ordered to; and so, almost by stealth, he was in the habit of doing it – not properly but as well as he dared. He even went to the length of occasionally buying a few sheets of glasspaper with his own money. (161–2)

For Jack Lindon, another worker,

> home and garden were his hobby: he was always doing something; painting, whitewashing, papering and so forth. The result was that although the house itself was not of much account he had managed to get it into very good order, and as a result it was very clean and comfortable.
>
> Another result of his industry was that – seeing the improved appearance of the place – the landlord had on two occasions raised the rent. (70)

In *The Ragged Trousered Philanthropists,* love of work, an instinctive resistance to rationalization or deskilling, *always* has an immediate economic consequence. When Owen has the opportunity to do intrinsically rewarding, minutely detailed, creative work – planning and draughting a paint job – he nearly loses his economic sensibility. Knowing that Owen feels 'an intense desire to do the work' (121), Rushton, his boss, attempts to take advantage of him. Because of 'the pleasure he experienced in the planning of the work,'

> The question, what personal advantage would be gained never once occurred to Owen. He simply wanted to do the work; and he was so fully occupied with thinking and planning how it was to be done that the question of profit was crowded out.
>
> But although this question of what profit could be made out of the work never occurred to Owen, it would in due course be fully considered by Mr. Rushton. In fact, it was the only thing about the work that Mr. Rushton would think of at all: how much money could be made out of it. This is what is meant by the oft-quoted saying, 'The men work with their hands – the master works with his brains.' (123)

The desire to work and the ideology of Work, Ruskin's in this case, are distinguished through the constant reminder that even satisfying work has an economic dimension and cannot be isolated from that dimension. Haywood somewhat dismissively treats the worker's desire to do creative work as part of the 'socialist orthodoxy that art can be defined as non-alienating labour' (31). That may be, but Tressell himself, at every opportunity, separates the dogma – the church is one of the strongest advocates of Carlylean Work, 'Work! for the night is coming' (157; see Carlyle, *Sartor Resartus* 149) – from a real need to resist work rationalization. Suffering economic injustice, the workers cannot believe in the ideal of Work: 'Extraordinary as it may appear, none of them took any pride in their work: they did not "love" it. They had no conception of that lofty ideal "work for work's sake," which is so popular with the people who do nothing' (93). But for Tressell, a worker himself, this rejection of work also has to be explained in terms of history and ideology. If work does not come naturally to workers, if it is a constructed desire, or if the rationalization of work overshadows any intrinsic value associable to Work, the rejection of it does not come naturally to them either. For Tressell, workers could and should enjoy work – 'all those who are capable of doing good work find pleasure and happiness in doing it, and have pride in it when done' (373) – but without the preconditions for satisfying work, without economic satisfaction, there is no Work satisfaction. In pointed contrast to Carlyle and Conrad, Tressell argues that modern economic conditions will and do preclude meaningful Work. As with pre-1850 working-class writers, Tressell does not represent workers – whether they are politically conscious or not – enjoying work under the economic conditions they find themselves in.

On the brink of being literally destroyed by economic conditions, Owen is saved by Barrington, who is not working class. The *deus ex machina* ending is often criticized: Haywood suggests that there is a 'tinge of hero-worship about the characterization' of Barrington (29). But Tressell is not condoning the conservative tradition in which the working class depends on a rebirth of the organicist/paternalist system in order to survive. Tressell's options were to kill off his hero or to construct a miracle resolution from within the system – the system he had represented as all-pervading and all-powerful. In order to avoid a scene where the underdog hero overcomes all odds to rise in the system that was his enemy, akin to workers gleaning intrinsically satisfying Work from laborious conditions, Tressell needed to introduce an external force. This is a working-class strategy we also saw in Cooper's 'Seth Thompson.'

Modernism

What was once a Gospel of Work becomes in modernism the apotheosis of culture. Culture now counters the apotheosis of work as contoured by the ascendant bourgeois class. The latter stood to gain extrinsically from proselytizing work as the labourer's keystone to intrinsic rewards, something the modernists cannot be accused of replicating. It seems everyone before the modernists and their direct predecessors, the *fin de siècle* aesthetes, represented work as noble and sacred: Conrad and conservatism to promote nonrationalized Work and a society modelled upon it (a 'moral economy,' artisanal, traditional, and socially rigid) and the bourgeois either to foster an ideology that mobilizes society towards production and has workers diligently labour or to promote their own image. Everyone, that is, except the economists. The money to be made by the middle class by capitalizing (on) Work meant that they had to go against the grain of economic theory, which argued that work was a disutility, that it was all just labour. This same group would go with the grain of economic reasoning when justifying working conditions that kept profits high and erased the possibility of an intrinsic reward.

But around the turn of the century a group of economists, the neoclassicalists, threw a spanner into these already cranky works. Before them 'economics' primarily signified the production of goods: value (of the product but with further-reaching cultural implications) was thought to be the result of the labour that was embodied in production. Instead of emphasizing production and assuming the consumer to be the mere means to further it, the neoclassicalists focused on theories of consumption. In *Consuming Desire* (1988), Lawrence Birken argues that 'value,' in economic theory and the dominant social outlook, became 'simply attached to objects by the subjective desire of consumers,' no longer the 'result of social labour nor of social need for products' (32). Though Carlyle and Conrad document a growth in consumerism by denigrating cheap merchandise and the rise of advertising, their assumptions are founded on a productivist theology – for classical economists, a productivist technology. If Smith, Ricardo, Mill, and Marx basically ignored demand, Carlyle and Conrad vilified it. The diversion away from production politics was twice as crippling for the advocates of Work as for the theorists of labour. The fascination with the consumer affected the social understanding of economic relations in such a way as to confirm the economic dismissal of Work even in such rarefied quarters as literary modernism.

The neoclassical view maintains that value proceeds from the satisfaction of individual desire or the subjective perception of need. It corresponds to the theory of marginal utility, which states that the least urgent, the last and least wanted, or the marginal need determines value. Value decreases with increasing availability so that the value of water at the margin, in its usual abundance, is low. In the desert the value of water is greater than the value of a diamond. In consumerist theories, neither labour or Work, mechanical or creative activity, nor the primary function of the object necessarily imparts value, whereas scarcity, psychology, theatrical display, fashion trends, culture, and individual taste do. *Homo consumeralis* replaces *homo faber* and *homo laborans* as the primary agent deciding value, not only price. This shift corresponds to the transition of an economy based on land and then trade to one based on finance. Economic savvy was no longer rooted in supplying basic needs ('useful' items), but in tracking the psychological and ideological flux of desire, or in manufacturing desire. David Trotter argues that the transition can be evidenced between 1880 and 1930 in the rise of popular phrases such as 'the age of demand,' 'the economy of abundance,' 'consumer capitalism,' or 'the retail revolution' (11). It is critically documented in *Tono-Bungay*. Though the politics of production did not disappear because attention had shifted to the consumer, and though it is not obvious that the majority of people in England in this period ever felt the Democratization of Luxury, the movement had cultural implications that were as far-reaching as utilitarianism.

Before examining the cultural and specifically literary consequences of the shift, I should say that the consumer revolution was not very revolutionary. Birken and Trotter are right to draw parallels between the innovations in economic theory and a twentieth-century preoccupation with subjectivity and psychology, but most economic models still presumed the predictable rationality of human behaviour and its fundamentally economic base. Consumers, as with producers in utilitarian theory, are thought to be rationally self-interested, always optimizing their interests. The 'Assumption of Non-Satiation' and the 'Diminishing Marginal Rate of Substitution' posit that if the consumer stops buying one good, he or she will or must buy more of another good in order to maintain the same total level of satisfaction. Marginal theory assumes that the consumer will buy until the cost of the last good bought equals the satisfaction or utility that will be rewarded by the purchase. The mechanical logic confirms the principle of maximization and the association of that maximization to 'rationality,' despite the new emphasis on the consumer's idiosyncratic desire. Neoclassical economists are no different from classical economists on the question of what determines this rationality – they simply dismiss the question.

Even Thorstein Veblen's famous *The Theory of the Leisure Class* (1899) assumes that the individual always acts so as to maximize or at least safeguard his or her interests, social standing, or reputation. Veblen, however, marks an important development in economic thought by showing that *homo economicus* is submerged in his social relations, in the need to display consumer power, and in the urge to employ leisure as a signature of success even to the point where his behaviour is nonrational in purely economic terms. Veblen's theory problematizes the function of objects from the consumer's point of view: a candle is not for light but for suggesting mood. Carlyle, on the other hand, problematizes the function of objects from the producer's or worker's point of view: making a candle allows for self-objectification and thus self-realization. Veblen, like Marx before him and Karl Polanyi after him, situates economics within the totality of society and assumes the basic non-economic nature of humankind. For my purposes, one of the more important implications of Veblen's thesis, given that he understands people to act rationally (to maximize) for 'irrational ends' (attracting a mate through conspicuous consumption) is to confirm Weber's thesis that formal rationality (the means) can lead to substantive irrationality (the end) – even though Veblen implies that formal rationality is irrational and substantive rationality (attracting a mate) is rational. If the free market operates rationally, then it does not follow that the ends are 'rational.'

But by assuming a general optimization hypothesis and a psychology of economic rationality, Veblen argues that anything desired and pursued that is not immediately necessary for basic life ought to be read as formal rationality, as maximizing self-interest. Not only is this conclusion precariously tautological, but it also imposes a strict homogeneity on behaviour. The question is not *whether* people conduct themselves as strategizing agents, but if they *always* do, and when they do, whether that behaviour is constructed, natural, chosen, or something not so neat. An even more relevant question might be whether or not people, and which people, have the information or could ever have all the information needed to be 'rational agents' (or if people have all the information needed to reject misinformation; e.g., advertisements). The theory of rational maximizing implies having complete and full knowledge of how to bring about an optimum outcome in any given transaction. It would do well to browse through the pages of literary theory and its general assumptions on the endless meanings of a text. Veblen assumes that people subordinate all other impulses or choices to pursue the maximization of their interests as a matter of nature, but also argues that culture or collective concepts give shape to those interests and that the operation of human reason (which in pure rational choice theories is not different from animal reason) must be situated in a broader discussion of ideology. But even then, under the assumption of rationality, culture is reduced to the obstacles that rationality negotiates in order to maximize; culture, while structuring all instinct, never fully prevails as a fateful determinant of human contingency because it parallels nature. Civilization, one can only imagine, is content.

Given that neoclassicism assumes rationality, Trotter's claim that modernism is 'the literary equivalent of the theory of marginal utility' (67) has to be severely qualified. He uses Birken's theory to argue that the shift in emphasis in economic theory from a nineteenth-century focus on society to a twentieth-century focus on the psychology of the individual can be found in the organizing principles of literary modernism after Conrad. Nineteenth-century British fiction, though frequently capitulating to or even promoting utilitarian theory, more often than not argues the detrimental effects of assuming that rationality as a process is applicable everywhere. Although modernism shares with neoclassicism a fascination with psychology and private motivations and abandons for the most part the drama of the producer, it also rejects the assumption of rationality, either as a process or an end. It has been part of my study to demonstrate that the relationship between a prevailing economic theory and the literature of a given period is an uneasy one. In trying to coordinate historical movements into an episteme, we too often ignore the maverick role art plays. Though the economic subject of consumerist theory is capricious, quickly shifting interest from one product to another, he or she always proceeds within the logic of the system, strategically. The subject in modernism is marked by fragmentariness, a seeming arbitrariness, an erratic logic, and disjunctions having little in common with economic 'whimsicality.' The literary subject does not proceed with purposefulness, with a calculated objective towards maximizing self-interest – if he or she does, it is emphatically not for a rational end. Kafka's resignation, Beckett's paralysis, Camus's indifference, Pound's multi-directionality of consciousness, and Joyce's wandering hero on the one hand or Eliot's and Yeats's myths and Woolf's flickering of intuitive and total vision on the other do not suggest subjectivity ceaselessly pursuing self-advancement. The portrayals of formal rationality, of Eliot's wasteland automatons, of Woolf's Mr Ramsay and his misguided ambition, of James's conniving villains, serve to illustrate the irrational (substantive) character of the established (formal) rationality. Modernism's layers of myth and symbolic codes challenge the science-like character (the language of mathematics, econometrics, matrix algebra, and what-have-you) economics was developing for itself as it turned away from defining itself within other disciplines. Even in realistic texts – in nearly all of Lawrence, in Joyce's *Ulysses* (1922), Forster's *A Passage to India* (1924), or Kipling's 'Mrs. Bathurst' (1904) –

the unknown, symbolism, Romance, epic forces, and the rituals then being investigated by anthropology, structuralism, and psychoanalysis penetrate and disperse rationalist causality and logic. Consumerist theories attempt to bring the idiosyncrasies of consciousness under rational control by finding economic logic, an economic man, in capriciousness. Literary modernism represents what cannot be assimilated into rationalist models.

Rejecting formal logic, an exaggerated faith in reason, the dominant individualism, and schemas for creating a predictable world, the counter-enlightenment movement in which literary modernism entrenched itself, however, retreated from the new economics and curled up in an anti-democratic, anti-industrial vision of society. Here culture, myth, and private reflection dominated society and a cultural elite dominated culture. The withdrawal from society may have been more extreme and complete than in earlier configurations, but withdrawal itself and even the opposition to democracy was nothing new. What was new was that in modernism society was no longer separated and removed from Work. For the most part, modernism bypassed the split between moral and pragmatic work where nineteenth-century writers and Conrad divided culture from society. Representations of work, moral or pragmatic, are conspicuously absent from the modernist canon, though modernists continued to segregate morality and rationality. The fact is that after Conrad something changed in the way in which literary writers and social commentators approached work. After the ambivalent Victorian-Conradian elevation of work (the unqualified representation of Work and the logic or practice of labour), and influenced by low modernism's growing suspicion of work and the *fin de siècle* rejection of it, the moderns were mostly silent when it came to effort or action, rewriting the term under which rationality was to be resisted as an exclusionary Culture. Culture opposed crass, trashy philistinism and materialism, but also threw the means to address economic life, or what T.S. Eliot would call 'Secularism,' *and* Work out with the proverbial bathwater.

Orwell indirectly criticizes modernism in 'Charles Dickens' (1940) and directly criticizes it in 'Inside the Whale' (1940). In the former he says that, 'All art is propaganda. Neither Dickens himself nor the majority of Victorian novelists would have thought of denying this' (*CEJL* 1: 448). In the latter he argues that 'what "purpose" [modernists] have is very much up in the air. There is no attention to the urgent problems of the moment, above all no politics in the narrower sense ... In "cultured" circles art-for-art's-saking extended practically to a worship of the meaningless. Literature was supposed to consist solely in the manipulation of words' (*CEJL* 1: 508). His attacks on modernism's claims to transcendence say as much about the politically active generation of the 1930s as they do about the writers of the 1920s. In the tradition of Carlyle and Conrad, Orwell uses Work almost symbolically to criticize industrial and social rationalization. But instead of a dialectical contest or contrast, he treats it as something to withdraw into, cut off from that rationalization. The anti-realist modernists turned to myth, aesthetics, and culture to censure rationalism in society, treating withdrawal itself as an alternative to rationalism. They struck out against the discourse of Evolution and Progress by representing atavism and degeneration. Their vantage point to criticize the fragmented, self-interested society was a transcendent, contemplative moral authority. Perhaps mixed up with their rejection of everything pre-modernist, Work was no longer part of the general opposition to society, labour, and economics. But the omission of Work entrained a rejection of the protest against the socially dominant form of labour and an acceptance of the economic assumption that work is necessarily a tedious routine, a disutility, a noncreative economic function, and unessential within the realm of the private self. Undifferentiated from labour, Work disappears into the dirty, crass, tawdry cheapness of modernity. Only contemplation, the *vita contemplativa*, withstands rationalism, bourgeois utilitarianism, and greedy materialism, or the degradation of violence, love, and mysticism that Eliot's juxtaposition of antiquity and contemporaneity attempts to invoke. The disappearance of Work, especially considering that modernism was largely open to the promise of order, hierarchy, and authoritarianism common to the Gospel, suggests either that the middle class had abused 'the work ethic' beyond repair, provoking Culture's dismissal, or that modernism felt the need to divide culture from society in a way that protected Culture from the influence of working-class or 'mass' culture. After introducing the proto-modern attitude towards work, which considered the Victorian Gospel a mere subterfuge for economic expediency and a reactionary fiat dictating moral duty, I will argue that modernism's cultural avant-garde evaporated Work into labour, consumerist vulgarity, and rationalism in order to preclude the rise of that other (largely theoretical) modern phenomenon, the democratization of luxury.

The modernist rejection of work was heralded by Samuel Butler's defence of luck in *The Way of All Flesh* (1903). Butler's very post-Victorian manner of undercutting the intransitiveness of a Victorian morality that demanded Duty to work and not duty to job 'x,' however, addressed the realm of necessity – something modernism, I argue, lumps in with materialism and rationalism. Around the turn of the century the floodgates opened. Oscar Wilde ('The Soul of Man under Socialism' [1891]) and Wells (*Men like Gods* [1923]), for example, question work in an age that promised machines to take care of unwanted labour so that everyone could devote their lives to leisure, art, or contemplation. Bertrand Russell shares their point of view but also directly attacks the Victorian code of Work in his 'In Praise of Idleness' (1932). Russell's essay combines equal parts of Freud (that the 'road to happiness' is signposted by the Pleasure Principle and therefore 'lies in an organized diminution of work' [12]) and Nietzsche (that the 'morality of work is the morality of slaves' [14]). Happily hedonistic, Russell assumes 'modern technique' will allow everyone the kind of leisure that only rulers had previously enjoyed. He understands all moralists as abusive elites, using the creed of Work as a means to induce others to labour for them. Yet despite his rejection of Work, necessity and history are not, as in high modernism, neglected. In fact, Russell very nearly bridges the concept of Work and the reality of labour, but for his denial that Work can be anything other than labour.

Out-and-out attacks on Work were first vogue for the Aesthetes of the 1890s. When Walter Pater declared that art was no longer to grapple with moral or pragmatic issues, that it strives to create a counterworld politically unconnected with the objective one, Work was first to the whipping post. Though claiming amorality through 'pure poetry' and an aspiration to music, Aestheticism and the entire concept of artistic self-sufficiency was still moral insofar as it critiqued the prevailing morality. Work was vilified because it was akin to the busybodiness of Victorian morality. Its overtones of order, strict behavioural codes and regulations, Action, and a gravity of purpose would not only pass judgment on sexual and lifestyle 'deviations' but would attempt to 'correct' them. The adoption of work by the bourgeois and Utilitarians, the way in which use-value was prostheticized onto it, also made it anathema to the Aesthetic cause, nonfunctionalism. In any case, Wilde's quip, 'Work is the curse of the drinking classes,' for example, has political content. Idleness, idealized in nearly all of his plays, shows the worthlessness of rationalist planning and attempts to expose the prudishness latent in proselytizing activity for activity's sake. Not only was flippancy an alternative to Work in the struggle against a hegemonic rationality, but *homo ludens* rose to challenge *homo economicus* and *homo faber* as if they were one. The post-Victorian rejection of Work was a rejection of the predictability and conformity created by rationalist societies, a society also rejected by Work enthusiasts, even though they meant to return to a traditional order and the Aesthetes meant to move far beyond it. Perhaps the advocates of art for art's sake could never tolerate the doctrine of work for work's sake because their creed also had a side – profit instead of labour – which they had to demarcate from their artistic claims in order to keep Aestheticism pure, just as Work cannot exist in a context of labour.

Lytton Strachey's suspicion of work and energy in *Eminent Victorians* (1918) is in some ways the Aesthetes' Gospel of Counter Work, though it also embodies the post-Work attitude of the Butler/Russell School. His dismissal of the Work Gospel echoes Nietzsche's contention that work 'keeps everyone in bounds' and reduces 'everything individual' (*Reader* 233). Strachey, Russell, and most of the post-Victorian thinkers owe a great deal to Nietzsche. Strachey's suspicion of religion is Nietzsche's suspicion, and his reproach of the Victorian age, where 'Even its atheists ... were religious' (Strachey, quoted in Sanders 171), is Nietzsche's reproach. Nietzsche abhors the façade of Christian sentiment that Strachey ridicules in *Eminent Victorians*. Nietzsche, however, was not beyond all Victorianisms, including a disjunctive attitude towards Work and labour. He argued that 'For all kinds of sadness and misery of soul we should first of all try a change of diet and severe manual labour' (*Dawn* 250–1). But he also argued that work is 'the best police' (*Dawn* 176) against self-realization. For the most part, he too had lost the meaning of Work, seeing it as the Master's ruse and heralding the neoclassical opposition of contemplation versus rationalized greed.

Strachey understands the conflation of work and morality as consolidating restrictions on all deviation from repressive norms and restraints. Thus he attacks Carlyle's 'unending energy' as facilitating a 'reckless moral sense' ('Carlyle,' 100, 102). And thus, in *Eminent Victorians*, all of his moral zealots are work zealots. Florence Nightingale, besides channelling libidinal energy into work, cannot separate her moral from her active self. Cardinal Manning's intolerance and rigidity parallel his 'zeal' and 'enthusiasm' (11). Dr Arnold's policy to initiate a return to religion and morality in the classroom, to restore 'family values,' is part and parcel of his insatiable work ethic. Mrs Arnold, mother of ten, 'no doubt' agrees with Carlyle that he has '"unhasting, unresting diligence"' (230), as Carlyle said of Arnold after visiting Rugby.

Strachey, however, targets the idea of providential callings in *Eminent Victorians* largely in order to indict a culture that permitted opportunism to validate itself as divinely sanctioned Progress. All of his subjects claim a matter-of-fact determinism and believe that they are 'allotted distinct work ... a destined goal' (General Gordon, quoted in *Eminent Victorians* 264). Manning 'decided that he had received a call from God'; General Gordon needs only 'to discover what were the Bible's instructions, and act to accordingly'; Nightingale must decipher 'that secret voice' and 'do her duty'; and Dr Newman cannot refuse the call to 'take part in a whole succession of schemes' (9, 258, 136, 82). Still, Manning 'decides,' Gordon 'discovers' the legibility of God's signs, Nightingale formulates and answers her own questions about duty before dressing for dinner, and Newman himself concocts the labyrinthine plot of an otherwise calculating divinity. In other words, the calling is not accompanied by a 'flash and a roar from heaven' (106) but is a rationalistic, self-motivated, self-interested call to enterprise and fame.

Though Strachey acknowledges that his figures believe or try to believe that they have a vocation, he reduces the work ethic and nonrationalist Work (the calling) to egocentric priggishness, superstitious self-delusion, spurious humility, self-righteous intolerance, and above all, greed. Again and again he refers to the Machiavellian manner in which they prey on whoever stands in the way of success. Manning and Nightingale are 'eagles' and she 'ravenous,' a 'tigress' (183, 173). Gordon seeks 'fame and influence' in the military world. In 'reality,' his 'desperate ... labour' is motivated by an attempt to position himself as if beside God – to be an earthly demigod ensuring '"Events ... go as God likes"' (260–1). Gordon, then, rationalizes 'violent excitements and extraordinary vicissitudes' in the name of complying with an inscrutable force (259).

The refutation of Work, eminence, and an endorsed vocation connotes a refutation of correct nature and conclusively normative sexualities not only because of Strachey's homosexuality but also because of the way in which he represents absurd retreats into sexual sublimation. Gordon redirects 'earthly desires and temporal temptations' (272) into a frenzied and fanatical work ethic. Nightingale's 'possessed' 'craving' for work more than suggests a displacement of 'passionate fires' (165). Her sublimation engenders a ruthless and demonic work ethic and a desire to manipulate to the detriment and even to the death of others (of Sidney Herbert). If Nightingale's calling to save lives eventually leads her to destroy other lives in part due to sexual repression, the criticism of a transcendental duty acts as a criticism, or acts simultaneously with a criticism, of the fear of sex and the subjugation of sexuality.

But Strachey's derision of work is pre-modern insofar as it is radically critical of order and custom and firmly based in history (i.e., an anti-metaphysical reality). The modernist project is often a search for an epistemological truth that would negate the passage of time, such as W.B. Yeats's apocalyptic fantasies or his and Eliot's juxtaposition of antiquity and contemporaneity. But myth was not invoked solely to foil social freedom; it was also made to confront the materialism and rationalism of modernity. Yeats's nationalistic or demarcated Jungianism, for example, depends on a contrast between a feudalistic and a capitalistic age. Yet it is not Work that initiates a withdrawal from modern life. His representations of a rural, traditional Irish peasantry might contrast work and money (the modern, rationalist devil), but the work itself is toil and only serves to contribute to the temptations of modernity. Spirituality, magic, literature, imagination, intuition, home, landscapes are the effective alternatives to rationalism. In Eliot's 'The Waste Land' (1922) modern rationalized work has led to an 'Unreal city,' with men dead in their spirituality mechanically flowing under brown fog. In a wasteland environment, work is reduced to industrial engineering, scheming, profiteering, and value-free instrumentalizing. This attitude towards rationalism speaks to a direct engagement with history, but again the alternative to spiritual dryness and corruption is spiritual contemplation, not Work. Anthropology, mysticism, and the Church replace Work as the contrary of rationalism, effectively negating any recourse to the discourse of economic practice. Whereas Carlyle, Conrad, and Orwell withdraw to Work against the tide of rationalist labour and economics, modernism retreats to culture and contemplation. There is no better evidence to show the emphasis on contemplation than the modernist subordination of events – action – to cerebral reactions. The exclusion of Work betrays an isolationism rife with a sense of entitlement far removed from the withdrawal and moral individualism underlying the division of Work and economics. Ironically, in 'The Waste Land,' withdrawal (contemplation) is made possible through a sharp, incongruous cut, a device Eliot uses in the rest of the poem to convey social fragmentation.

In *Literary Modernism and the Transformation of Work* (1988), James Knapp skillfully argues that modernism was a 'powerful kind of social analysis, rather than a quasi-religious escape from the hopeless condition of modern history' (3). He suggests that scientific management and modernist fragmentation 'might be brought together in ways which call into question the view that modernist writing tended to suppress historical reference and engagements' (14). Though he admits that Eliot evades history and that Ezra Pound abuses history, his argument is tenable insofar as, one, modernists were as vocal in their critique of a rationalist society as the Victorians before them, and, two, sensuous, complex language does not necessarily signify the whitewashing of history. But he does not mention James, Beckett, Woolf, Forster, Hulme, or discuss Yeats. More important, he does not come to terms with the absence of Work in modernism, even though he focuses on its technical rationalization. Modernism may have been sensitive to the fragmentation of modern labour practices, but the fragmentariness of the style, considering the glaring absence of Work, is much more likely to represent a general fragmentariness in society (caused by secularism, for example) than work rationalization.

It is possible that Samuel Beckett had rationalized labour on his mind when in nearly all of his plays his characters strive to find or insert a bit of variation into the repetitiveness of their lives, or be defeated by that repetition. In *Quad* (1984), for example, slight changes in the performers' routines act as to resist the mechanized, machine-like repetition that seems to resemble factory work. But the protest against rationalism is not specifically directed at work rationalization: political fascism or simply the philosophical struggle against habit is more likely to be placed in contrast with a need for variation than the daily grind of the working class. Whereas Carlyle finds in habit the 'source of all Working, and all Apprenticeship, of all Practice and all Learning' (*Past* 129), Beckett finds only 'the ballast that chains the dog to his vomit' (*Proust* 8). Beckett is not the best example of a modernist who spurns the proliferation of consumers, where this discussion on the disappearance of Work is leading, but his attitude towards work is typical of the modernists' bent for contemplation. Belacqua finds that the 'antidote' of work, 'depending on its efficaciousness on mere physical exhaustion,' deserves 'the greatest contempt' ('Ding-Dong' 40).

Notwithstanding a brilliant chapter on *Ulysses*, Knapp is so involved in a Foucauldian search for a 'subtle, calculated technology of subjection' (Foucault, quoted in Knapp 11) that he ignores the obvious absence of Work in modernism and the attitude, which Virginia Woolf epitomizes, of having outgrown social criticism. Though it is true that, as Lukács had said, the modern critique of machine production must confront 'the subtler dangers of a more pervasive, inward redefinition of the very subjectivity of ... workers' (Knapp 11), one must begin by representing workers to see their subjectivity redefined. And it was *not* the nineteenth century that exclusively limited debate to the moral and aesthetic consequences of work rationalization. Rationalism in *Hard Times*, for example, is all-pervasive, and whether it was born in the factory and seeped outside or vice versa, it dilates into nearly every aspect of Coketown, including consciousness. Modernism's complaint against ugliness, on the other hand, is primarily directed at the size and impact of mass culture; a complaint against the effects of class elision as much as against the effects of rationalized industry. Carlyle and Conrad are nostalgic for morality structures that would circumvent the proliferation of cheap goods. They also treat the effacement of class division and the spread of rationalism as one and the same, as would the modernists. Carlyle shares Yeats's and Eliot's complaint (in 'Meditations in Time of Civil War' [1928] or 'Sweeney Erect' [1920] for example) that violence was losing its greatness, its class, its stability and with Eliot felt that it had declined into an ugly state of mechanical and indifferent brutality (*Past* 191). But in his recensions of the past, say in *Past and Present*, which are as reactionary as in modernism, Carlyle represents Work as the alternative to rationalism, implying that anti-rationalism is fundamental to the working class and making it accessible to them. Orwell, as I will attempt to show in the next chapter, goes further than most in championing working-class culture precisely because and only as far as it is anti-rational. Carlyle, Conrad, and Orwell all depict the working class as having special insights into Work. In modernism the alternative to rationalism is Art, and specifically art that was alien to the mainstream population. If modernism raises the question of modern work, it is only to censure the proliferation of its aesthetic shortcomings, which modernists yoke to a mobocracy dictating the market. The proliferation of consumers and not the work rationalization takes the brunt of the criticism.

The threat of the consuming mass, a group ratified in neoclassical theory by the 'fact' of their purchasing power, was mostly a perceived threat: the mass was still mostly poor (Trotter 11). But unlike the Aesthetes who welcomed this perceived change in consumerism (a change largely ushered in by economic theory) because it promised an always-right consumer who ignored use-value and bought for the sake of buying (the necessary flipside and precondition to art for art's sake), the modernists downgraded the new consumer into a parvenu. Modernism's objective was to sell its items on its own terms, to challenge the expansion of the marketplace but still make a buck. Perceiving that the new, 'vulgar' consumer – a post-working superclass made up of the traditional working class (or 'proletariat'), the lower-middle class (retailers, bureaucrats, etc.), and the bourgeois, all of which are in some way defined by work or a Gospel of Work – could determine the cultural marketplace, modernism was to rarefy itself beyond quick consumption. Its value was to be defined by its rarity, in creating a higher demand by making the supply of meaning low. Instead of serving the 'tawdry' mass market, it would meet its needs by creating specialty markets. The democratization of luxury implies that the working class, or at least those who were once the working class and became the 'mass,' was the new consumer. Validating Work, a fixture of working-class culture, would be the equivalent of validating the consumer. No distinctions were made between Work and labour because even though they are the opposite sides of the same coin, that was not the coin, the purchasing power, modernism wanted to earn.

In other words, the highly specialized, opaque, and deliberately difficult style and subject matter of high modernism were not merely the aesthetes' distaste for the language and manifestation of capitalism or a disguise and denial of its own commodity status. Modernism's formal experiments with language and material target the quantitative increase in commodities available to the 'masses' and indicate a bitter refusal to allow everyone into the market where they shopped. Ironically, modernism's position was part of the same epistemological movement as marginal theory, an auxiliary to consumerist theory. As said, marginal theory argues that value decreases with increasing availability. Modernism, not readily available or retail-friendly, positioned itself as the glass of water in the middle of the arid desert so that it could sell at an inflated price.

Modernism failed to acknowledge Work when it presented culture as an alternative to the individualism, rationalism, materialism, commercialism, and all that is vulgar, degenerating, transitory, fragmentary, and dirty in modern life. They guard against the rationalization of human relations, but where is there Work in James or Woolf? For that matter, where is there labour? Henry James repeatedly implies in his essays that 'centres of consciousness,' insofar as they are to be 'lucid reflectors,' must have the kind of refined sensibility not available to the lower classes, even if the centres are to be slightly bewildered. He argues, for example, that the 'immediate' drama of 'getting through a job' is not the 'affair of the painter' ('Preface' 65). Orwell, always deeply pragmatic when handling specific subjects, argues that

> even the best writers of the time can be convicted of a too Olympian attitude, a too great readiness to wash their hands of the immediate practi-

cal problem. They see life very comprehensively, much more so than those who come immediately before or after them, but they see it through the wrong end of the telescope. (*CEJL* 1: 510)

Though the economic does not become entirely invisible in the modernist focus on the private and mythological (even if it could be wiped clean from the art, it can never be wiped clean from all interpretations of the art), economics – class, wages, relations of production, and so forth – were folded into culture's antithesis. The same, I have argued, is true for Carlyle and Conrad: they also strictly demarcate economics and antirationalism. But Work was included in the sealed-off compartments of culture, which, if it accommodates the economic-as-is, does not seal off the working class, the majority, from culture.

The two poles of the modernist evasion of history, the retreat to eternity, myth, and a sanitized antiquity on the one side and the withdrawal to an inner self on the other both assume that economics, which is not distinguished from Work, erodes and vulgarizes culture in the same way that Carlyle's and Conrad's withdrawal into Work assumes that labour and economics erode Work. But Carlyle and Conrad not only included Work in culture, they practised a discourse of labour in its own specific terms. If the trend in Edwardian fiction was to be informed by some kind of exploration of the various strata of class and their potential to determine consciousness, Woolf's complaint against Wells, Bennett, and Galsworthy might have less to do with a supposed reduction of character to the 'fabric of things' than with the rooting of fiction to an economic dimension. Her representation of the unknowability of subjectivity and the eternal is not reducible to, but certainly related to, an attempt to transcend class, specifically, the lower class. Her complaint against materialism is a complaint against the representation of white-collar, lower-middle-class shopkeepers and clerks. The near refusal to depict character in an economic and social situation in order to find the *essential thing*, to absolutely divide essentialism from environment, to downplay background, material circumstances, and whether or not Mrs Brown works in 'Doulton's factory' ('Brown' 327) – Woolf's Mrs Brown would not – suggests that her agenda to shape the common reader included the denial of the common consumer. Woolf's initial reaction to *Ulysses* – 'An illiterate, underbred book it seems to me; the book of a self taught working man, and we all know how distressing they are, how egotistic, insistent, raw, striking, and ultimately nauseating' (*Writer's* 46) – does not document her snobbery as much as it reflects modernism's anxiety about the perceived tawdriness of cultures based on work. She rejected a realism dominated by male perspectives and chose a literary form that emphasizes subjectivity and allows a female voice to be as experienced as any male voice that had come into direct contact with public work. Work, then, would be downplayed. But if form, literature, can have political content, then why criticize Wells for attempting to do the work of the government (someone's got to do it)? Her elevation of the private life draws lines between literature and the rest of the world that would dramatically reduce the importance of her own writings. Woolf was politically committed to left-wing progress. That she was wellnigh preoccupied by the private, psychological dimension of experience in her novels suggests that modernism made elitism and the disappearance of the consumer, labourer, and Worker its mandate.

The ebbing of Work under the anti-humanist, anti-Enlightenment school of T.E. Hulme and Eliot also involved vitiating Work and the activities of the working class and compartmentalizing them with crass materialism. By refuting the exaltation of the individual and insisting that 'man' is essentially bad, Eliot and Hulme divorced themselves from the rationalism or rational progress that the dominant social forces connected to work, but also from the idea that Work leads to intrinsic gain. Hulme thought that poetry should contain itself, soberly express a 'holding back' and avoid the 'infinite,' metaphors of flight and so on. Eliot added the doctrine of impersonality, conscious design, and confirmed the ban on spontaneous emotion. 'High' art was to force attention on to the work of art itself, art for its own sake. This is exactly what Work does: directs attention away from the production process. Yet Eliot's insistence that the work of art ought not to contain the personality of the artist counters Carlyle's and Romanticism's, or Marx's and Lukács's, idea that in the object of work lies the expression, objectification, realization, and development of the worker. Lukács contends that the working class sees an object as a process, the coming together of parts, whereas the bourgeois see the object as static, a purchased item. Opposing Work in this way is to judge all work as rationalized labour, as the attempt to maximize one's interests in the temporal world and through temporal world standards. For Eliot and Hulme, only the spiritual world is anti-rational. But, ironically, opposing Work as the means to self-realization is also reconcilable with Enlightenment scepticism, insofar as Enlightenment phenomenology claims the importance of seeing the object as it really is. Eliot and Hulme reject the principles of rationalism, not its sobriety, not its supposed antipathy to the values of working-class culture. They show a willingness to accept rationalism as a process but not as a conclusion.

To be fair, modernism's rejection of work and economics was not due solely to a stubborn elitism. If the Victorian and Edwardian, realist or naturalist writer tried to convey human experience by representing work, the most ordinary of experiences, the modernist writer tried to convey the difficulty of representation itself, that the thing written is not the real thing. Since reality was no longer considered to be a self-evident construct, the emphasis on Work as that which structures reality had to be quashed. Even if, as in Woolf's *Orlando* (1928), a 'single self, a real self' (196) is still available, it is not susceptible to objectification through Work as with Carlyle or Marx. The development of character into a coherent self by a well-made narrative of Work – such as in the smooth, linear development of a *bildungsroman* (naturalism depends on a narrative of labour) – is turned inside out by the new emphasis on the fragility of consciousness. If Work had once fixed identity, it had to be silenced, disappeared, in order to convey that identity is made up from random 'scores upon the consciousness.' Carlylean and Conradian Work obviates or precludes modernism's interrogation of subjectivity, making the abdication of Work a precondition for the rendering of consciousness as volatile, fragmentary, purposeless, and multidirectional. Arnold Bennett's work ethic, his obsessive/compulsive tracking of the number of words he wrote daily and annually, along with his total yearly earnings, for example, suggests a sense of will power, self-control, and purpose that goes against modernism's scepticism about the stability of selfhood, the security of a reliable epistemology, and the possibility of rendering experience in its fullness. But if the subject who receives, shapes, and assesses 'myriad impressions' is also shaped or framed by those impressions, why does modernism exclude work as a fundamental part of those impressions? Orwell hazards an answer: 'Was it not, after all, because these people were writing in an exceptionally comfortable epoch? It is just in such times that "cosmic despair" can flourish. People with empty bellies never despair of the universe, nor even think about the universe, for that matter' (*CEJL* 1: 509). Yet it was not simply the realm of necessity that modernism ignored or denied, it was also working-class culture. Modernism ignored Work because from its position that was a realm of freedom reserved for the working class.

CHAPTER THREE

George Orwell

The difference between George Orwell's withdrawal from and modernism's aversion to society is not merely one of degree, but of kind. His reaction to the new technologies of human interaction revolves around an essentially Victorian, not a classical past. Whereas Orwell finds refuge from rationalism in Work and the folksy traditionalism of the 'common man,' modernist transcendence looks towards enforcing a revival of the spiritual/corporeal divide. I have argued that as Work – the most common point of departure from society for Carlyle and Conrad – is treated as if separate from its context and effects, a real submission and benefaction to the very economic structures and agents its advocates deplore is inevitable but suppressed. Withdrawing into Work is different from any other utopian gesture, spiritual high, Cultural retreat, or totalizing refusal of modernity insofar as work is an active ingredient in the rationalized world. In order not to become economistic myself, however, I avoid the argument that every time a worker smiles he or she is contributing to his or her own exploitation or that every time a writer represents Work he or she is engaged in some sinister mystification of rationalist capitalism. The writers of Work I have identified also grapple with economics, debate specific issues, and get their hands dirty over specific ills. But to do so they are forced to adapt to the language and terms of rationalist economics, revealing preconceptions about the inevitable structure of the economic: presuppositions that deny Work and that would never produce Work relations. Between Work and economics there is no middle ground and no dialectical confrontation. The dichotomy points towards, or leads Orwell towards, an affirmation of a moral intransitiveness: the individual manages to find Work despite economism, despite an overwhelming and ubiquitous rationalism, the acknowledged but compartmentalized rule of labour that refuses to dignify individuality.

Orwell inherited from Carlyle and Conrad not only the tendency to buffer Work from economics but also the related tendency to associate the working class with special insights into the world of Work and nonrationalism. Reacting against economism they are suspicious of all economic negotiating and praise the working class because of its supposed ignorance of labour issues. The other, pragmatic, discourse, even when uttered on behalf of the working class, confirms that the working class itself remains impervious to economic thinking. Orwell goes further than his predecessors in linking Work to the working classes (or the lower middle classes) and, as a result, declaring them in particular to be moral individuals able to wrest Work from situations he identifies as rationalized work sites. Carlyle and Conrad often link Work to the working class in order to make way for a conservative agenda of rekindling feudalistic relations between 'masters' and 'men.' The working class know only Work; it needs 'natural superiors' to manage economic matters. Orwell's attitude towards Work and the working class follows this pattern, but contradictions overwhelm his writing because his pragmatism is as acute as his moralism. That pragmatism nevertheless has the gritty, concrete, inductive, stopgap, anti-theoretical attributes that are coincident with the logic of immediacy and that intermittently characterize Carlyle and Conrad. Orwell epitomizes this dualism not only because he intermittently pays homage to the Gospel of Work and then denounces it, but because he swings harder, faster, and further than those before him between claiming the unqualified abstract and negotiating the problematic concrete, between representing work as subjectively good and objectively perverted. As I am treating Orwell as sharing the logic of the Victorian age, and in some ways epitomizing or amplifying it, this entire chapter is devoted to his work and ignores his contemporaries.

The differences between Orwell and Carlyle or Conrad cannot be overestimated. Though the belief in Work is remarkably similar, the pragmatism Orwell demonstrates has less to do with endorsing the economic-as-is than Carlyle's or Conrad's pragmatism. His politics, if not socialistic or working-class, are egalitarian. Though he shows the imprint of Carlylean nationalism when he argues that the English people 'must breed faster, work harder, and probably live more simply' (*CEJL* 3: 37), his acceptance of the logic of conventional economic and social structures is based on his perceptions of the immediate needs of the lower classes. Whereas Carlyle repeatedly states that the 'only happiness a brave man ever troubled himself with asking much about was, happiness enough to get his work done. Not "I can't eat!" but "I can't work"' (*Past* 157; see also 38, 155), Orwell says 'when one's belly is empty, one's only problem is an empty belly' (*CEJL* 3: 103). Conrad, emphasizing Work in an illusory realm of freedom, but recognizing that it is illusory, is somewhere between the two. We should be careful not to minimize the validity of Orwell's reference to the immediate needs of the working class. If it precludes a truly revolutionary consciousness and ignores 'the system' (which is a point that needs to be debated, not taken as obvious), it at least takes place on the front lines of the struggle and has a direct impact on human suffering. However, such a gritty position unravels Orwell's loftier ideas about Work, or would if they were opposed to each other.

Bernard Crick simply refers to 'English socialism' when diagramming Orwell's ethical, anti-theoretical, non-Marxian, libertarian politics. Describing Orwell and English socialism, Crick identifies a fundamental rift:

> on the one hand a sensibility and perception that is close to observable experience and intensely practical, but on the other hand Pilgrim with his eyes raised towards Zion, head-in-the-air while feet necessarily tramp through the slough of Despond and Vanity Fair. But perhaps only the plodding Pilgrim could sustain the idealistic Pilgrim through the hard work and daily disappointment that gradualism is heir to. ('English' 19)

Orwell scholars often allude to Orwell's central place in a distinctly English socialism: George Woodcock argues that its chief characteristic is that it looks back in time to shape its values (*Crystal* 234); Stephen Ingle relates it to a suspicion of intellectuals and the overvaluation of abstract, intellectual work (*Political* 95). These are features of a long-standing anti-utilitarian tradition. Orwell also epitomizes English socialism by combining radical strands of socialism with traditionalism, by generally blurring ideological orientations, by maintaining peculiarly Victorian moral and pragmatic sensibilities, and by proudly defending his inconsistencies as a feature of a fully human individual. Orwell differs from Carlyle and Conrad insofar as he is more likely to face the whale, to get inside of it, and to struggle inside of it when there. As well, he is more likely than them to offer a real challenge – albeit gradualist and piecemeal – to the economic-as-is. Orwell's working classes, in contrast to Carlyle's and Conrad's workers, frequently deliberate on day-to-day economics, though never on long-term economic or political interests. The 'genuine working man' is 'seldom or never a Socialist' (*Road* 154), in terms of having a vision for transforming society or the worker's place in it. Orwell's approach to the working class is ultimately paternalistic and his characterization of it ultimately revolves around dependency. Insight into the economic would be atypical of workers, leaving Orwell to improvise on their behalf. His concept of the individual, the dualism of his anti-rationalism and his day-to-day pragmatism, and especially his aversion to accepting a politics that would resolve the tension between Work and labour also resemble the radical conservatism of Carlyle and Conrad.

The inherent conservatism but dramatic inconsistencies in Orwell's work have generally been recognized. Few commentators, however, including both his apologists and adversaries, point out that an author of a column entitled 'As I Please' would intentionally flaunt antinomies. Woodcock, who understands Orwell well, is an exception. He thinks Orwell 'tended to glory in his contradictions and in the unsystematic nature of his thought' (*Crystal* 55). Head-spinning inconsistencies, so much the more audacious for being very clearly stated, preclude automatic allegiances to Orwell the man, forcing conversation to organize itself over ideas, perhaps over the idea of 'Orwell.' But Woodcock also reads in the inconsistencies a 'shift in his attitude which took place whenever the subject moved from the abstract and general to the concrete and personal' (*Crystal* 56). The implication is that Orwell's contradictory style gets away from him, that it is deeply rooted in an epistemological discontinuity. Dan Jacobson has recently reformulated Woodcock's analysis of an a priori/a posteriori shift by noting that Orwell, when generalizing, ridicules homosexuals, vegetarians, and middle-class intellectuals, for example, but supports 'them in directly *political* terms' (4). Orwell, notwithstanding the Celia Kirwan list, would defend individuals persecuted by organized factions even as he derides who they are or what they represent. That is, he thinks differently depending on his proximity to people and events.

When speaking in abstract terms Orwell resists the strictures of rationalism – depicting work as a good in itself and money as the root of all evil, rejecting technology, and attesting to the sanctity of tradition. When speaking in concrete terms he concedes to rationalism – ridiculing the representation of work as anything but a means to satisfy economic need, and money as anything but the root of all good, admitting the necessity of technology, and vilifying a romanticized past. In his denial of rationalism he never abandons reason, promotes mysticism, or psychologizes for a return to behaviour guided by instinct. To argue that only his resignation to rationalism is a 'concrete' response to the modern organization of work, or society, is to imply that his resistance to it is merely an antiquated, utopian idealism. His resistance to rationalism is only utopian insofar as it is not opposed to his pragmatism. Negotiating the terms of rationalized work does not make for a monopoly on the down-to-earth. Orwell is clearly right to argue that the unemployed need work for non-economic reasons. He also says that the unemployed need only money. These views compete under the single category of the 'concrete,' the real needs of a particular individual. To apply the abstract concrete distinction unconditionally and suggest that only arbitrating the details of labour is *real* would be to ratify the assumption that the resistance to a rationalization of work is not 'useful,' a utilitarian and capitalist tautology. This would be to prejudge Orwell's contradictions from a fully rationalist point of view. It is also to dismiss the relevance of the contradiction.

At the same time, the distinction between Work and labour is fundamental to any analysis of Orwell's contradictory attitudes. Most critics point out an inconsistency. For Raymond Williams and Terry Eagleton, Orwell's 'double vision' (*Orwell* 19), or the 'tensions and contradictions' (*Exiles* 86) in his work, reveal the untenable assumptions of his conservatism. For Daphne Patai he is not merely contradictory, but 'equally simplistic and extreme at each end of the spectrum' (7). For Richard Hoggart the 'contradictory mixture' includes a 'toughness in manner' and a warm, gentle tolerance ('Introduction' 37). Beatrix Campbell comes close to my own formulation of the dualism when she concludes that 'Orwell moves between these great moral virtues and the private, commonsense morality of decency' (218). Alok Rai identifies a 'schizoid affiliation' to middle-class literati and their notions of value and an aesthetic and moral bond with the people he wrote about (31). In a similar way, Ingle argues that in *Down and Out* Orwell 'continuously switches from identifying with the poor and writing about society from their point of view to identifying with "society" and writing about the poor as a social problem' (*Political* 25). Some critics judge Orwell's writings by the standards of coherency, treating the contradictions in themselves as evidence of artistic and theoretical failure. More often than not this comes across as purely evaluative, formalist, ideological, and self-defensive attempts to expose inauthenticity, dishonesty, or a lack of decency and to deflate what Orwell's popularity might represent.

Orwell's vacillations go beyond the quasi-aristocratic, individualistic whimsicality of a title such as 'As I Please,' the general/concrete split, or the superficial vagaries coincident with nonpartisanship. Neither can the cause of the contradictions be reduced to a varied occupational history or his interaction with different social classes. Orwell was a revolutionary and a traditionalist, a radical and a conservative, an ironist and a sentimentalist; he wore political labels and was anti-sectarian; he was a propagandist of feel-good optimism, a hater of Jeremiahs, and a gloomy pessimist; he was 'dominator and dominated' (Williams, *Orwell* 19); authoritarian and rebel; a moralist who believed change begins with the individual and a socialist who contributed to a bleak theory of constructivism; synchronic and diachronic; a liberal and liberalism's critic; and finally, a humanist and someone who envisioned the ultimate collapse of human subjectivity. Jeffrey Meyers comments that 'Orwell never could – perhaps never wanted to – resolve the contradictions in his elusive character: Etonian prole, anti-colonial policeman, bourgeois bum, Tory anarchist, Leftist critic of the Left, puritanical lecher, kindly autocrat' (168). Orwell's thought was both inside and outside the whale: caught between history, specificity, and variability on the one hand and the desperate plea for the final knowledge of 'culture' on the other. The paradox of Orwell's inconsistency is best seen as he rocks back and forth between adopting a romantic vision of Work and integrating himself into the capitalist whale. In this divergence work is either exalted to be innocent of its purpose, origin, and effect or reduced to its instrumental purposes, origins, and effects.

Though I am not treating Orwell's prose and fiction differently, I will begin by demonstrating this divergence with reference to his prose, especially *Down and Out in Paris and London* (1933) and *The Road to Wigan Pier* (1937). Before doing so I should point out that it is also impossible simply to bypass Orwell's defence of inconstancy. Instead of claiming that a 'deficiency resides in the fact that he was not a theoretician' (Kubal 50; see also Williams, *Orwell* 27; and Karl 159), we should accept Orwell's 'perfect horror of a dictatorship of theorists' and 'absurdly consistent' *intégristes* (*CEJL* 1: 532; *Road* 156). Inconsistency is still the best weapon against accusations of ideological prescriptions. Whether 'ideology' means systematic partisanship, a cultural worldview, or mystified tractability, inconsistency eats into the basic idea of conformity. It is also a tool that checks idealizing, the dream of a utopian wellness, for it provides a reminder of the specificity and complexity of any human situation. In this study the inconsistent has a special relevance as it is the product of Work, displaying individualized thought, just as Ruskin claims inconstant Gothic architecture displays a nonmechanical, nonrationalist, free expression of the worker's independence. Variation, again, is in itself irreverent towards systemization. Orwell condemns theory as grossly totalizing; as imposing on and limiting human behaviour (not merely analyzing it) for the sake of neatness and a latent rationalism; as experientially void, casuistic, impotently discursive, elitist, alienating, and private (empiricism would be public). For Orwell, any categorical allegiance, philosophical or ideological absolute, any organizing grid (any organization), or any orthodoxy creates sectarian values elevating the sect over the circumstance. Theory itself rationalizes; it thematizes, reducing centrifugal elements to calculable exigencies and distorting spontaneous irregularities into the logical and predictable forms of an organizing principle. Orwell treats theory as Ruskin treats rationalized work. By claiming that 'only the "educated" man ... knows how to be a bigot' (*Road* 156), Orwell may idealize the working class and his own autodidactic independence, but he also situates himself primarily as a moralist against organized morality. Education for Orwell paradoxically engenders both ideological partisanship and freewheeling relativism, both of which preclude argumentation and pragmatic activism.

The blatant Orwellian contradiction asserts an independence of mind even as he admits that he has internalized middle-class values. He twists the tension between his affiliation to working-class values and his filiation to the middle class into a proud contradiction that galvanizes and reconfirms autonomy or the ability to think outside class prescriptions. Yet, even when taking into account his objection to the 'absurdly consistent,' Orwell vacillates between hard and firm approaches to work. His traditionalistic link to a moral conception of Work is loudly pronounced, especially considering the poverty-ridden time in which he wrote. But Orwell, with a sociologist's eye for detail, also outlines the value of work as a means to make money, period. Though a vaguely discernible sense that Eric Blair was comfortable constructing a Janus-faced George Orwell might provide an out against both formalist and politically mandated critiques of the contradiction, the flagrant split between Work and labour is itself consistent with the two strains of thought that frame and motivate Carlyle and Conrad.

Perhaps Orwell began to believe that English character was particular to workers because he was engaged with that specific line of 'English letters.' Perhaps he equated the working class with verve and vitality because as a child his parents forbade contact with the men working in their neighbourhood. Perhaps it was somehow related to the desire to expiate the guilt of being a police officer in poverty-ridden Burma, or originated in the streets of Paris, London, and Wigan. In any case, he certainly represents the working class as possessing special emotional virtues. His portrait of Wigan shows the drudgery of work in an industrial town, especially the impossible hardship of mining, the physical decay of the workers, the degradation of menial work and poverty, and the economic stress accompanying unemployment. Yet these images are of a piece with a celebration of Work and an insistence on the moral superiority of the working class partly because they maintain dignity, humanity, volition, a sense of domesticity and community, and a belief in Work while shuffling through the ugliness of industrialism. Labour and Work are effectively isolated.

At various points, mining in *The Road to Wigan Pier* represents working-class Work. Mining positions endurance and *dureté* against great odds, involves an organic setting, and allows for a confrontation with the basic elements. One of the basic concepts of Work to which Orwell subscribes is that Work occurs when a subject encounters something outside himself or herself from the natural world that first withstands and then yields to effort. There is joy in work because one feels victorious in overcoming the resistance offered by the external object. The environmentalism central to the concept of Work is based not only on an aesthetic reaction to industrialism, but also on the idea that the subject is in a state of dependence on nature as it provides the objects that are the source of his or her joy (Applebaum 462). 'Work,' says Carlyle, '*is* in communication with Nature' (*Past* 196). Mining has a special place in the arts (Zola, Lawrence) because it is central to both labour and Work: it was the keystone to industrial development but is also rich in metaphorical or figurative potential. The image of mining, more visibly than in other occupations, opens up to a display of symbolic self-determination, the hammering-out of identity through a physical encounter with nature. Orwell's miner 'contemplates himself in a world that he has created' (Marx, 'Economic' 76). Working, the miners become 'hammered iron statues' (*Road* 21). The gruelling, backbreaking conditions they endure, conditions that are rightly a fact of labour, become the opportunity to show how tough and virile they are, how stable and honourable because they can and do 'take it.' I am not denying that physical work confirms a sense of identity demanded by either external (cultural) or internal forces. People look for hard work outside of their employment all the time, especially if their employment does not allow them the opportunity to use their hands. But Orwell's narrative of Work, confirming the miner's physical and moral strength – 'the arms and belly muscles of steel' and 'the extraordinary courtesy and good nature' (31, 65) – displaces the case he makes about the conditions the miners endure as labourers.

By emphasizing the 'most noble bodies,' the 'splendour of their bodies,' and by representing the polite, patient, kind humanity of the miners – 'the people, not the scenery' (21, 32, 65–6) – Orwell counters the Marxist dictum that alienation occurs in harsh, alienating conditions or when the worker is robbed of the product created and the right to control the productive activity. His miners have the capacity to resist alienation, a capacity that seemingly comes from the work itself. For both Marx and Orwell alienation is the opposite and negation of self-realization because the worker cannot 'affirm himself in his work.' Work thus becomes labour, 'not voluntary, but coerced; it is *forced labour*'; 'not the satisfaction of a need; it is merely a *means* to satisfy needs external to [the labourer]' (Marx, 'Economic' 74). Neither Marx nor Orwell is distinguishing between biological needs and cultural prescriptions, between needs and norms. At other times, both identify the philosophy behind the intrinsic need to Work as the machinations of the ruling class. The concept of alienation presupposes an internal, natural need to work. If there was not that need, alienated workers ought to reconcile themselves to alienating work, quit protesting except for increased wages and job security, and renounce any desire for better working conditions and work fulfillment. The difference between Marx's and Orwell's attitudes toward work is that the latter represents intrinsically valuable, self-realizing Work, without the worker being duped or suffering adaptation, in a rationalist/capitalist economic system, and Marx does not. Orwell, in fact, often points his blaming finger at Marxist-Socialism instead of at the managers and owners of the mines who profit from exploiting the vestiges of Work in the conditions of labour. At other times, describing in detail the low standard of living, the cruelty of the slumlords, the Corporate houses, the haughty middle-class discrimination that deprecates the miners on a daily basis; the impossible, unsafe, monotonous, and dehumanizing labour that the miners do for the benefit of others; and the 'system' in general, he adopts a unified discourse of labour. His indebtedness to *The Condition of the Working Class in England* (1845), or at least his genealogical ties to Engels's classic, underscores a suspicion of Work. But he treats the effects of the 'system,' of infrastructures and superstructures alike, of economics itself, as something foreign *to the workers.* Every time Orwell shows a 'pang of envy for [the miners'] toughness'

(20) and represents their steadfast commitment to their jobs or the artisanship of their Work, their elaborate and specialized skills, he separates the miners from their labour, just as Conrad's best workers aboard the *Narcissus*, with their manly bodies, are separated from their labour.

Perhaps because Orwell, Carlyle, and Conrad found themselves in between class cultures, distanced but with direct connections to working people, they fluctuate between perspectives that either participate in or merely observe the working world. Reflecting on the working class, representing it from the outside, Orwell adopts an analytical, specific, labour-oriented discourse that refutes or dismisses the concept of Work. But when adjacent to the working class, when attempting to share its experiences, he embraces a generalizing discourse that elides economic questions. His critique of working conditions is not made when he is in close proximity to the working class. Orwell's worker can then be instinctual and integral despite the work environment. It is as if he is a moral Worker first and a paid employee, a wage earner and a labourer, a distant second – and even then, only through Orwell's mediation. Even when Orwell recognizes the rationalized economic structure, and argues that the miners are underpaid and that the work is overtaxing, the Workers he represents do not complain. Orwell's discourse of labour, spoken on behalf of the miners, is cut off from the representation of the miners who Work. They are mute when it comes to low wages, unfair treatment, or unsafe working conditions. The reader is forced to accept that the miners, insofar as they are at all conscious of it, view the roughness of their work as only confirming a manliness or resoluteness of character, that hard work is their lot, or that they ought to have a very humble sense of self-entitlement. There is little evidence, on the contrary, to suggest that the working class ever in fact embraced this isolated idea of Work. In fact, never in John Burnett's collection of working-class journals does a miner or for that matter a housemaid refer to the internal rewards of Work. Union members are especially notorious for downplaying Work. Gus Tyler reports that 'there probably is not a single [union] that refers to the "work ethic"' (197). Though Orwell would probably respond by saying that a union member is not the right person to survey, that the unemployed would have a different answer, his miners act as if above and beyond the realm of need, or as if dependent upon an external (and paternal) voice to deal with the messy economic matters. Orwell's tendency to protect the workers from hard economics explains his chivalric, indeed his erotic, language when describing the miners – a language reminiscent of a man admiring a woman's impeccable beauty.

Besides denying that the miners might have an interest in their own labour, Orwell fails to express that 'there are economic conditions for the awareness of economic conditions' (Bourdieu, 'Disenchantment' 56). Pierre Bourdieu's 'old-fashioned peasant' and his 'sub-proletariat' share a good deal in common with Orwell's working-class worker, especially in their traditionalistic resistance to rationalism. But in Bourdieu's anthropological reading of working-class activity he argues,

> It is only because profitable work is closed to them that the sub-proletarians renounce economic satisfaction and fall back on occupations whose principal, if not exclusive, function is merely to provide a justification in the eyes of the group. Everything takes place as if they were forced by circumstances to dissociate work from its economic result, to understand it not so much in relation to its product as in opposition to non-work. ('Disenchantment' 42)

Orwell's working class also dissociates work from its economic context and creates codes that measure success in non-economic terms. But Orwell, here, does not offer an explanation of working-class culture and behaviour that references economics. In fact, he offers no reason for working-class traditionalism that cannot be attributed to super-historical virtues. If indeed the miners were focused on Work to the point of being ignorant of their labour, then, according to Bourdieu, there would be economic forces driving that preoccupation with Work. Orwell also recognizes the forces that generate or indeed attempt to cultivate Work instincts (or, alternately, that neuter a consciousness of labour), but not when he is immersed in the working class. What Bourdieu says about his working class – the 'most improbable practices are therefore excluded, as unthinkable, by a kind of immediate submission to order that inclines agents to make a virtue of necessity, that is, to refuse what is anyway denied and to will the inevitable' (*Logic* 54) – corresponds precisely to Orwell's description of the miners.

It is not my intention to assert that the miners could not be content and unmystified: I only want to establish that the narrative of Work Orwell creates for them is divided from Orwell's discourse of labour. The miners Orwell depicts were carefully selected to not reveal signs of alienation and to embody the nonrationalized values he sought to promote. Both Williams and Kay Ekevall, independently, point out that many of the miners Orwell represents were in fact socialists, if not confirmed Marxists (*Orwell* 51; Wadhams 59). Orwell's miners are not representative and mining is not a sociologically accurate overview of the work that takes place in an industrial town if only because of the unique strength of their union (Crick, *Life* 291; Hoggart, 'Introduction' 39). The miners' interest in the *labour* they do, their economic negotiating, is not represented in *The Road to Wigan Pier*. In its physicality, its demand for total engagement, its social usefulness, its community, its demand for 'manly' strength, its direct involvement with the land and solid materials, and in the image of self-realization it confirms, mining encapsulates nonrationalized Work, an idea Orwell isolates and protects. Mining also provides a sharp contrast to the economic maximizing of bourgeois work or the cerebral work of the intelligentsia. That Orwell includes himself in the latter effete group, saying 'if there is one type of man to whom I do feel myself inferior, it is a coal-miner' (*Road* 102), ought not to detract from the central point that physical, nonrationalized Work for Orwell is *real* work. Despite being slightly disingenuous (the reader is constantly reminded that the writer's authority comes from his proximity to the work), by dissociating himself from the working class and the Work it does, Orwell confirms the moral superiority of nonrationalist, Carlylean Work with proper biographical humility and shelters Work from his own critique of labour. But by intuiting working-class life, as with any act of intuition, he denies the differences between himself, the observer, and the observed.

Despite Orwell's expressed attempts not to idealize the working class, the absence of any mimetic representation of violence in the home or pub, for example, as opposed to the diegetic references to its toughness and what its members would do to interfering middle-class observers, undermines that effort. Orwell means to validate a specific kind of English socialism, a cultural socialism that clings to nonrationalist or traditionalist values – such as an emotional, visceral understanding of the difference between right and wrong. He contrasts the 'self-made man' who has only 'a talent for making money' (*Road* 101) to the working class in order to show that the values of nonrationalism belong to the working class. Frederick Karl argues that Orwell turns the structure of the nineteenth-century *bildungsroman*, especially as mastered by Dickens, 'upside-down' (151). (If not strictly of that genre, Orwell's prose is certainly concerned with the education or development of a central figure, most often Orwell himself.) Instead of having the moral growth of the hero correspond to economic improvement, verifying the bourgeois code of self-starting industriousness and frugality, Orwell shows the morality of those who do not grow socially or financially. In fact, he reserves a particularly vicious invective for those of the working class who attempt social mobility – in spite of his Dickensian belief in effort, the will, and the individual (we are better off to distinguish the Orwell of *The Road to Wigan Pier* from the later Orwell of *Nineteen Eighty-Four* [1949]). The miners resist bourgeoisification partly because of their geographical distance from the urban entrappings of fast-paced commercialism and partly because of the work they do, work that in itself satisfies their needs and furnishes its own substantive justification. By representing a working class indifferent to making money, and in order to discredit bourgeois desire, Orwell has the working class validate Work. Orwell's working class lives qualitatively; a rationalized conception of work – whether that means economic maximizing (or even 'satisficing') or acknowledging the conditions they work in – is alien to the best of them.

In *Down and Out* Orwell suggests that society 'despises' the tramps only because they do not make money and 'Money has become the grand test of virtue' (155). Society is rationalized, as it judges its subjects by their capacity for 'profitable' activity. But Orwell counters the notion that 'work' is only paid work and that paid employment is the only source of value. It is important not to blow off this notion as mere ideology or mythology. Patrick Joyce, a work theorist who recognizes that the meanings of work are historic or 'socially produced,' still accepts that 'At all levels of skill, even the lowest, work may denote special meanings, such as those to do with rites of passage, with handling danger and with testing identity ... workers in "menial" jobs may attach the utmost significance to their work' (14, 22). But there can only be therapy or satisfaction in hard work if all other things, economic things, are right. At this point I am only describing the length to which Orwell goes in order to resist rationalism. In other sections of his writing he concedes to the everyday world, arguing that tramps tramp only because they cannot find paid work, and that they are ready to fill the imperative of earning a living and taking 'a respectable place in society' (184).

Nonetheless, Orwell insists that tramping is 'work' (Work), and as such it equips tramps with morality. In *Down and Out* he describes the abject conditions of poverty *and* the kindness flourishing within those conditions by segregating a discourse of Work from one of labour, just as the workers of *The Road to Wigan Pier* are immune to their surroundings. The 'envious' tramp with a 'jackal's character' is nevertheless 'a good fellow, generous by nature and capable of sharing his last crust with a friend' (136). Throughout the text Orwell manages to find a code of well-being – camaraderie, generosity – among the decay. This code is inextricably interwoven with the survival of 'character' or personal identity. No matter how debilitating poverty, underemployment, or degrading work may be, *Down and Out* represents highly individuated, non-rationalistic, and idiosyncratic 'characters' connected by a common code of *caritas*. Bozo, the screever (sidewalk painter), asserts 'that poverty did not matter' (147), that with the moral and spiritual (or psychological) confirmation of a willed work ethic he could survive the indifferent world. He may be an 'exceptional man,' but it is precisely that quality that Orwell admires and that constitutes the underdog hero, and in this case almost the entire cast of the book. Those who break the code are secretly bourgeoisie or merely ideological fundamentalists: Jules, who hates work and sounds like Paul Lafargue, echoes the worst kind of Marxist rhetoric. Maintaining a personal identity, the more eccentric or nonrational the more personalized, is to maintain the code, as if selfhood is a moral virtue in itself. The code nourishes a sense of both individuality and solidarity. When Boris gets work, he walks three kilometres after a twelve-hour shift, says to Orwell 'we're saved,' shares his food, and makes plans to steal more for them the following day. When Orwell receives some money while tramping with Paddy, he is overcome by an instinctive urge to share it. Later, when Paddy finds some money, he does the same (48–9, 161, 166).

Nevertheless, it is a provisional code that can be subordinated to the demands of necessity. At least at one point in *Down and Out* Work and labour do clash. Orwell's 'first lesson in *plongeur* morality' is to drop his scruples while interacting with 'quite merciless' employers and to learn that he cannot 'afford a sense of honour' (53–4). However, most of the time when he describes the actual nature of the work taking place, the discourse of Work abruptly disappears, is sealed off at the introduction of labour, or politely stands by. At other times, when Orwell is describing the working class as a participant in its culture, Work dominates. The point of *Down and Out* is not that abject conditions make for abject morality or that middle-class notions of the sanguine worker easily crack when tested; rather, Orwell is saying that self-imposed regulating codes of pre-capitalist behaviour survive: one for *plongeurs*, one for cooks, one for waiters, one for tramps. *Down and Out* is a history of Orwell's initiation into various codes, the idea of the code itself amounting to inviolate Work, to individual morality sustaining group morality, and vice versa. The workers who abuse each other at work drink and sing together at the end of the shift. Reprising cliché imagery of an earthy, rough-and-ready, carnivalistic, working-class fraternal code, Orwell attempts to reconstruct an age when workers did not consider their labour solely as a commodity or a rationalized activity, but as a self-defining, community-building expression of meaningful living. The work itself, the endless hours spent dripping in slime while scrubbing pots for the bourgeoisie, is swept up into a folkloric tradition of vague resistance and dissent: a snub against economic activity and the rationalisms behind it.

Part of Orwell's subscription to the act of physical work in itself stems from a quasi-Puritan, post-Protestant tradition. His anti-hedonism, his fear of centralized power, and his championing of the underdog also relate to a Protestant heritage. When Orwell identifies Dickens as being 'part of the English puritan tradition, which is not dead even at this day,' he is certainly, as Woodcock first noted, demonstrating similarities between Dickens and himself. Is it Dickens or Orwell 'who is always fighting against something, but who fights in the open'? Who is a 'liberal, a free intelligence, a type hated with equal hatred by all the smelly little orthodoxies which are now contending for our souls' (*CEJL*, 1: 429, 460)? Alan Sandison argues that this is the image of Protestant individualism, the heretic. Orwell, says Sandison, 'out-Protestants the Protestants' insofar as he disparages half-hearted commitment, avoids institutions, prefers simple truths, favours self-sufficiency, and believes that work in conjunction with the physical world is the means to, if not a spiritual end, a nonrationalized end (6). But Orwell's celebration of the folksy rough-and-tumble habits of working-class culture suggests that his ethos was also made up from traditions far removed from Puritanism and Protestantism. Protestantism, according to Weber and Tawney, also lends itself to individual ambition and the cult of success. The Work glorified by Orwell and represented as particular to the working class is certainly not. It is in as many ways antagonistic towards Protestantism and the course of its development as it resembles Protestantism.

The images of camaraderie also incorporate and endorse a tradition of male bonding that functions to ratify Orwell's nostalgia for an understood rigidity in gender roles. I will discuss issues surrounding Orwell's androcentricism later, treating it in the meantime as a symptom of his traditionalism and his traditionalism as an aspect of his resistance to rationalism, especially work rationalization. *The Road to Wigan Pier*, however, is less about work (or socialism) than unemployment. Yet interpolated between documenting the economic conditions of the 1930s and emphasizing that work is the means to obtain the wherewithal needed to live, Orwell represents work with a Carlylean belief in intrinsic value. He states: 'Cease to use your hands, and you have lopped off a huge chunk of your consciousness' (173). This not only recalls Carlyle's belief that physical work is the expression of an independent human spirit and the means to secure psychological stability, but also echoes his rhetoric. In response to the efforts made to combat unemployment (occupational centres), Orwell suggests that a man be allowed the opportunity of 'using his hands and making furniture and so forth for his own home'; he proposes to give the unemployed 'a patch of ground and free tools' so they might 'have the chance to grow vegetables for their families' (75). Even if one disregards the fact that carpentry and gardening were two of Orwell's most cherished pastimes (Crick, *Life* 411), the opportunity for simple, physical, self-governed Work represents a traditional, independent, and essentially ideal life attainable for the unemployed, for those outside the sphere of rationalized work. Orwell, however, is 'torn both ways' over the centres: his anti-rationalist side rejects the notion as liberalist planning, answering all social problems through organization, or as a means to prevent working-class culture; his pragmatic side recognizes that something immediate and concrete needs to be done.

But by suggesting that the moral and psychological effects of unemployment are 'far worse than any hardship' (77) – worse, that is, than financial burdens or the struggles endemic to poverty (which, of course, Orwell had experienced) – Orwell again offers a temple of Work as an asylum from the realm of necessity. By no means do I intend to belittle the psychological effects of unemployment or suggest that its economic effects can be segregated from its psychological effects. Rather, I wish only to point out the problematic consequences of having the unemployed define work in terms other than employment. The unemployed individual 'needs work and usually looks for it, though he may not call it work.' 'He,' apparently adopting the Conradian view that Orwell also shares, recognizes that 'life has got to be lived largely in terms of effort' (173). At this point, 'he' ignores or can ignore that life, certainly when unemployed, is lived in terms of needs. The unemployed in the London of the 1930s might question the usefulness of a 'patch of ground and free tools.' Orwell is right to answer his own question of 'what is work and what is not work?' by suggesting that one person's work is another person's leisure. But the separation of the psychological from the economic effects of unemployment is a permutation of the disjunctive schism between Work and labour that reinforces self-sufficient moralism at the expense of the unemployed Orwell means to support.

Orwell, offering gardening to the unemployed, also means to curb the definition of work as exclusively an instrument for economic gain. He reproduces John Beevers's hyper-rationalized approach to work in order to take the stuffing out of it. Beevers writes:

> It is so damn silly to cry out about the civilizing effects of work in the fields and farmyards as against that done in a big locomotive works or an automobile factory. Work is a nuisance. We work because we have to and all work is done to provide us with leisure and the means of spending that leisure as enjoyably as possible. (168)

Beevers's attitude is hedonistic. As Sean Sayers explains, according to a

> hedonist account of human nature, which underlies utilitarianism and classical economics ... the pursuit of pleasure and the avoidance of pain are the sole motive forces of human life. Work involves painful exertion and the deferral of gratification; we undertake it only because we are forced to, as a means to satisfy our [external] needs. (723)

Orwell resists the gap between private (leisure) and public (work) selfhood. He rejects the idea that work is a burden. He opposes the idea that life is about the pursuit of pleasure and that work is a mere means, not 'life.' From this Carlylean or Conradian attitude towards work, Orwell challenges definitions that restrict it to pure marketable production, to exchange, or to the means to ensure consumption. But in doing so he makes Work an opposing term to economic activity, even when addressing unemployment.

Orwell also ridicules Beevers because the latter 'claims, or rather screams, that he is thoroughly at home in the modern mechanized world' (168). Orwell is clearly not. He in fact adulates the home to express a traditionalism fundamental to his concept of Work. In *The Road to Wigan Pier*, Orwell draws together patriarchal, communal, familial, and nonrational values, Work values, by representing an inviolate working-class home. Woodcock is correct to identify the relationship between Orwell's vision of an ideal home and stock Victorian scenes of blissful domestic life (*Crystal* 63). Actually, both Orwell's workers and Woodcock's Victorians wax nostalgic over a pastoral retreat where 'the old communal way of life has not yet broken up, tradition is still strong and almost everyone has a family' (*Road* 71). The difference between the pastoral trope and Orwell's retreat is that Orwell escapes from the speed and transience of an encroaching modernity but remains in industrial Lancashire. This is not the only instance in which he appropriates generic Victorian values and relocates them in the working class of the twentieth century. And this is not the only instance in which Work and labour exist side by side without recognizing each other's existence, without being embroiled in conflict.

Many things have been said about the romanticized working-class home in *The Road to Wigan Pier*; most of them have been appropriately critical. Here again is the home:

> In a working-class home – I am not thinking at the moment of the unemployed, but of comparatively prosperous homes – you breathe a warm, decent, deeply human atmosphere which it is not so easy to find elsewhere. I should say that a manual worker, if he is in steady work and drawing good wages – an 'if' which gets bigger and bigger – has a better chance of being happy than an 'educated' man. His home life seems to fall more naturally into a sane and comely shape. I have often been struck by the peculiar easy completeness, the perfect symmetry as it were, of a working-class interior at its best. Especially on winter evenings after tea, when the fire glows in the open range and dances mirrored in the steel fender, when Father, in shirtsleeves, sits in the rocking chair at one side of the fire reading the racing finals, and Mother sits on the other with her sewing, and the children are happy with a pennorth of mint humbugs, and the dog lolls roasting himself on the rag mat – it is a good place to be in, provided that you can be not only in it but sufficiently *of* it to be taken for granted.
>
> This scene is still reduplicated in a majority of English homes ... (*Road* 104–5)

Crick's defence of this scene, on the basis that it illustrates 'fraternal virtues which contrast vividly with both middle-class acquisitiveness, competitiveness and propriety and with the restless power-hungry arrogance of the intellectuals' (*Life* 288), correctly identifies Orwell's resistance to rationalism but does not actually examine the scene itself. Lisa Jardine and Julia Swindells point out that the scene 'wipes women from the landscape of class, poverty and struggle' (118). Woodcock calls it 'impossibly idyllic' (*Crystal* 65). The sentimentality and unreality of the scene are hardly mitigated by the stipulation that the man must be in work, that it underlines the effects of unemployment. Here, as in most of Orwell's writings, the representation of the ideal is completely cut off from his political and critical discourse. As Crick says, the home is meant to censure the ambitions of the middle class (this is one way to read 'completeness'), but the contrast between the appeals to permanence (another way to read 'completeness') and the stated intention of the book to expose the hardships and insufferable conditions of the working class, including their living conditions, augments the division between moral from pragmatic values, while giving the moral individual a physical sanctuary. Orwell's home obviates change at both abstract and concrete levels of work. The same is true for Orwell's direct aggrandizement of Work: both Work and the concept of the working-class nuclear family remain entirely isolated from history and politics, from time and technology, from labour.

Orwell's working class is remarkably similar to Hoggart's version of it in *The Uses of Literacy* (1957). Both Orwell and Hoggart emphasize cozy, warm homes with well-defined gender and age roles. Hoggart characterizes working-class culture as stressing tightly knit communities, solidarity, tradition, and home cooking. Its relaxed attitude towards time or 'wasting time' underlines its pre-capitalist character. It is replete with emotional life, gregariousness, rituals, superstitions but common sense, and anti-intellectualism. Because the working class adopts a general 'acceptance of life as hard, with nothing to be done about it,' they seek immediate gratifications, have their 'sights fixed at a short distance' (78, 77). Hoggart's working classes do not save money or plan out their lives. Nor do they have a pressing sense of their own political situation. Neither Hoggart's nor Orwell's working class, absorbed in custom and traditional living, have any consciousness of the world of labour except to passively accept the idea that life is based on a daily struggle. There is no sense of injustice within the working class itself, no concept of alternatives, no sense of the economic beyond short-term consumption and the need to endure. There is also no sense of the ideological formation of its consciousness, if indeed this is working-class consciousness, in Hoggart's or Orwell's commentaries, or that such pragmatism can be more than just a day-to-day survival tactic. In Orwell's case, working-class traditionalism is represented as an alternative to bourgeois acquisitiveness to the point where his working class become oblivious to or would deny its own economic conditions, precisely what is taking place in his representation of the 'average' working-class home. At other times, Orwell starkly represents those conditions and remarks that there are other long-term economic conditions that create the Work-related ideology that 'life is a struggle' – and that capitalist agents embrace the ideology for their own ends – but not when he blankets himself in working-class culture and is bent on juxtaposing it with middle-class ascendancy or its preoccupation with economics.

The distinction between the *gemeinschaft* and the *gesellschaft*, between a spontaneously arising, organic, and harmonious community and a rationally developed, mechanistic, and impersonal society, is as central to Orwell as it is to Carlyle and Conrad as they confront and repudiate rationalization. Yet none of them – despite their ideas about *gemeinschaft* communities, mutual obligations, and the communal values generated by Work – would ever conceive of or favour a 'Blithedale' commune. Their pragmatic, anti-romantic sides would, in fact, deflate any gesture of easy social harmony. In his pragmatic 'mode,' Orwell lists the benefits and argues in favour of 'rationalizing the interiors of our houses' with machines. Here he looks forward to machines that would make for 'very little work' (*CEJL* 3: 330). It is a completely different attitude than the one shown by fearing a future of 'no manual labour,' every household thing cold and made of rubber (*Road* 105). In that section of *The Road to Wigan Pier*, 'poverty' is listed among dogs and big families as a traditional thing of value disappearing in the rationalized world:

> In that age when there is no manual labour and everyone is 'educated,' it is hardly likely that Father will still be a rough man with enlarged hands who likes to sit in shirt-sleeves and says 'Ah wur coomin' oop street.' And there won't be a coal fire in the grate, only some kind of invisible heater. The furniture will be made of rubber, glass, and steel. If there are still such things as evening papers there will certainly be no racing news in them, for gambling will be meaningless in a world where there is no poverty and the horse will have vanished from the face of the earth. Dogs, too, will have been suppressed on grounds of hygiene. And there won't be so many children, either, if the birth-controllers have their way. (105)

This is not his political, pragmatic 'mode' that addresses the problems of labour. Orwell may not romanticize poverty, but he invests in images of struggle and hardship the capacity to signify anti-rationalist value, a strategy that contradicts his more concrete side. In the 1945 'As I Please' article, where he accepts 'rationalizing,' he is searching for practical solutions to the labour involved in 'washing up':

> Like sweeping, scrubbing and dusting, it is of its nature an uncreative and life-wasting job. You cannot make an art out of it as you can out of cooking or gardening. What, then, is to be done about it? Well, this whole problem of housework has three possible solutions. One is to simplify our way of living very greatly; another is to assume, as our ancestors did, that life on

earth is inherently miserable, and that it is entirely natural for the average woman to be a broken-down drudge at the age of thirty; and the other is to devote as much intelligence to rationalizing the interiors of our houses as we have devoted to transport and communications.

I fancy we shall choose the third alternative. (*CEJL* 3: 330)

When in his Work, nonrationalist, moral 'mode,' Orwell will explicitly make the case to simplify, as he does describing the working-class home in *The Road to Wigan Pier*, or he will adopt the Conradian position that life is inherently hard and tragic, as in his representation of the miners' attitude towards their lives. The world of Work, of nonrationalism, competes for space with the world of labour, the need to pragmatically respond to labour, but without confrontation.

Not unexpectedly, the traditional home in *The Road to Wigan Pier* is directly related to Work. Both represent qualitative living, not quantitative pursuit, and a refuge away from the alienating and atomizing effects of rationalization. Joyce confirms that by the late nineteenth century, as 'Satisfactions and needs were increasingly identified as coming out of non-work time ... the cult of family and home became established' (24). As the assent to economic rationalization became naturalized, the home and work were more and more differentiated. But for Orwell, the values generated and needs satisfied in the home are exactly the same as those generated and satisfied by Work. What he says about the working-class home corresponds to what he says about Work.

Orwell's home is also designed to equate the sanctity of homelife to liberty, the notion that 'the Englishman's home is his castle' (*CEJL* 3: 11–12). Connecting the home and freedom argues that property, ownership, and privacy form the basis of freedom and individuality. Orwell's equation, however, is less a valorization of private property than it is a valuation of an establishment that supposedly separates individuals from consensual habits, just as nonrationalized Work supposedly promotes self-realized and personal identity. But the image of a home with 'sane' and 'perfect symmetry' appeals to order and hierarchy, not liberty, or at least not liberty for all. The representation of the home with the man firmly lionized by his having employment echoes Friedrich Engels's concept of the family in capitalism. Engels writes, 'As wealth increased, it ... gave the man a more important status in the family than the woman' and in 'the family, [the man] is the bourgeois; the wife represents the proletariat' ('Origin' 735, 744). The difference is that whereas Engels condemns a Victorian middle-class family, Orwell condones a working-class one. For Engels, 'the last remnants of male domination in the proletariat home have lost all foundation' because there is 'no stimulus whatever here to assert male domination' ('Origin' 742). Orwell and Engels are involved in very different kinds of idealization. Orwell superimposes middle-class Victorian imagery onto the twentieth-century working-class home in order to recover rigid Victorian morality and epistemology and locate them in the working class.

Orwell, though by no means in dialogue with Engels, is also counteracting the heavily ascetic Marxist assumption that the working class has been led to 'moral ruin' (Engels, *Condition* 71). Basically, Marxists take this position because they believe that with capitalism, so with its conscripted constituents, 'it is not possible for a single human sentiment or opinion to remain untainted' (Engels, *Condition* 275). According to rhetorical convention, working-class homes in *The Condition of the Working Class in England* and *The Road to Wigan Pier* reflect their occupants. Engels observed decency but emphasizes squalor. Orwell, though not consistently, observes squalor and emphasizes decency. Whereas Engels represents the effects of 'the system,' Orwell represents the individual rising above that system.

What Orwell admires in the working-class home, why the middle class 'can learn a great deal' from it (*Road* 103), is its resistance to change, or that it is less susceptible to change (it is not clear that the working classes play an active role in preserving their culture). Orwell's working class is closer to the Gospel of Work than any other class. Its values are the values of Work, from a lack of whining when faced with rough work, an instinct to sacrifice themselves or at least approach a task with as much effort as possible, to an enthusiasm for home life and traditional morality. Finishing up his description of the home, he says, 'our age has not been altogether a bad one to live in' (*Road* 105). 'Our age' is not 1937, the year of *The Road to Wigan Pier.* It is apparently not an era of rationalism but a largely imagined Victorian age of Work. But Orwell is also very much integrated into the real politics of his age. As an observer, from a remote, analytical point of view, he represents the working class as only labouring because of necessity, insisting that those would be the reasonable parameters of its thought, that pragmatics is simple decency. Under that modus vivendi – a manner of living based on practical compromise – Orwell treats Work as rubbish, as a mystification, a blinding ideology that attempts to mitigate a consciousness of extrinsic, economic needs.

Orwell's attraction to the working class comes down to his understanding that it is 'generally more conservative than the bourgeoisie' (*Road* 114). Orwell's conservatism is a strange, unsteady creature that irks conservatives. In general, it relates to his traditionalism and a reluctance to accept rationalization and modernization. This makes for an odd confluence of ideational habits, but one typical of Carlyle and radical conservatism in general. To resist rationalism is to combine conservative and nonconformist ideas. I said earlier that Orwell is more likely to resist rationalism when speaking generally and abstractly than when speaking personally and concretely. Paradoxically, when Orwell distances himself from working-class culture, when he speaks analytically about the specific, day-to-day lives of the working class from an economic point of view, he also speaks in 'personal' terms. When he speaks as if in or *of* the working class, he speaks in general and abstract terms. Orwell is a 'conservative' when he speaks in a general mode, and a pragmatist when he speaks in personal terms. When he speaks in personal terms is also when he thinks inside the whale of rationalism. The identity he creates for himself is the exact opposite of the so-called armchair Marxist or parlour-room rebel who is anti-conformist in theory, when speaking generally, and absent in practice.

It is with Work that Orwell best expresses his nostalgia for traditional things and his rejection and denial of the positivistic, quantitative, impersonal, and functional aspects of rationalism. Modern rationalism begins or is always coincident with an approach to work, for work is the means to the fetishized, maximizing end. Rationalized work, if not setting the stage for functionalism in society, for utilitarianism and economism, for systematizing in thought, is in collusion with other clinical rationalisms (scientism, positivism, business). Yet it is with work that we see the other side of Orwell's dual habit of mind, the side that pushes away romantic images and concepts of Work and deals pragmatically with the terms defined by a rationalist social order. Orwell demonstrates a degree of faith in the intrinsic value of Work and the work ethic that needs to isolate Work from the issues surrounding labour, the realm of necessity and the real. But he also maintains that one cannot separate work from external necessity and to do so would be to perpetuate a sham myth that romanticizes work for the benefit of the ruling class and conceals the inexorable realities of the rationalized world that the working class have to accept. Richard Rees identifies this competing loyalty as two different Orwells: the 'rationalist Orwell, the tenacious heir of eighteenth-century *Éclaircissement*,' and the 'romantic' Orwell, 'a lover of the past ... of old-fashioned customs and old-fashioned people' (6). The 'different Orwells' are best identified at sites in which non-economic (moral, psychological, social) and economic imperatives would clash, should clash, but do not.

Contrary to his representation of Work, a dissimilar Orwell argues that the last word on work has to consider survival, 'the really basic thing' (*Road* 82). Much of *The Road to Wigan Pier* and *Down and Out* is thus devoted to nutrition rather than abstractions, notes on shelters rather than general ethics. He elides the concept that the worker needs work for its intrinsic value by saying that the stigmatization hovering over the unemployed is entirely socially constructed (*Road* 78). He insists that modern work is tolerable if 'your spare time is your own' (*CEJL* 3: 12), differentiating a leisure-self from a work-self and confirming the idea that work is a disutility, or acceptable as one. At one point in *Down and Out*, he identifies a 'solution' to pauperism, the social apparatuses that would allow the homeless to lead a 'settled life.' Though other parts of the text are by no means a defence of nomadism, the invocation to bourgeoisie stability jars against the idiosyncratic portraits of the tramps – the dignity of their social marginality, the legitimacy of the effort they give and the work they do, their community and their spirit of sharing, and their prerogative to impish, antisocial peccadilloes. He derides the work ethic, the sanguine attitude that steadfastly posits that the cure for social or psychological ailments is to 'get our shoulders to the wheel.' He calls it 'pernicious rubbish' (*Road* 141). He cannot separate the act of work from the act of paid employment. In 'Charles Dickens' (1940), Orwell understands that when Dickens's Snodgrass '"purchased and cultivated a small farm, more for occupation than profit"' it is not 'work' but a 'sort of radiant idleness' (*CEJL* 1: 446). This is an altered Orwell, not the one who equates rough hands to self-realization and idealizes the miners because they are economically disinterested. This is an Orwell engaged in concrete economic realities, who is only concerned with the struggle against the specific but inevitable aspects of the rationalized world, not the struggle against economism or a general and inevitable struggle with life, given 'life is a struggle.' It is a reformist Orwell who calls for 'better wages and shorter hours and nobody bossing you about ... justice and common decency' (*Road* 154). Long-run considerations are suspect if there is no immediate effect or benefit. His characterization of the working class, in turn, centres on its preoccupation with day-to-day economic calculations. It is not concerned with Work *or* social change, but with 'getting by': those instincts, in fact, constitute a good deal of its 'decency.' By no means do I wish to imply that by yielding to material relations Orwell wrongly apostatizes or endorses the economic-as-is in the same way that Carlyle and Conrad do. The representation of a world revolving around immediate economic interests underlies a solidly ethical starting point. To resign oneself to rationalism (such as with Gordon Comstock in *Keep the Aspidistra Flying* [1936], or the 'common stock' in general) is only as problematical as its isolation.

Still, the mandate for economic awareness is in striking contrast to Orwell's nonrationalist ideas about Work. In *Down and Out* he protests that only 'comfortably situated people' would claim 'work in itself is good' (106). The rhetoric of work as its own end allows for the capitalist class to reap the benefits from the workers' surplus value; it increases the surplus. Turning a full 180 degrees from his own idealization of work, he argues that the dominant social voices 'have made a sort of fetish of manual work.' The ruling capitalist class calls 'hard and disagreeable' work 'honest' in order to mobilize the workers to endure their agenda (*Down* 104). That agenda is to cultivate power, not necessarily to make economic gain (and here this Orwell differs from the Marxist tradition). The issues of power will be dealt with elsewhere; here I only want to emphasize Orwell's dual habit of mind.

Orwell epitomizes the indeterminable ideological frame of radical conservative thinkers such as Carlyle or Conrad not because he splits Work and the realm of necessity – that is, I argue, central to it – but because when he turns towards economics and pragmatics, he actually mocks the concept of Work and the moralism surrounding it. In 'The English Tradition' (1944), Orwell contends the work ethic is 'forced upon the working class' in order to 'get more out of him [the working man] for less money' (*CEJL* 3: 10). In contrast to the representations of a morally fit working class, in a 1944 'As I Please' article he writes, 'that this business about the moral superiority of the poor is one of the deadliest forms of escapism the ruling class have evolved.' The article is brilliant, but it contradicts all of what we have seen in Orwell's attitude towards Work. The ruling class, by means of the popular media, convinces the working public that as a result of their poverty 'you are superior to your oppressors' (*CEJL* 3: 197). The rich man in popular art is always the 'bad' man. Orwell calls the formula whereby the good poor man defeats the rich bad man a 'sublimation of the class struggle. So long as you can dream of yourself as a "strong hard-working garage hand" giving some moneyed crook a sock on the jaw, the *real* facts can be forgotten. That is a cleverer dodge than wealth fantasy' (*CEJL* 3:198).

But we have seen in *The Road to Wigan Pier* and in *Down and Out* that

Orwell himself idealizes the manual worker – the strong, hard-working hand – and represents Work as a source of identity and pride. He even invests poverty with a moral cachet. Despite the fact that the restaurant workers are 'underpaid workmen' drinking in order to compensate for abject working conditions, there is the 'pride of the drudge.' Enjoying the 'frantic' restaurant work, Orwell insists that a 'sense of honour' accompanies 'the man who is equal to no matter what quantity of work' (*Down* 70). The 'pride of the drudge' is not represented as inurement or ideology: it is a thrill, a nonrational emotion. But Orwell also describes a lack or an impossibility of pride when working in degrading conditions. The employees at the Hotel X who 'take a genuine pride in their work' are the same ones who provide only 'an imitation of good service' (67, 71), as they themselves proliferate filth. The Work ethic, the pride of the drudge, manifesting itself when Orwell participates among the working class, is at best a private affair. An employee might Work, but that is an individual matter; the employees are labourers, and labour is a self-estranging activity that excludes pride. The shift from labour to Work allows subjectivity to be preserved. Still, Orwell's alliance to Work always ends abruptly. Distanced from the people and the events, observing the working class critically, identifying immediate needs, relating minute details through charts and diagrams, and addressing wages, expenses, and standards of living, he denies and derides Work. Orwell then depicts working-class culture as fixated on the daily struggle to survive and validates that economic short-sightedness. In this way he goes further than Carlyle or Conrad, who only imagine and condone a working-class culture glued to Work. The two distinct and competing systems of thought and discourse, his disjunctive reasoning and the hard and fast swing within it, the change in attitude depending upon his proximity to the working class, the way in which he strictly disavows any value that might inhere in work when he addresses labour in its economic details, and the huge gap between a mimetic representation of Work and a diegetic analysis of economic conditions amount to an extreme configuration of Carlylean or Conradian radicalism.

Part of the reason why Orwell feels 'contentment' as a *plongeur* is that it is accompanied by admission into a solidarity, a 'scene,' or a boys' club. The feeling is also relative to the devastating poverty he previously endured. But the stupefying work and lifestyle of restaurant work – wash, bistro, sleep – nonetheless satisfies. Comparing himself, a Worker, to an exhausted 'well-fed beast' (*Down* 81) has greater implications than the Hardyesque tropes of 'the harder the work the heavier the sleep' and 'time off is enjoyed when there is little of it.' The goodness of physical labour is problematic in that in a nondialectical relationship with pragmatism it sweeps in a program for the working classes to remain uneducated, economically obtuse (whether it is abstract or concrete economics), and incapable of autonomy: to remain virtually unconscious. This is exactly the dupe he accuses the ruling class of perpetuating. Though Orwell calls him who raises his consciousness while continuing to work 'one of the finest types of man we have' (*Road* 143), Work and education are emphatically polarized. He echoes Carlyle's admiration for the 'stupid,' 'thickest-skinned,' and conservative John Bull threatening the feeble Man of Theory (*Past* 159–66). The boy is 'manly' and 'happy' because he chooses 'real work,' and the man is 'unmanly,' 'sickly and debilitating,' because he chooses to study (*Road* 104). Orwell follows the formula whereby intellectualization fosters rationality, a disenchantment with nonscientific claims to knowledge. Gone are the *feelings* of morality and intrinsic Work satisfaction. He also privileges manual work that brings about intellectual limitations because he understands the manual worker will retain a *basic* 'decency,' be wary of new ideas, and will not harbour secret desires to accumulate power if he remains simple.

For Orwell, any social advancement in a rationalized economic and political structure is cause for suspicion (though he is perfectly comfortable with workers who participate in that structure on a day-by-day basis). Reflecting on his experiences in Burma, he says, 'At that time failure seemed to me to be the only virtue. Every suspicion of self-advancement, even to "succeed" in life to the extent of making a few hundreds a year, seemed to me spiritually ugly, a species of bullying' (*Road* 130). Though Orwell's pragmatic realist is cleared of that suspicion, Orwell himself developed an unflinching support for the underdog as long as he remained the underdog. Contentment with social position, satisfying needs and not maximizing gains, are qualities he sees in or projects onto the English working class, and by extension the English people. Because the impetus to maximize financial gains is the same as the drive to maximize power, he amplifies his already substantial rhetoric of satisfying needs, the rhetoric of nonrationalist Work. If England is not to fall to fascism, Work for Work's sake. Only the educated, the rationalist, and the ambitious can abstract the irrationality of fascism into something that looks decent. His often harsh attitude towards Marxists stems from his understanding that they had no mechanism to account for the psychological network that desires power or to internally check their own motives. By claiming that the working classes were better off uneducated and at

Work, Orwell was also expressing a fear of its 'bourgeoisification.' The Dickens novel goes 'wrong' when it abandons traditional values and professes the 'gospel according to Smiles.' Orwell speaks of *David Copperfield*'s last chapters as vitiated 'by the cult of success' (*CEJL* 1: 458); self-aggrandizement and self-helping buccaneerism are not to be part of the English ethos, of a cultural socialism. The rags-to-riches story is best to collapse before the riches, as it does in Orwell's stories.

Williams for one would not be satisfied with this answer to Orwell's valorization of the supposed simplicity or intellectual shortcomings of the working class. He would probably be unsatisfied with Crick's analysis of an Orwell who 'never seemed to ask too much of ordinary people' as well (*Life* 19). (Though if Crick is hinting at a paternalistic attitude towards the working class, he may in fact be quite close to Williams's view of Orwell.) Williams argues that Orwell saw the working classes as 'stupid, strong, and kind' – proles incapable of shaping their own future. Orwell says as much when he argues that the middle class is necessary to lead them into a new society. The model for this society is a working-class, not a middle-class culture, with working-class attitudes towards Work. Despite some sadness accompanying his belief that the working class cannot write its own future, he does not see that it is his own rhetoric of a content and uneducated working class that insists on its dependency and lack of revolutionary initiative (Williams, *Orwell* 78–9).

The problems of treating Work as a welcomed agent of stupefaction are all the more complex because Orwell himself underwrites the unwelcomed consequences of servility and stupefaction, of work that gets workers 'trapped by a routine which makes thought impossible' (*Down* 104). The thrilling adventure of Work and the satisfied exhaustion it offers is laid aside and in its place is the argument that the 'instinct to perpetuate useless work is, at bottom, simply fear of the mob' (*Down* 106). Nothing has changed in the nature of the work that once brought pride, but now it is labour, a tool for social engineering, and deemed 'useless.' In *The Road to Wigan Pier*, Orwell suggests that unemployment centres are 'a device to keep the unemployed quiet and give them the illusion that something is being done for them. Undoubtedly that *is* the underlying motive. Keep a man busy mending boots and he is less likely to read the *Daily Worker*' (74). Later Orwell rages against temperance societies and in *Down and Out* against the Salvation Army for bribing the desperate and hungry with bits of food in return for their pacification, humility, servility, and abdication of a right to overthrow systems of repression (including those very societies). He shows how the unemployed are taught to blame themselves for being out of work whereas in reality unemployment is endemic to capitalism (*Road* 76–7). He pulverizes the middle-class myth that the poor have grown accustomed to menial work, that they 'don't mind that kind of thing' (*Road* 56). Finally, he says that if it is not the institutions of the social net that 'press a working man down into a *passive* role' (*Road* 43) it is the working class that internalizes the idioms that paint it as deservedly servile. Tramps especially become 'docile,' allowing themselves to be repeatedly swindled.

These are critiques that disappear during the representation of Work, the kind of work that denies introspection and reflection, the kind of Carlylean work he endorses at other times. On the one hand, the capitalist class is seen to strip away any pleasure or intrinsic benefit in work by overworking labourers with humiliating and useless work in order that the 'mob' becomes a stupefied 'flock' and in order for labourers to learn that work is a drudgery, the first premise of classical economic theory. On the other hand, Orwell shows that demanding, even burdensome and stupefying Work is a good in itself. Orwell never advocates for working-class servility, recklessly promotes an intransitive Duty, or calls for a dumb acceptance of harsh working conditions. But he inherited certain ideas from the Victorian idealization of Work that clash with the rationalized world in which he found himself. The suppression of that potential dialectic is a central feature of Carlylean or Conradian work. Orwell writes about character, about individuals being individuals in a setting that disallows individuals – a setting that he underlines. The contradiction between moral Work and the effects of rationalist labour is never resolved. The lack of any real tension between the two, or any acknowledgment of tension, guarantees that he would not have to endorse the kind or degree of structural change that his vision of Work implies but that he is not able or prepared to make.

The gap between the treatment of labour and Work, 'between the scientific point of view of the historian and the moral point of view of the prophet,' to use Edmund Wilson's famous phrase, also materializes in Orwell's style. Yet this formal split between a grammar of labour and an aesthetic of Work is never as pronounced as the thematic split between the negotiation of labour and the apotheosis of Work. Orwell's style, for example – concrete, specific, and direct – nearly always has the attributes of a pragmatic approach to labour, and Carlyle's style – deductive, generalizing, and sermonizing – nearly always has the attributes of a Gospelized approach to Work. But though the shift in rhetorical character is small compared with the thematic shift, it nonetheless exists, evidencing not only a split in attitude, knowledge, and social history, but also cracks in the premeditated persona of the writer.

For Orwell, encountering the concrete is a value in itself. If the sections of *Down and Out* and *The Road to Wigan Pier* that deride Work and negotiate labour or economic circumstance argue any one thing it is the value of the specific and material. His prose style, famously lucid, non-jargonistic, precise, and direct, imitates and amplifies his focus on the concrete. He insists on using words that 'point to any discoverable object' (*CEJL* 4: 132). The themes of anti-intellectualism, empiricism, pragmatic politics, confrontation, and the everyday lives of everyday people are all paralleled in the stylistic emphasis on physical detail, journalistic fact, and demotic bluntness. His style conveys the importance of having a direct impact, and if it does not necessarily suggest the virtues of physical or material acts in themselves, it accents the importance of discussing concrete and immediate social, economic, or political facts. Just as Carlyle uses style to shorten the distance between the Writer and the Worker, to be a participant, Orwell uses style to connect with the working class, but his appeal is rather to the simple, anti-theoretical pragmatism he associates with it. Orwell uses mostly short, exclamatory, basic words and avoids euphemisms and grandiose words: he describes things as 'good' or 'bad' and 'right' or 'wrong.' The violence or abrasiveness of his rhetoric, its urgency, its transitiveness, straightforwardness, and unapologetic detail, correspond to the recognition of the inexorable world of labour.

The diction and the rhythm of his sentences are informal but not particularly casual: they abide to laws of clarity and hypotactic syntax. Typically, Orwell begins a passage with a personal experience, places it in a sequential and causal narrative, and then develops an argument based on the description. He organizes detailed and elaborate images into purportedly objective or sociological snapshots of the day-to-day experiences of the working and lower-middle class, focusing on minute-by-minute accounts of their labour, unemployment, and street life. He uses description as a way into prescription and pragmatic criticisms. His social critique is often made through a personalized attack on an identifiable enemy or wrongdoer. Woodcock notes that Orwell's concrete point of view also forms the basis of his literary criticism. Orwell, he suggests, 'can never resist thinking of another writer as a person and trying to see him in his mind's eye' (*Crystal* 332). Orwell finds in Dickens an 'impressionistic touch' because Dickens, he thought, did not have a firm grasp on how people make a living (*CEJL* 1: 443–5). He saw Dickens living comfortably. Grounded in the realism of pragmatic labour or economic necessity, Orwell sought concreteness in his images and language. His rhetoric, for rhetoric it is – punctuated with statistics, appeals to 'transparent' veracity, specific and itemized 'case studies,' statements of historical data, and the anti-theoretical materialism of prices, wages, living conditions, and so on – repeats the step-by-step, piecemeal logic of Orwell's pragmatic negotiation with labour.

Orwell's language of labour would be frustrated by suspicions that representation cannot be objective or made from neutral ground with neutral language. Orwell defends objective truth, first and foremost, to insist on a distinction between language that leads to equivocal, duplicitous argument and graphic, gritty language that leads to pointed argument, assertions of injustice (that injustice or cruelty truly occur), and a changeable object. In 'Why I Write' (1947), Orwell maintains that his 'starting point is always a feeling of partisanship, a sense of injustice' (*CEJL* 1: 6). Objectivity does not mean suspending one's biases or suppressing the urge to editorialize and argue a point of view. Objectivity in Orwell's school of thought means disclosing your objective to your audience (and yourself) and, as he said several times before *Nineteen Eighty-Four*, that $2 + 2 = 4$. Using numbers or an equation to express the case for empirical truths speaks to the nonessentialist, non-Carlylean character of his truths and the centrality of Orwell's pragmatic inclinations. The idea that truths can be independent of language and are not merely the function of the rest of one's beliefs is an essential presupposition for the pragmatic reformer who sees things politically.

Orwell's language is not only political; it is grounded in *realpolitik*. His main argument against unnecessarily complicated, abstract language and particularly nomenclature, apart from alienating 'everyday people,' is that power-mongers and the politically or ideologically orthodox use it to deny brutal truths. Nearly everything Orwell said about the political content of language, from Newspeak to how language will construct 'your thoughts for you' (*CEJL* 4: 135) to Professor Laski's pomp, has the left wing's flirtation with totalitarianism and Russia as a definite point of reference. Still one of the most important critics of 'the automatic way in which people go on repeating certain phrases' (*CEJL* 3: 145), his argument that language precedes knowledge does not contradict his argument that language can express clear truths when it itself is clear. Because he thought politically before he thought aesthetically (or historically), he feared how language could create meanings as opposed to being tantalized by the fact. His argument about the politics of language, despite the emphasis on precision, directness, and rules, expresses the same kind of support for a linguistic subversion of and dissent from centralized systems of discourse as Mikhail Bakhtin's theory of the novel articulates.

On the other side of Orwell's diegesis – his logical categorizing and bottom-line utility scrutinizing – is his high valuation of aesthetic, mimetic language. I will not argue that Orwell slips into purple passages when discussing Work and its attendant moralism, or even when discussing his love of nature and dislike of technology. He is more likely, however, to qualify, hesitate, circumscribe, specify, and be characteristically Orwellian when he speaks about economic matters than when he apotheosizes Work. When negotiating labour he refers to statistics, makes charts, and lists the incomes and expenses of the working class. He takes account of the minute details of their experiences as a social scientist might. He also grudgingly accepts technology and rejects, for example, William Morris's romanticism. But when speaking from an involved, generalizing perspective that embraces Work (and wholly rejects machine production), he follows Carlyle and Conrad in rejecting statistics, scientific facts, and compromises.

Woodcock reproduces three passages from Orwell's prose and fiction to show that Orwell progresses towards a greater and greater degree of blunt, unadorned, political (or labour-centred) diction as he matures as a writer. His point is valid and confirmed by Orwell himself, who wrote in 1947, 'of late years I have tried to write less picturesquely and more exactly' (*CEJL* 1: 7). As Orwell matured as a writer he spent less time directly participating in working-class culture and thus spoke less in a language of Work. One can, however, notice a shift in tone and style when looking at two passages from the same text or written in the same year. Here are two scenes from *Down and Out*. In the first, Orwell is a participant, celebrating working-class culture and the accoutrements of Work (the camaraderie that follows 'the pride of the drudge'). The second example is of Orwell summing up his social experiment.

> The brick-floored room, fifteen feet square, was packed with twenty people, and the air dim with smoke. The noise was deafening, for everyone was either talking at the top of his voice or singing. Sometimes it was just a confused din of voices; sometimes everyone would burst out together in the same song – the 'Marseillaise,' or the 'Internationale,' or 'Madelon,' or 'Les Fraises et les Framboises.' Azaya, a great clumping peasant girl who worked

fourteen hours a day in a glass factory, sang a song about, '*Il a perdu ses pantelons, tout en dansant le Charleston.*' Her friend Marinette, a thin, dark Corsican girl of obstinate virtue, tied her knees together and danced the *danse du ventre*. The old Rougiers wandered in and out, cadging drinks and trying to tell a long, involved story about someone who had once cheated them over a bedstead. R., cadaverous and silent, sat in his corner quietly boozing. Charlie, drunk, half danced, half staggered to and fro with a glass of sham absinthe balanced in one fat hand, pinching the women's breasts and declaiming poetry. People played darts and diced for drinks. Manuel, a Spaniard, dragged the girls to the bar and shook the dice-box against their bellies, for luck. Madame F. stood at the bar rapidly pouring *chopines* of wine through the pewter funnel, with a wet dishcloth always handy, because every man in the room tried to make love to her. Two children, bastards of big Louis the bricklayer, sat in a corner sharing a glass of *sirop*. Everyone was very happy, overwhelmingly certain that the world was a good place and we a notable set of people. (82–3)

This is description for description's sake. It is deliberately atmospheric and visual: half sentimental, half sensationalist, and probably a quarter factual. Insofar as there is an objective in this passage, it is to enjoy the setting. The sentences are elaborate, the diction less than plain. Nearly every noun is modified by an expressive adjective. Compare it to the language of labour:

> To sum up. A *plongeur* is a slave, and a wasted slave, doing stupid and unnecessary work. He is kept at work, ultimately, because of a vague feeling that he would be dangerous if he had leisure. And educated people, who should be on his side, acquiesce in the process, because they know nothing about him and consequently are afraid of him. I say this of the *plongeur* because it is his case I have been considering; it would apply equally to numberless other types of worker. These are only my ideas about the basic facts of a *plongeur's* life, made without reference to immediate economic questions, and no doubt largely platitudes. I present them as a sample of the thoughts that are put into one's head by working in an hotel. (108)

The sentences are shorter, the diction more terse, direct, analytical, and dressed down. It is especially important to note that he *had* explicitly referred to immediate economic questions but denies it in order to emphasize the shortcomings of a nonsociological point of view. In this passage Orwell appeals to reportage, objectivity, and to the impossibility of the grand, omniscient vision (the kind of vision he has in the earlier passage). One might also examine the linguistic shifts in *The Road to Wigan Pier*, from lyrical passages on the miners' strength and the gushing descriptions of working-class homes to statistical passages on unemployment and the standard of living in Lancashire. Orwell writes differently about the working class and its culture depending on his proximity to it, on whether or not he directly experiences it. Even in 'Such, Such Were the Joys' (1947), which comes relatively late in his career, Orwell oscillates between elaborately descriptive passages couched in narrative – when caught up in the moment of representing his childhood – and argumentative statements in response to those scenes – analytical observations about the effects of childhood or the point of reminiscing.

Still, the split is not exact or final: Orwell's style favours the concrete and precise, which is an attribute of negotiating labour, not a feature of intransitive Work. Even the whimsical 'A Nice Cup of Tea' (1946) proceeds in a methodic and orderly fashion. It includes a list of 'eleven rules' on how to make a nice cup, making it easy to forget that the point of the whimsicality is to censure utilitarian writing (*CEJL* 3: 41). He has the Victorian habit of classifying and categorizing (Mayhew, Ruskin, Philip Henry Gosse [Edmund's father], and so on), a gesture of imposing order on a world that seemed less than orderly. The split seems larger than it actually is, however, because Orwell himself frequently commented on it (or on variations of it). In 'Why I Write' (1947) he wrote:

> I write because there is some lie that I want to expose, some fact to which I want to draw attention, and my initial concern is to get a hearing. But I could not do the work of writing a book, or even a long magazine article, if it were not also an aesthetic experience ... So long as I remain alive and well I shall continue to feel strongly about prose style, to love the surface of the earth, and to take pleasure in solid objects and scraps of useless information. It is of no use trying to suppress that side of myself. (*CEJL* 1: 6)

John Rodden thus talks about Orwell's 'split self' (175) and Simon Dentith identifies 'varying emphases in the course of [Orwell's] writing, allowing him at one time to praise good writing as an independent value, and at other times to suggest that he sees it as no more than a frill tacked onto the real business of getting the meaning across' (205). In *Orwell* (1971), Williams, following the argument of *Culture and Society* (1958), argues that Orwell shifts between thinking that all important writing is a form of journalism or pamphleteerism and praising it precisely for its lack of utility. Orwell, he suggests, was caught in a struggle between writing *about* something, as Orwell would put it, and the 'higher' art for art's sake movement, which desired to distinguish itself from utilitarianism and commodification – between 'society' and 'culture' (29–40). Williams and the others are not wrong, though I think it is important to point out, as I do in my formulation of this divide as determined by an oppositional approach to labour and Work, that Orwell primarily favoured what he called 'political' language. Carlyle, who also oscillates between poles of labour and Work, favours the other side, the side of Work. The difference between the two writers is one of degree, or sides, not of kind. Both of them embrace a discourse, the language of labour or the language of Work, without squaring off one lexicon against the other.

The gap between labour and Work materializes again in Orwell's attitude towards gender, specifically in the way he links Work and masculinity. Orwell amplifies or is certainly attracted to 'an aesthetic of working-class manliness' (Jardine and Swindells 117); a gender ideology mediates his representations of nonrationalized Work and the culture of the working class. Daphne Patai correctly identifies *Down and Out* and *The Road to Wigan Pier* as 'narratives of a process of masculine self-affirmation' (54). Boris and Mario are admired for their soldierly approaches to poverty and overtaxing work, and the miners are stronger – not management more culpable – for facing life-threatening dangers. Orwell also celebrates in working-class culture the idea that a worker can work all day and have all the more energy for doing so. The Arabs in *Down and Out* are 'lucky men' because they 'had the power of working all day and drinking all night' (81). When he is bonding with the working class, Work and manliness become synonymous. But when Orwell discusses issues surrounding labour he dismisses the mythology that a difficult life corresponds to sexual strength. The two 'great evil[s]' of a tramp's life are 'enforced idleness' and the loss of the 'sexual impulse' (*Down* 181; see also 136). Relating the loss of sexual energy to poverty counters Zolaesque romanticism and operates to undo the myth of lower-class sexual stamina. A nonrepressed libido (a close proximity to nature) is supposed to compensate for or complement a lack of worldly goods (also a close proximity to nature) and suggest an advantage over the bourgeoisie, who care too much about appearances for any sexual pleasure. Orwell's analysis also counters the Marxist idea, used to warrant their asceticism, that the lower classes 'concentrate their whole energy' on sex, thereby guaranteeing an unconsciousness of their class position (Engels, *Condition* 153). When observing the working class from an outsider's point of view, a position that is amenable to the world of labour, he deflates the idea that being of the lower class engenders good, 'manly' sex.

Notwithstanding the argument that poverty amounts to a loss of the sexual appetite, Orwell prefers the exclusion of women from men's lives. Feeling pleased because he had been called 'mate' for the first time by one tramp recognizing another, he immediately comments that women 'shudder away' from the poor because of their appearance. He had just expressed enjoyment about having that appearance (*Down* 115). Not only are men the centre of all activity, all reality, but Orwell is not even comfortable with women on the margins. The nonrational tradition, the tradition Orwell paints as a working-class tradition, pivots on patriarchy. Because rationalism or capitalism, in theory, would bypass any regard for gender (or ethnicity), with the maximization of profit overriding all prejudice (the idea that economics, the free market, is blind), anti-rationalism digs deeper into traditional patriarchy. Resisting the dehumanizing effects of an advanced rationalization of work becomes a resistance to the largely imagined sissifying effects of modernity. In fact, when Orwell initially speaks of the emasculating effects of poverty, of his own experience, he moves the narrative from the first to the second person (*Down* 15–18). Moreover, it is likely that he entrenched himself in the harsh climate of Jura when he was very ill because it represented to him the opportunity to get stronger. It is a more likely theory than the theory that Orwell's trip was part of a suicidal impulse. He deliberately sought physical, existential, and perhaps even psychological hardship to prove to himself that he could stand extreme situations, such as tramping, and because he believed they would make him stronger. Yet, the affirmation of self based on toughness contradicts his stand against the 'survival of the fittest' mentality that dominated laissez-faire capitalism, power politics, and imperialism (*CEJL* 4: 27). His machismo, an attitude inseparably linked to Work, is mitigated when he thinks in concrete political terms, the terms of labour.

But Orwell admires physical work because it prevents men from getting 'soft.' He fetishizes the miner's 'toughness,' how they 'look and work as though they were made of iron' (*Road* 21). Though Orwell would never indulge in the kind of soft/female/mine – hard/male/worker imagery or any of the kinds of phallocentric imagery that came so easily to D.H. Lawrence (he often expresses distaste for Lawrentian imagery), he does share Lawrence's awe of the ostensibly transcendental, subsequently structuralist, connections between archetypes, the earth, and 'naturally' prescribed human roles. Though he admits that it 'seems a little unfair' that an unemployed man would not help with the housework, he uses the 'fact' that both husbands and wives 'feel that a man would lose his manhood if, merely because he was out of work, he developed into a "Mary Ann,"' to naturalize gendered relations (*Road* 73). Apart from being tautological and speaking of those relations as if sanctioned by common sense, Orwell ignores that what ought to be at issue are not the 'facts' but the factors that create those feelings and perpetuate those states of relations.

By revisiting Lancashire, Beatrix Campbell discovered that Orwell in his day suppressed the participation of women in the workforce, in fact suppressing history – relations of production, social hierarchies, social constructions and attempts to challenge those constructions, and so on. She also argues that 'the equation between work and masculinity depends on an exclusion – women' (99). Orwell, however, does represent women working and women in poverty. The portraits of female workers are made with feelings of authentic – patriarchal and paternal to be sure, but genuine – sadness, indignation, and concern. Emmie works for starvation wages in a mill only to return to the 'bondage' of housework (*Road* 11). The 'slum-girl' sees Orwell and makes Orwell see in himself that the greatest difference between them is that he can escape the 'drudgery' and she cannot (*Road* 16–17). The housewife of Lancashire is always 'muddling among an infinity of jobs' (*Road* 52). He replaces a 'horribly bullied' female dishwasher (*Down* 62). But such representations only illustrate victimization: they do not insist that the women also need to realize themselves through effort, confrontation, and activity. Orwell never idealizes the workplace – it is a rationalized site. The male worker is idealized; he is nonrational (he works because work is a good in itself, using the separation between Work and labour as if to turn labour into Work). The female worker is a victim of rationalization, not a hero despite of it, not engaged in an ennobling struggle against it: she cannot be the moral individual determining reality. Orwell can sympathize with the working woman but simply cannot empathize with her.

The linking of Work and identity, manliness, is bound to be followed by a censure of technical 'progress.' It also follows that Orwell would connect the mechanistic historical narrative of socialist doctrine, the 'pea-and-thimble trick' of dialectical reasoning, to a faith in machine technology (*Road* 155). Socialism, according to Orwell, is yoked to a 'completely mechanized, immensely organized' rational thought-machine (*Road* 165). His complaints about socialism/Marxism are broad. Socialism is 'glued to economic facts.' It is impersonal, trans-individualized, scientific, rationalized. It assumes 'man has no soul' or character or idiosyncratic vigour (*Road* 188). Orwell's attack on socialism is so angry that it is easy to forget that he is arguing in favour of it. In order to attract the decent, traditional, machine-resisting working class, socialism has to lose its misguided legacy of mechanization and embrace the values of Work. Marxism is mere economism: an overemphasized, cold, rationalist scientism and the child, however recalcitrant, of classical political economy. When submerged in a discourse of labour, his complaint against Marxism was that lost in abstract economics it had no direct effect on workers' lives. Poverty, unemployment, or the specific conditions that the working class were forced to endure were not abstract issues, nor could they wait for capitalism to self-destruct or surrender to theory before they were properly addressed. 'Poverty is poverty' (*Road* 201): immediate material realities must guide any sociology, economics, or politics. For Orwell, the established left was just too rationalistic in every way except in its failure to deal directly with the rationalized world.

But when Orwell says that 'the Socialist is always in favour of mechanization, rationalization, modernization' (*Road* 176), he is speaking of the nuts-and-bolts machines that sever humans from the need to Work. Machines 'frustrate the human need for effort and creation' (*Road* 176). The demise of *homo faber* means nothing short of the demise of humankind. Carlyle's interjection is the same as Orwell's: 'human things do require to have ... some soul in them' (*Past* 190). But for Orwell, 'machine-civilization *is here*, and it can only be criticized from the inside, because all of us are inside it' (*Road* 192). Only 'romantic fools' and 'the he-man' attempt to live outside of the rationalized world. The contradictions fuelled by his resistance to rationalism while inside the rationalist whale, contradictions between abstract and concrete points of view, between traditionalism and pragmatism, Work and labour, are never as evident as they are in Orwell's attitudes toward the machine.

Orwell's argument with machines is that they make 'a fully human life impossible' (*Road* 167). Again we are asked to reduce 'human' to 'man.' Orwell repeatedly associates machines with the making of softness and physical, *real* work with 'monstrous men with chests like barrels and moustaches like the wings of eagles' (*Road* 88). He asks 'Where are the monstrous men?' in what appears to be an attempt to echo Yeatsian machismo, imagery, and the poet's glorification of the past via a lamentation of the genetic deterioration of the male physique in the present.

Sharing with Yeats a fear of 'some frightful subhuman depth of softness and helplessness' (*Road* 176), a yearning for a previous age, for manliness, for things natural and handcrafted, and for the soil (especially of a particular country), perhaps contributed to Orwell's rather soft criticism of him, as Conor Cruise O'Brien suggests (42). Orwell's somewhat forgiving attitude towards Yeats, and modernism in general, relates to a mutual appreciation of traditional systems of order, cultural stasis, a tough and neatly violent past, and a dislike of new, urban things.

The binary Orwell creates excludes any admission of degrees: either the man is 'safe and soft' or 'brave and hard' and life ought to be 'harder instead of softer' (*Road* 170, 184). Peter Stearns points out that the coal mine was 'one of the real tests of nineteenth-century masculinity' (39). Not only would men be drawn to mining because of its relatively secure pay, the strong union, or the lack of alternatives in a mining town – three items Orwell fails to mention in *The Road to Wigan Pier* – but they would also pursue mining because it provided a challenge by which notions of masculinity could be tested. Stearns also argues that mechanization lightened the tasks demanded of the physical labourer, but heightened the rigidity and importance of gender roles because men feeling bossed around by employers, and now machines, tried to preserve their threatened masculinities more aggressively outside of the workplace. Orwell fears and predicts just the opposite, that when work becomes easier men will become less manly in all situations. Instead of seeking alternatives to the 'test' of work in their leisure activities, they would seek safer lifestyles, they would seek 'safer cars' and so on. This is an appeal to an underdog mentality, for men to express their manliness at all times – while the attributes of manliness are reduced to violent self-determination (as with mining), to hardness, and to the rejection of softness – because it is becoming increasingly impossible to do so.

The implied attack on women and the feminization of the world is coupled with an explicit fear of the slippery slope that would proceed from mechanization to human automation. Orwell derives his critique from the tradition of Carlyle, who also complained about 'the Age of Machinery in every outward and inward sense of that word' ('Signs' 226). Carlyle and Orwell emphasize the vitalistic man rather than a deterministic infrastructure, but the force of their argument is towards identifying and circumscribing a construction of consciousness. The problem with machines is not only that they are 'ugly' but also that they produce 'warped lives' (*Road* 97). Thus, when faced with a 'job of work,' the modern 'habit of mind' (*Road* 180, 182) is to look to technology. The trend towards making life safe has the 'status of an instinct.' Not only does technology mean technocrats and an elite class of experts, but it also allows for the conditions in which individuals blindly begin to follow leaders. By extension, people automatically repeat what they hear, be it a 'worn-out metaphor' or a slogan inculcated through a megaphone. 'Mechanization has itself become a machine,' whose primary function is to be 'habit-forming' (*Road* 182, 178), to overtake subjectivity for the sake of overtaking subjectivity. At the same time, he fears the machine because it cuts individuals off from the time when hardship was endured and people knew that life was laborious (*Road* 180). This is profound traditionalism, close to a Puritan ontology mixed with a Conradian sense of the human tragedy. It petrifies Work absolutely and forever as nonamenable to the arbitrations of labour. Since socialism aligns itself with the machine, the true working-class reaction will be a 'spiritual recoil from Socialism' (*Road* 164). The 'spirit' comes from Victorian epistemology; Orwell again is attempting to marry the working class to a distinctly nineteenth-century refusal of rationalism. He fears the machine because it undermines craftsmanship and manliness, because it ushers in a 'paradise of little fat men' (*Road* 169), because it means a society oriented towards the consumer and not producers, and because it cuts one 'off from the chance of working – that is, of living' (*Road* 173).

But Orwell has to accept that the 'machine has come to stay' (*Road* 178). The Orwell who concerns himself with concrete, material problems and not abstract and moral ones recognizes that machines make for greater economic freedom and safer conditions. In any case, the machine is here, it 'has got to be accepted' (*Road* 178). Regardless that it ought to be accepted 'grudgingly and suspiciously' – he is not a Luddite – in order to have an impact on how the machine is used, Orwell cannot simply dismiss it. In 'Inside the Whale' (1940), itself an apology for pragmatism, he criticizes Lawrence on the grounds that 'what he is demanding is a movement away from our mechanized civilization, which is not going to happen, and which he knows is not going to happen' (*CEJL* 1: 507). In 'The English People' (1944), he insists that the English should not listen 'to those who tell them that the England of the past can return' (*CEJL* 3: 37). At the end of *The Road to Wigan Pier* he throws a spanner into that work by saying, 'if you give me to understand that in some subtle way I am an inferior person because I have never worked with my hands, you will only succeed in antagonizing me' (201). He even adopts the cynical overtones of the twentieth-century rationalist when he pursues the anachronistic place of the call to Work in the modern age:

> Deliberately to revert to primitive methods to use archaic tools, to put silly little difficulties in your own way, would be a piece of dilettantism, of pretty-pretty arty and craftiness. It would be like solemnly sitting down to eat your dinner with stone implements. Revert to handwork in a machine age, and you are back in Ye Olde Tea Shoppe or the Tudor villa with the sham beams tacked to the wall. (*Road* 175–6)

Orwell negotiates rationalism, and derides Work, because he is taking into account the daily routines of the modern. The two sides of Orwell, the one glorifying Work and the other coming to terms with labour, are not forced to confront each other. Against the 'frightful debauchery of taste that has already been effected by a century of mechanization,' the 'fish-and-chip standard' of the lower classes, is the recognition that a cheap consumer good 'compensates you for a great deal' (*Road* 179, 79–80). Orwell rejected the liberal idea of the cultural improvement or education of the working class. But rationalisms meet and confirm each other when he says that 'cheap palliatives' have the beneficial effect of placating the masses into rejecting 'insurrections,' beneficial because insurrection only means being massacred by the police (*Road* 80–1). These are the same cheap goods, lottery tickets, and what-have-yous that the ruling class uses to 'hold the unemployed down' (*Road* 80). The two contradictory positions exist side by side because they are never dialectically opposed. In a discourse of Work, he rants against the cheap goods produced under the tactics of rationalism, quantity over quality. But when under a discourse of labour, he moderates his confrontational tactics and goes along with the short-term benefits accrued by the fast production of consumer goods because the working class would and do appreciate a *real* – concrete and tangible – change, a *substantially* improved standard of living. Under such a position, capital and business make enormous profits and wealth continues to be unfairly distributed; such a concession, in fact, as with the 'growth agreement' between labour unions and capital, the labour/business truce, allows for capital (and capitalism) to renew itself and even gain ethical credibility. But Orwell looks towards the immediate and real conditions of the worker, the lower class, the underdog – an aspect of the radical conservative tradition he more than all others stood hard by – as much as he embraces the rarefied rejection of capitalism that looks towards Work.

Orwell was a nostalgist who forced himself to face harsh modern realities. Those realities offered no support for his hypertrophied traditionalism but could not be ignored or denied, only compartmentalized.

Contradictions occur frequently because he adamantly documents life 'inside the whale' of rationalism but had charged into it, and thus saw it, with a great deal of Victorian moralism and Work sentimentalism. One final example: speaking in general terms, in idealist terms, Orwell admonishes the working classes for a diet that 'rejects good food almost automatically' (*Road* 89). But answering the question of why the lower classes do not eat better, he changes his position: 'the point is that no ordinary human being is ever going to do such a thing' (*Road* 86). Orwell rarely moralizes against the lower classes and makes every attempt to accommodate their culture intact, though it often goes against the grain of his own culture. Bad dietary habits, however, cause harm to workers. When hearing about an institution designed to teach the lower classes about nutrition and the best way to organize on a limited budget, he is 'torn both ways' (*Road* 89) – and not for the first time.

The ongoing crossover between a refusal of rationalism and a pragmatic acceptance of it, primarily a contest over the nature of work, is not reducible to Orwell's personal history. Rather it is an intensified expression of the contradiction proceeding from the transition between nonrationalized views of Work and a rationalist economy. The dichotomization and the unresolved tension between Work and labour are as prominent in his novels as they are in his prose. Williams finds that the fiction and prose are reducible to one, to intrapersonal documentary in which crafted, self-exiled, and nonconformist versions of Orwell submit to more powerful social forces (*Orwell* 41). But only the final novels condemn the self-exiled, nonconformist heroes to utter defeat. Only the final novels end the oscillation between the success and defeat of the subject, the survival of the moral self and the submission to rationalism, that propels the earlier works and the prose. By that time Orwell was no longer participating in working-class culture, his inspiration for moral Work and indeed moral individualism. The later prose also shows less influence of working-class culture, however projected it may be, than *The Road to Wigan Pier* or *Down and Out*. The early prose and fiction vacillate between showing passive, resigned identities inexorably absorbed into a rationalist society that refuses expressions of individuality and representing moral idiosyncrasy. Though the early novels conclude by leaning towards pragmatic realism – an absorption into rationalist society – and not moral individualism, both the early fiction and prose shift between a world of Work and independence on the one side and a world of economics and necessity on the other – in the fiction often an inside world and an outside one. Only the late fiction decides once and for all that life in the outside, rationalized world makes any other kind of existence impossible. The later novels represent complete defeat, submission, failure, and total capitulation to the rationalized world. The early fiction is also essentially defeatist, conceding to the world of labour, but the concession also involves a moral victory of sorts. *Animal Farm* (1945) and *Nineteen Eighty-Four* (1949) depict a process of rebellion and independence as if only to set up a final statement of inescapable defeat, of a world where the past has lost all of its meaning. Though little pockets of anti-rational individualism survive in these texts, they can be distinguished from the early prose and novels by the fact of their unequivocal devastation.

The early novels, on the other hand, presuppose that society offers nothing in the way of support, stimulation, or non-economic affirmation to the individual – just the opposite most of the time – and yet insist that some form of selfless decency survives. To write the survival of decency in indecent conditions is to attempt to imagine a working-class version of the Victorian self-made man myth, a popular variant of the underdog story. Notwithstanding Orwell's clear revulsion for the middle-class narrative (as in *The Road to Wigan Pier*, 101–2), both Orwell's storyline and the self-made man myth represent society as an obstacle overcome by joining it. His characters do not gain the kind of ascendancy, success, respect, and happiness through self-help, an ethical steadiness, perseverance, and work that constitutes the self-made man story, but through self-motivated endurance and work they maintain moral integrity. All the novels end by insisting that life is lived, has to be lived, within the rationalized order, but only the early ones treat submission as an awakening. All of Orwell's novels end in the defeat of a rebel, of an outsider reconciling or being forced to reconcile himself or herself (or itself in the case of *Animal Farm*) with the aggregate (with the exception of *Burmese Days* [1934], which ends in Flory's suicide). But the final scenes of capitulation and defeat in *A Clergyman's Daughter* (1935) and *Keep the Aspidistra Flying* (1936) – where existence is reduced to negotiating the conditions of labour or submitting to the whale of rationalism – also represent hope, humanity, and common decency, and suggest that a kind of steadfast nobility can flourish within a corrupt society. If Dorothy Hare and Gordon Comstock compromise themselves, embrace the world they had previously tried to escape, they achieve a moral, nonrationalist independence that contradicts the callous, rationalist, or individualist society they join. Accepting the 'pragmatic realism' of the texts, reading that Dorothy and Gordon abandon their struggle against the world that demands conformity (a very compelling reading in light of Orwell's later fiction), does not contradict the concept of moral individualism: Dorothy and Gordon learn that they cannot change the world, yes, but they nevertheless manage to change some part of their inner states, their way of perceiving and negotiating the world. They can live decent lives and be decent people despite the rationalistic, capitalistic, economistic, and *deterministic* world that had previously received their and their creator's wrath – or at least triggered their evasion, as in Dorothy's case. Common decency, in defiance of an all-engulfing rationalism, is affirmed even though nothing shores it up but individual effort. That what I have called pragmatic realism and moral individualism can exist side by side shows that the world of labour and the world of Work are never made to confront one another. I am not discussing *Burmese Days* because it would involve an analysis of colonialism, a topic too large in itself to introduce at this point. I am also not discussing *Animal Farm* because its themes and mood can be seen in *Nineteen Eighty-Four*.

A Clergyman's Daughter

Not only does *A Clergyman's Daughter* end by confirming a swing-with-the-punches theme hard to square with the critical tenor of the novel, but it also contains the most ambivalent or contradictory attitude towards work in Orwell's fiction. No matter if she is cooking, cleaning, scavenging for her father, slaving as a volunteer, hop-picking, or teaching, Dorothy suffers economic deprivation, physical abuse, and, in a word, the effects of labour. Yet in each of these roles or episodes, the work, ultimately, is or can be internally rewarding, gratifying, and character-building or at least an opportunity to locate or ground identity. What P.J. Keating said of Dickens, that he 'emphasized certain moral positives in working-class life which he shows as flourishing in even the foulest rookery' (22), is even more pronounced in Orwell.

When the novel begins, Dorothy is overwhelmed and undervalued mostly by her father, though she also seems to give herself as a willing slave to the entire East Anglian parish. Unconsciously in need of escape, she gets amnesia and becomes the wandering Protestant, first headed towards the Kentish hopfields. The hop-picking episode is the most autobiographical and documental episode in the text. Joining a band of migrant pickers, Dorothy has a glimpse of the redeeming value of Work, which she again endorses at the end of the novel. The difference is that as a hop-picker she experiences Work as a social glue and at the end of the novel she feels the experience of Work as a social glue without being part of an integrated community. The hop-pickers sing as they work; they are 'happy,' 'sitting round the fires with their cans of tea and their hunks of bread and bacon, in the smell of hops and wood smoke!' (97–8). Orwell's picaresque working-class home gone mobile segregates, filters out, or erases the representation of an otherwise (and understandably) economically preoccupied crowd. Moreover, it is as if the Proudhonian universe of a just and stable social order organized around Work and mutualism, the *gemeinschaft* community, were faster to arise under economic injustice than in the world of regulated contracts, once that injustice has been rearticulated and dislocated into the terms of hard, demanding, physically exhausting Work. With proper naturalistic/economistic detail, Orwell outlines how pickers deal with the harshness of their work and living arrangements, the physical wear and tear, the lowness of the pay, and the lack of a defence against thieving farmers. Yet despite overwork, poverty, fatigue, undernourishment, and lice,

> you were happy, with an unreasonable happiness. The work took hold of you and absorbed you. It was stupid work, mechanical, exhausting, and every day more painful to the hands, and yet you never wearied of it; when the weather was fine and the hops were good you had the feeling that you could go on picking for ever and for ever. It gave you a physical joy, a warm satisfied feeling inside you, to stand there hour after hour, tearing off the heavy clusters and watching the pale green pile grow higher and higher in your bin, every bushel twopence in your pocket. (105)

Having twopence in the pocket is no longer an economic fact, but part of a romantic underdog image of the swaggering worker doing an honest day's Work. Even the gypsy thieves are heroes and morally solid. Being cheated by a farmer is written into a game where the pickers exact justice by stealing apples from other farmers. Saturated in the culture of the workers, Orwell only represents Work. Just as Work becomes the means by which Dorothy seals off her deprived, draughty, and drudging life at the novel's end, in the hop-picking scene Work displaces economics, minimizes the struggle over reaching the wherewithal to live, and compartmentalizes the complex politics of survival that it is one of Orwell's impulses to represent as the bottom line. By keeping the conflict between Work and labour at bay, by stepping out of the economic context and having his working class so easily do the same, Orwell undermines his own sociology, trivializes the inequities that the workers face, and negates the tenets of his reformism – just as his capitulation to existing economic structures negates the radicalism implicit in Work.

The morality of Orwell's migrant workers is internally managed, even though he takes great pains to describe the ugliness of the external conditions and seems set on emphasizing the subjective effects of those objective conditions. Karl suggests that this internal, sacrosanct morality can be related to Orwell's proximity to the 'romantic tradition.' He suggests that Orwell's

> books suggest a kind of civilized pastoral in which man fulfills himself through work and sex without regard for money, competition, and self-seeking. Like William Morris' Utopia, Orwell's socialistic state is tinged with this nostalgia for a past that the latter is surely too astute to believe ever existed outside of man's imagination. (164)

Orwell in fact derided Morris's vision and the fundamental goodness of 'man' it implies. But he swings hard and fast between a naturalism that deflates the pastoral vision and a romantic view of working-class culture that resurrects it. The vacuum produced by this split undermines the principled criticisms that are his greatest strength as a writer, whether they are moral or pragmatic principles.

I have little to say about the underworld descent scene in *A Clergyman's Daughter* because it has little to do with Work or labour. It does show, however, Dorothy's ability to remain unscathed in a 'naturalist environment' of slums and prostitution. The chapter is a complete failure, of interest to the reader only for imagining why Orwell would attempt it or for observing the speed at which he moves from it, a Joycean experiment, to a Dickensian critique of rationalist education.

The episode at Ringwood House, the private school, also stands out in Orwell's writings insofar as *it involves a dialectical contest between Work and economics*. As a teacher, Dorothy is tremendously successful, creating enthusiasm in her students and actually teaching them something. But due to corruption and rationalist ideologies, analogous to the economic real world she faces when hop-picking or the oppressive work she does for her father, she is forced into 'Practical work,' 'figuring and handwriting' not poetry and creativity: teaching by the numbers and conceding to the 'eleventh Commandment,' 'Thou shall not lose thy job' (211). Confronted by economic reality, Dorothy's nonrationalist approach to teaching, the Work she does, comes undone. The difference between this and the hop-picking scene is that while hop-picking Dorothy experiences labour but engenders Work for herself and while teaching she experiences Work but is confronted by economic reality.

The teaching scene, the contest between Work and rationalist economics and the final depiction of the impossibility of Work in the modern world, is a lot less ambiguous than the infamously vague and equivocal scene that concludes the novel. That scene also sees Dorothy coming to terms with pragmatism but in a way that does not jeopardize the meanings of Work. In one way, Dorothy is defeated at the end of *A Clergyman's Daughter*. Eagleton argues that 'the movement to freedom and renewal, here as in all Orwell's novels, ends in failure. Life is hopeless and sterile, but the worst false consciousness is to think you can change it' (*Exiles* 89). Dorothy is hauled back into service for her father and the unthankful recipients of her philanthropy, reduced to the same 'discouraging,' 'futile' work that unconsciously drove her to leave the Rectory (48), left bereft and divorced from the *gemeinschaft* community that made the labour of hop-picking such a petty problem, and saddened or hardened by her experiences and her loss of faith. *A Clergyman's Daughter*, like all of Orwell's novels, is tinged with an anti-Victorian sense of futility and resignation that goes against the grain of, for example, the family romance or the recapturing of an all-important social identity typical of nineteenth-century literature. The image of a still-passive Dorothy finding comfort in labour and duty, in 'what is customary, useful and acceptable' (261), is not very different from the image of Winston Smith drinking Victory Gin and smiling happily at Big Brother, an unequivocal image of utter defeat.

But the same image of Dorothy 'working on' is in another way a victory, a moral affirmation of the self in the face of a failure to change the world. This reading, not a difficult one to make, has Orwell reintroduce the Carlylean resolve to bypass introspection and the impossibility of faith by turning towards Work. She embraces the Gospel of Work written for the working class: not the 'bourgeois work ethic' that values ascendancy, but the other Victorian Gospel that values endurance. Such a reading also confirms the Conradian 'saving illusion' by implying that Orwell assumes the value of devoting oneself to immediate tasks despite a consciousness of their moral emptiness or a half-conscious knowledge of their part in the perpetuation of corrupt systems. In other words, Dorothy, like the Marlow of *Heart of Darkness*, knows the world is valueless, but finds inner strength to act as if it were not and thereby consolidate and augment inner strength – a nonvicious cycle. Philip Rieff reads the conclusion of *A Clergyman's Daughter* as an 'ethic for liberals in a meaningless world,' an affirmation of the verb 'to do' that might ward off metaphysical and social despair. Dorothy, then, uses 'the exhaustion of activity [to] counter the exhaustion of morality' (56–7). Sandison critiques Rieff's analysis because he is determined to argue that Orwell never fully relinquishes the culture of Protestant individualism (which in itself is probably true) and therefore never assumes a Godless universe (not at all a corollary). Such a critique is off the mark. In *A Clergyman's Daughter* Orwell explicitly treats Work, 'glue,' as a substitute for religion. Dorothy has a 'need for faith' that cannot be found in the church (or in going too far towards a hedonistic belief in 'paganism' or too far towards a rationalist belief in 'Progress'), but that is satisfied by the 'smell of glue,' of getting to Work. With Carlylean confidence, Dorothy makes Work 'the answer to her prayer' (261). As both a social and psychological glue, Work becomes a Religion of Humanity, a Feuerbachian rediscovery in Man of the moral imperatives that were previously thought to follow from the concept of God. In Dorothy's case, her Eliotic (George) humanism finds her masochistically abasing herself to Man instead of masochistically abasing herself to God. *A Clergyman's Daughter* preaches duty and Work: Orwell is never more Victorian than when he affirms the theme of endurance. Dorothy gives into the whale, 'saying in effect, "What the hell is all this about? God knows. All we can do is to endure"' (*CEJL* 1: 501). In the novel, Orwell attempts to echo the theme he understood James Joyce was getting at in *Ulysses* (1922). Orwell thought that 'What Joyce is saying is "Here is life without God. Just look at it!"' (*CEJL* 1: 508) and in *A Clergyman's Daughter,* Orwell – sketching out the theme of resignation he was to pursue for years to come – tries to do the same. But whereas Joyce in a Nietzsche-cum-Chaplin pose mocks the solace that the substitution of one form of faith for another is supposed to accrue in modernity, Orwell returns to a Victorian or Carlylean affirmation of Work, the Master Narrative. Orwell suggests that the devil finds activity for idle hands, even if the devil is dead.

Sandison is correct to point out, however, that there is 'an ambiguity in Dorothy's attitude which suggests that she may not in fact be morally exhausted' (50). Her return to the Rectory can be read, as I have suggested, as both a counter-Victorian defeat and a very Victorian confirmation of autonomous or self-made morality. That she does not despair or deceive herself about her situation, or the prospects for the future, is itself an affirmation of self-sufficiency, that she will get by on inner strength. Though she rejects the provincial and religious guilt that demands that she work, she determinably returns to work under the same conditions of economic inequality, abuse, ennui, and vacuousness – labour – that define her initial pre-amnesiac situation. As Eagleton explains, the Dorothy Orwell satirizes for sacrificing herself to self-flagellating habits is nonetheless endorsed by the plot's resolution (*Exiles* 89). Dorothy's devotion to duty validates her older habits, even if they are divorced from her latent desire for a nun's habit, and assumes that she can find affirmation in herself. That affirmation comes at the expense of the novel's greater criticisms of the exploitation and corruption that Dorothy's laborious, unrewarded life represents. Dorothy finds internal strength in 'some inner part of the soul that does not change' (258). She perseveres for its own sake and by doing so accepts that 'the mere outward things like poverty and drudgery, and even loneliness, don't matter in themselves' (257–8).

This brand of moral individualism is made possible by an undialectical approach to Work and economic oppression: Dorothy's inner self (which Works) and her outer identity (which labours) are not forced to confront each other, and neither is made to bend to the weight of the other. Rather, the two sides exist as if unrelated. But by affirming intransitive Work – 'that if one gets on with the job that lies to hand, the ultimate purpose of the job fades into insignificance' (261) – Dorothy withdraws from the knowledge that she labours for others, an oppression that Orwell had acknowledged and condemned. In other words, *A Clergyman's Daughter* repeats the pattern of splitting Work from labour that pervades the prose. By keeping work intransitive, Orwell keeps it and the idea of the inner self inviolable. In doing so, he denies that Work in the conditions of labour exculpates and exacerbates those conditions. The work that Dorothy withdraws into is not Work; it is labour: invented Work or inverted labour. Dorothy wrests from the labour she does for others – the same demeaning work that unconsciously drove her to escape the Rectory – the rewards of anti-rationalist Work.

The novel repeats this dualistic pattern several times. Dorothy spends a good deal of the novel avoiding, evading, or escaping her slavish duties, driven by an unconscious (justified and authorially endorsed) desire to be free of those duties. Whether she is drifting from her father's rule or recoiling from metaphysical questions of deeper meaning through Work, both the economic and the spiritual problems raised by the novel are sidestepped. Yet the novel is about the moral value of refusing escape. Not only does she return to her drudging routine, but she also refuses, with a decisive authorial endorsement, to indulge in the hedonism Warburton makes available to her. Warburton is ambiguously drawn: both a hedonistic rake and a liberated alternative to Dorothy's sexual repression. Whereas he and Dorothy both accept the meaninglessness of the universe, only Dorothy's refusal to abandon responsibility is condoned. Dorothy's frigidity is at first parodied, but as she recovers redeeming value through a dutiful commitment to the task at hand, it is affirmed. The sexual repression and the ambiguously treated alleviation of that repression through work parallel Dorothea's conflict in Eliot's *Middlemarch* (1871–2). Warburton is a sexual threat to her just as Henry James's Warburton is a threat to Isabel Archer, an earlier rewriting of Dorothea in *The Portrait of a Lady* (1881). The dualisms in *A Clergyman's Daughter* correspond to the distance between the Orwell who has a fiery hatred of hedonism and the Orwell who has an equally passionate allegiance to common simplicity and uncalculated day-tripping, the kind of playfulness that 'Some Thoughts on the Common Toad' (1946) expresses. Orwell writes between a contingent decency and a complete morality, creating a tension that is only 'resolved' by keeping them strictly divided.

Keep the Aspidistra Flying

In general, Orwell's lower- or working-class characters yield themselves subjectively to the logic of rationalism. For the most part, however, submission merely entails a willed retreat into a private, inner, purifying sanctum. The innermost selves of the characters remain undefiled or actually refreshed despite the gook they surround themselves in, just as values of Work are wrested from conditions of labour. *Keep the Aspidistra Flying*'s Gordon Comstock eventually yields himself completely to modern rationality. At first, however, he is disgusted by the money god, renounces the world of bourgeois business, attempts to 'escape the money code,' and seeks a 'bad job' (57, 60). His judgment and rejection of day-to-day conventional society, the ideology of 'getting on' or even of getting up (Gordon's politically oriented laziness and self-exile pre-echo the slacker's creed), takes him to the brink of complete self-alienation, to a no man's land of dogmatic negativity that refutes idyllic withdrawal and political engagement. His capitulation to conventional normality, losing his 'soul' to an advertising company, an industry that greases the consumerism he initially vilifies, could be read to signify defeat or pragmatic realism. He forgoes his youthful and rebellious pride, and his obstinate desire for autonomy, to the lower-middle-class humdrum life of wives, babies, and aspidistras. His abandonment to expediency and pragmatism, to the comfort of going with the grain, is tinged with a sense of self-betrayal and failure that subverts the many stubbornly vitalistic readings of the text. Bernard Crick, who is not ideologically bent on asserting Orwellian vitalism, suggests that Orwell despised the materialist or money monomania that defines the modern age, but 'like Gordon Comstock' 'realized that independence for a writer depended on earning some [money]' (*Life* 67). Though Orwell, in his specific, concrete, pragmatic 'mode,' makes the point often enough that the artist, and in fact everyone, needs a full belly in order to best find expression, Gordon does not gain independence after his acquiescence to 'the system'; he even ceases to be an independent writer.

However, Williams, for one, is in uncertain territory when he suggests that Orwell's characters, and especially Gordon Comstock, are exiles who do not integrate themselves with society 'in any positive way,' and in that manner mirror Orwell himself (*Culture* 291). Williams steadfastly maintains that a defeatist, surrender theme permeates all of Orwell's novels, that characters eventually submit to the corrupt society at large. Winston Smith's acceptance of society may be entirely void of positivity, but the value of Gordon Comstock's surrender is much more ambiguous. Gordon abandons his principles and bows down to the money god at the end of *Keep the Aspidistra Flying*, but he is an exile when he clings to those principles, when he rejects that god. Stephen Ingle nails it perfectly when he suggests that Gordon becomes 'anti-Polly' (*Socialist* 53): the self-chosen economic outcast who then finds and engenders value by embracing the economic society. *Keep the Aspidistra Flying*, unlike *The History of Mr. Polly*, uses pragmatism as a corrective to anti-social, high-minded moralism.

All of Orwell's anti-heroes end up submitting to economic reality because for Orwell such was the experience of the common man who cannot live life on moral principles. If one reads his novels in sequence, one finds resistance to the corrupt social world starting afresh from one novel to the next, though in a diminished state from novel to novel as the worlds become increasingly corrupt. The same hard swing between seeing wholly and pragmatically that characterizes the prose then rises to the surface. Just because Gordon chooses conformity over the puerile romance of anti-social nonactivity or has that choice forced upon him, Orwell never ceases to rotate between the two visions of moral and pragmatic imperatives. As with *A Clergyman's Daughter*, the ending of *Keep the Aspidistra Flying* is not necessarily defeatist. In many ways it is precisely the opposite. The ambiguity of its ending, and of the value of Gordon

Comstock-as-rebel, is never finally resolved. The question of whether Gordon Comstock the outcast or Gordon Comstock the up-and-comer at the New Albion Publicity Company is our hero is never finally answered.

The discrepancy between Nicholas Guild's reading of *Keep the Aspidistra Flying*, in which Gordon's capitulation to convention is definitely 'something of which his creator approves' (144) and Richard Rees's version of it, where in 'the end [Gordon] is a disastrously defeated rebel' (32), for example, testifies to the ambiguity of the novel's final swing towards the logic of pragmatism. Perhaps it is impossible to see Gordon's transition to the money world as anything but the right, proper decision because the rebel Gordon is insufferable. Gordon may begin by rejecting the 'money-stink,' but he is nonetheless obsessed with it. When Orwell insists that a lack of money leads to 'Social failure, artistic failure, sexual failure' (*Aspidistra* 84), he incisively touches upon an expansive reading of economic determinism. But when the same critique comes out as whining complaint or self-pity, it translates into an entirely different and unsympathetic gesture. Gordon uses poverty to excuse his brutal treatment of Rosemary and his failure to write poetry. He amplifies his isolation, imagines he is snubbed when he is not. Even when he foolishly blows the slight fortune he stumbles upon, in itself not a condemnable act, he blames it on his lack of economic training, declaring that the 'rich don't behave like that' (199). He is too preoccupied with economics – even his poetry is about the effects of poverty – to notice the decency of Ravelston, Julia, or Rosemary. When Gordon sheds his self-pitying it is almost impossible not to read his new job, new outlook, and so forth, as a victory, an authorially approved submission to the artificial, to the grip of the new economic order.

But just as Dorothy's 'action of going to the scullery' ends her 'self-pity' (260), utilizing the classic antidote of Work when in fact she returns to rationalist labour, Gordon's return to the advertising agency, which he excels at because he proceeds mechanically, is written as a return to Work. Gordon's awakened devotion to activity, like Dorothy's before him, is a testament to the individual's ability to find value in the valueless. Gordon, in this way, is a hero for shedding his Byronic, Swiftian pose, for becoming a social being: he even gets the girl. It would be hard to maintain that Gordon is less decent at the novel's end as someone who has joined the money world and validated the corruption of pure morality that it represents than as an entirely negative, self-pitying, but unflinching moralist.

Becoming decent in the corrupt economic world underlines the foremost characteristic of moralism, in which subjective value is created through individual effort despite the overwhelmingly corruptible objective world. Gordon's criticisms of a society based on money, the cash nexus, and self-interest, criticisms that Orwell himself endorses, unravel as he discovers in himself the decency that survives the rationalist, petty bourgeoisie world of moneyed relations. The traditional values Orwell raises to nostalgic heights, such as fatherhood and family, are conflated with the acceptance of mediocrity and aspidistras, with a sensual appreciation for the feel of money (259), and with mild bourgeoisie rationality. The rebel Gordon turns out to have been merely a self-centred, whining, callow, *mistaken* brat: 'Failure' turns out to be 'as great a swindle as success' (63). In between criticisms of the day-to-day rationalist world and locating value in that world lies moral individualism. The baby to be born at the end of the novel is inside a womb and Gordon is inside the whale of modern labour, which Orwell also calls a womb (*CEJL*, 1: 521). The new Gordon, then, is 'alive and stirring' (264), as innocent and vital as a newborn. But the miracle of Gordon is that he can be alive and stirring while fully embracing and participating in a world that readers were led to believe stifles life. Instead of trying to change the world, ultimately written as a preordained failure reducible to youth and angst, Gordon successfully changes himself and his relationship with the world, gleaning decency and nobility where decency and nobility had been absent. Between total moral commitment and the pragmatic strategies necessary to make a buck is an undialectical non-event, the surpassing of the moral limitations of pragmatism through a retreat to an inner, unassailable morality. Eagleton's assessment of Gordon's transformation, that 'the novel finally perceives the humanity which remains at the heart of capitalism' (*Exiles* 99), is only slightly inaccurate. The humanity exists in the heart of the individual who, while participating in it, can and does elevate himself above capitalism. Capitalism turns out to be insurmountable in all ways but in its moral or subjective effects, and the radical criticisms of the text – not of marriage and paternity but of the rationalist concessions needed to support them – are withdrawn. Orwell did not believe the working class (the proles of *Nineteen Eighty-Four*, for example) or the lower-middle class (men like George Bowling or Gordon Comstock) could or would change the world. He does not blame Gordon – the common stock – for abandoning his principles because survival itself is a value and despair is valueless. Gordon, by focusing on the immediate, turns work into a palliative even though that very type of rationalist work had received nothing but his, and Orwell's, condemnation from a moral point of view. Work becomes an intransitive item, its rationalism rationalized by its identity-fixing function, albeit the identity of the pragmatist.

Coming Up for Air

After one has examined Carlyle's *Past and Present*, the juxtaposition of a pre-rationalist past, where life is a 'natural process,' with a 'mechanical' present (and dismal-looking future) in *Coming Up for Air* (1939) can seem almost hackneyed or rudimentary. But it is also a cliché to critique how every generation hearkens back to a time when the grass was greener: Orwell for the days of Conrad, Conrad for the days of Carlyle, Carlyle for the days of yore. When the pragmatic, concrete Orwell admits that 'Progress does happen' (*CEJL* 3: 57) or sympathizes with George Bowling for proceeding one repetitive day at a time, he goes against the grain of a convention that the moral, generalist Orwell fully endorses in *Coming Up for Air*. But in this text it becomes very difficult for the reader to distinguish between an animadversion on modernity and an entirely subjective nostalgia for the lost days of youth. George Bowling's yearning for the 'civilization which I grew up in' (*Air* 74) is indiscernible from his fond memories of being a boy, effectively reducing the story to a lower-middle-class man's middle-age crises. The psychological drama in which George conflates 'getting on' in the business world with getting on in years may be absolutely necessary for the integrity of the novel, but it sets up an unbridgeable chasm between what was and what is. The chasm between youth and age slides into a chasm between the past and present, or between that which they represent. Intrinsically satisfying Work on the one hand and pragmatism on the other are then irrevocably polarized according to the model of youth and age, with the only recourse to Work (or youth) under the inexorable and complete reality of labour (or age) being through an imaginative repossession of identity. In George's modern reality, Work or nonrationalism are as unattainable as youth, establishing a disjunction between morality and practicality that makes for a nearly ahistorical past and a nearly amoral present.

George remembers ponds with fish in them (as opposed to the rubbish dumps of industrial expansion), innocent and naive women (as opposed to economically savvy wives), strong beer, and Work. When he is recalling the past, the representation of economics is certainly not absent – George's father, for example, has financial difficulties – but economics do not affect the spirit of the age. George remembers his uneducated Uncle Ezekiel quoting Carlyle. He bristles when describing how 'man's work' and 'woman's work' were well defined (49–50). And he emphasizes for nearly an entire section (two) that everyone worked all the time as a way of life: not between certain paid hours for an indexed paycheque, but as an activity fundamental to a sense of identity, purpose, belonging, self-respect, honour, and so forth. His present, on the other hand, is not merely a Wellsian world of shopkeepers and petty bourgeoisie traffickers but a Joycean world of demoralizing urban work (21). Drab economic survival suffuses every aspect of life, and getting a job means that the *job gets you* (85). George's present is a *gesellschaft*, a rationalized world where 'recreations are provided' and the potent sense of a life-affirming vitalism (especially feelings of manhood and self-sufficiency) is subordinated to the 'struggle to sell things' (86, 128). George has a working-class past, a working-class inner identity, and a bourgeois present and appearance.

Economic reality is far from absent in the representation of George's past, but the point is that though economic pressures existed, though class boundaries were severe, and in fact though 'People on the whole worked harder, lived less comfortably, and died more painfully,' a 'feeling of security' and a 'feeling of continuity' (106, 107) effectively displaced the hardship. When Orwell speaks in general terms, he describes the working or lower classes as suffering an inevitably tragic life, but remaining mentally, morally, and spiritually healthy. When prioritizing economics and speaking about specifics from the point of view of an observer and not a participant, his working class suffer physically and undergo complete psychological (and sexual) malfunctions. In *Coming Up for Air*, the separation of the moral past and economic present is written as an irrevocable either/or, essentialist/historicist rift because Work makes economics impossible and economics makes Work impossible. Pre-capitalist adventures are made available to the 'modern' George only through an imaginative revival of an inner self, a self that struggles against or contradicts the naturalist conventions Orwell follows and the hyper-extended economism that the older George projects onto the world. When the older George displays the characteristics of an earlier time, is an imaginative participant in working-class life, when he claims that he has 'more the prole's attitude towards money' as 'Life's here to be lived' (137), it counters the otherwise uncheckable forces of bourgeois determination that the novel insists upon by strictly dividing the spirit of the past from the demands of the present.

Critics such as Patrick Reilly who seem obsessed with emphasizing the consistent humanism and vitalism in Orwell's canon and who argue that George refuses 'to submit to the bleak banality of the world' (218) may impose an optimistic ideology on Orwell's worldview in order to protect something they themselves value and believe in, but they are nonetheless feeding off a solid foundation in moral individualism – ideas about the power to withdraw into an uncorrupted, nonrational world of Work. Even under the weight of despondency, despair, and the threat of war (as the novel's refrain goes, 'it's all going to happen'), Orwell affirms that even the stereotypical bourgeoisie has an inviolate moral centre. Nothing hinders the individuated subject's capacity to locate and retreat into value in a valueless world. Unlike Leopold Bloom, George Bowling is not written ironically or as a contradictory, ideologically ridden (or narratologically ridden) character who is rationalist bourgeoisie at one time and romantic escapist at another. Rather, George's rationalist, modern self is always represented as external to his inner identity and, furthermore, under the control of the moral, inner individual. The super-economic self can step out of his life to critically assess and respond to it. George admits he is 'vulgar,' 'insensitive' – 'I fit in with my environment' (23) – but in doing so he has already distinguished himself from his environment. His external life, however, is written as socially constructed according to the conventions of the naturalist tradition. Again, I am not insisting that George should be contained by his situation, his bourgeoisie environment, but insofar as he is able to jump from a rationalist to a nonrationalist world, a world incommensurable with his contemporary one and the naturalist structure of the text, he is the moral individual, able to keep himself – the place where he withdraws into – defiantly inviolable.

For Orwell, total submission to the rationalized world, pragmatic realism, does not entrain the corruption or social rationalization of the individual, though it theoretically would if it were to be dialectically opposed to the individual, if Orwell's 'economic fatalism' were opposed to his 'ethical utopianism.' Submission, doing whatever it takes to get by, according to Orwell's own definition, is a central fact of working-class decency; Orwell's pragmatic class is a modern version of the Carlylean and Conradian worker, validated by the degree to which they accept their subordination and rely on paternalism to organize systems of labour. The worthy worker is always the nonpolitical worker. In 'Inside the Whale' (1940) Orwell apologizes for quietism and accepting the 'thing-as-it-is,' albeit 'decay,' on the grounds that it is the reasonable choice of 'a voice from the crowd, from the underling, from the third-class carriage, from the ordinary, non-political, non-moral, passive man' (*CEJL* 1: 501). This is the Conradian or Carlylean tragic sensibility firmly implanted in modern times. It is worth noting that Orwell's common man has little to do with today's average Westerner, whose sense of self-entitlement demands a great deal more than what the tragic sensibility will offer. Still, what I have called moral individualism is evidenced when Orwell's characters submit to an all-encompassing whale but find the means to remain impervious to its effects. Moral individualism exists in the fact that by 'accepting' the comfort of the whale's insides, being 'irresponsible' by giving up the struggle against rationality or tyranny, being 'completely negative, unconstructive, [and] amoral,' even a 'Whitman among the corpses' (*CEJL* 1: 527), the subject only gains decency. Orwell is not necessarily wrong: submitting to and negotiating actuality might lead to decency. Because one has a job in the modern world one will not necessarily carry the imprint of a cruel capitalism. But the moral individualism implied here undercuts and dissolves the radical critical sensibility underlying both intransitive Work and the more political strains of his economic sensibility: it is, as he says, 'non-political, non-moral.' The moral individual is kept entirely but magically removed from his or her situation because the idea of a moral individual and the idea of an immoral determining structure erase each other out. The typical Orwellian novel includes unmitigated criticisms of the rationalized world, including dismissive criticisms of those who are cogs in it or do not challenge it, sympathy for those who are swallowed up by it, and space for those who can withdraw from it.

In *Coming Up for Air* Orwell borrows Eliot's wasteland imagery of an English Walking Dead, but he also sees the decency that outlasts the transfixing rationalism and that takes place despite the unambiguous dismissal of them as bourgeois zombies in other parts of the novel. Succumbing to the world as it is, George Bowling, one of the Dead, abandons the social critique implicit in his nostalgia for the past. He concedes that 'if a factory isn't in one place it'll be in another' (209). He accepts living in a spiritual vacuum, relinquishing his idealized past and his prophetic fear of the future for the comfort of blending in under the cloak of mediocrity: 'What's the future got to do with chaps like you and me? Holding down our jobs – that's our future' (225). This is the 'voice of the belly protesting against the soul,' the 'little fat man who sees very clearly the advantages of staying alive with a whole skin' (*CEJL* 2: 192). It is the voice of pragmatism or pragmatic realism abandoning or segregating the dream of Work. But in spite of his effete and passive acceptance of the terror the future promises to bring, a vestige of the little thin man survives inside the whale of the fat one, entirely swallowed up but inviolate, a 'real me' saturated in an unforgiving universe of fatty, naturalist determination. The split between an inner self who is in touch with the world of Work and an outer self who knows only that he lives in the conditions of labour corresponds to Orwell thinking inside and outside of working-class culture and experience, participating in it or observing and dissecting it.

The oddity of a very active Orwell, an Orwell who fought in Spain and was a political advocate for the working class, repeating the Victorian creed of endurance and tolerance, virtues of the ruled, and expanding on the myth of a working-class tragic sensibility demonstrates the reach and force of an organicist ideology. His central characters are always associated with the working class in one way or another. They also submit to a tragic fate, whether it is the whale of rationalism or the hard life (as with his miners). Orwell himself would resist and struggle against modern rationality: he forgives his lower-middle and working classes for submitting to necessity, sees decency in their concessions, because the paternalist vision demands helpless common folk. He re-creates a structure of dependence common to Carlyle and Conrad in which lower classes do not or cannot address their economic or political situations, relying instead on the patronage of others (the same attitude he has towards his miners and tramps). Williams is certainly right to point out similarities between Orwell and his main characters. But there is at least this one difference between creator and created: all Orwell's characters betray themselves or are betrayed to various forms of cold, rational management; Orwell himself, forgiving of the 'little man,' did not position himself as someone who abandons himself to fate, economic or otherwise. He struggles against the rationalization of human relations for the benefit of those he believed could not. Behind Orwell's refusal to grant autonomy to the average working man or woman lie the residuals of a paternalistic authoritarianism unequivocally pronounced in the Carlylean or Conradian attitude towards work. The egalitarian feelings and philosophy expressed in *Homage to Catalonia* (1938) are undoubtedly genuine; Orwell's authoritarianism is a subtle, unconscious remnant of the hierarchical structure of thought that surrounds even the mutualistic elements of organicism.

Discussing the British adoption and adaptation of the naturalist novel from continental Europe, Terry Eagleton argues that

For the naturalist novelist, men are capable of a limited transcendence of their determining environments – they can, if they are sufficiently sensitive, identify and fight its sterility – but it is part of the philosophical assumptions of naturalism, which the English novel ... inherits, that men are passively bound to their situations by only partially controllable forces. (*Exiles* 73–4)

In Orwell's version of the naturalist novel, the truth of small things and a faith in large ones are at odds. History and essentialism are at odds: economics and Work would attempt to expose each other as a gesture of escape or a trivial commonplace. The two sides of the antinomy are compartmentalized and the final victory of material circumstances becomes shrouded in qualifications and ambiguity, even though it is clear that he attempts to show, as Georg Lukács said of realism, economics 'as immediate forms of existence of human life' (*Historical* 354–5). *Coming Up for Air*, *A Clergyman's Daughter*, and *Keep the Aspidistra Flying* are all undecided, unresolved novels: George, Dorothy, and Gordon are defeated and heroic characters. The ambiguity of the novels, in which morality or decency are seemingly gained by capitulating to amorality or indecency, in which the characters are irrevocably determined by but also fundamentally independent of or different from society, reflects a hard, undialectical split between history and humanity.

Nineteen Eighty-Four

Still, as Williams points out, the defining moment of 'George Orwell' begins with a cold day in April, the clocks striking thirteen (*Culture* 285). The bleakness of Orwell's final vision has nothing to do with moral individualism, the world of intransitive Work, self-sufficiency, or any hint of a possible transgression against or withdrawal from the rationalized order. However, there may still be some decency in Winston's defeat. Even if his betrayal of Julia marks the end of his humanity, his final submission to the Party is very human insofar as Orwell defines humanness. For Orwell, being 'defeated and broken up by life' is the 'essence of being human' when one fastens 'one's love upon other human individuals' (*CEJL* 4: 467). *Nineteen Eighty-Four*, as with so much of Orwell's writing, reenacts the argument of 'Inside the Whale,' though it goes a great deal further than any other expression of pragmatic realism. Whether or not he endorses compliance or inertia, he allows himself to be understood as at least sympathizing with those who submit to or passively accept the way of the world, if only because the path of least resistance is the most common path. *Nineteen Eighty-Four* is unique if only because of the way the futuristic world aggressively hunts down anyone who steps off the path. Winston Smith is never the last man in Europe or anywhere else, never independent. His 'rebellion' is always under the scrutiny of O'Brien. From the beginning it is merely the result of a seed planted in his head by O'Brien 'to meet in the place where there is no darkness' (27, 256). Representing the totalitarian state must do one thing: represent total control and total submission to that control. Julia, who expresses her anti-rationalism through sex, is the only rebel in the novel, but Orwell simply could not imagine a last woman in Europe. But even her autonomy is questionable: if it were her story it seems likely that she, as with Winston, would also have turned out to be a confirmed experiment. In any case, neither she nor Winston is able to stay even partially autonomous. The novel goes way beyond pragmatic realism: Winston and Julia concede to the rationality of the world, but there is little left to pragmatically negotiate except saving their own hides.

Nineteen Eighty-Four differs from Orwell's other fiction or prose insofar as it *resolves* and is depressingly consistent. The rationality of the futuristic world, in which military music is music, statistics are empiricism, and a glass ornament is forbidden 'because of its apparent uselessness' (99), is absolute. The Party is rationalist politics gone berserk. If modern governments try to impose homogeneous desires on the public because a sameness of predictable preferences, in theory, might maximize support for them (if two people want two different things, the government will anger one person by favouring the second person's desires), the Party standardizes preferences and the whole population as a matter of course. *Nineteen Eighty-Four* is not simply an anti-government textbook. Orwell also held that a rationalist, 'free' market and private ownership in general lead to 'tyranny' (*CEJL* 3: 118). He wanted to show that power, not only economic power, but the attempt to maximize power for its own sake – formal political rationality – leads to or is abuse. The defeat of the moral individual who cannot change himself let alone the system is a commentary on the system, not on the individual. Whether the final defeat of moral individualism and the final success of rationality have to do with Orwell's growing depression over his health or the rise of centralized governments, it is contrary to Carlyle's, Conrad's, and his own earlier writing. The world of nonrationalism, the golden country, and the world of rationalism are still split, but the latter is now completely victorious.

Hyper-rationalized, each and every article in Winston's world could act as a kind of microcosm of it, but his workplace suggests one of the more prophetically frightening aspects of *Nineteen Eighty-Four*. The severe bureaucratic rule of invisible bosses, the electronic and panoptical-type surveillance, the standardization of routines, the paper-pushing, and the anonymity in Winston's workplace are all nearer to the contemporary world than any other 'big brother' scenario of the novel. Today, interfaced computer technology allows for a greater amount of surveillance or impersonal activity tracking than ever before (Sennett 59). Contract-driven work eliminates the chance of fostering a work community (not to mention worker solidarity), and the absence of visible authority, *a boss*, allows corporations to reorganize, hire, and fire without having to consider or hear about the employees' individual situations. But Winston's work, albeit a 'tedious routine,' is his 'greatest pleasure in life' because the 'jobs [are] so difficult and intricate you could lose yourself in them' (46). (The more-physical Julia enjoys her work because it is mindless and she can use her hands [136].) It is as if some residual anti-rationalism survives despite Orwell's determination to create a world where it cannot. I will not argue that anti-rationalism or moral individualism ever prevails in *Nineteen Eighty-Four* in a meaningful way. In *Coming Up for Air*, *A Clergyman's Daughter*, and *Keep the Aspidistra Flying* a certain part of George's, Dorothy's, and Gordon's subjectivity remains in contrast with the world they submit to or join. Up until *Nineteen Eighty-Four*, defeat, submitting to the rational world, did not mean the end of decency or the still-individuated person's capacity to remain good while inside the whale that otherwise overwhelms. Not only is any type of escape impossible in *Nineteen Eighty-Four*, no inviolate humanity is possible. The idea of a Two Minute Hate, the emotional exercise of *Nineteen Eighty-Four*, does not mark the end of humanist sentiment because people are expressing hatred, but because their emotional life has been rationalized into a time-based, systematic order.

But Winston's work, despite being incredibly dismal and intensely rationalized, is still satisfying. The proles work harder and in worse and more primitive conditions than even Winston does, but as with the working class of the earlier fiction, they are of superior morality, almost gleaning their morality from those conditions or from their ignorance of the economic structure. Throughout his fiction and prose, Orwell jumps from depicting people who are economically disenfranchised, and who work harder physically, as internally better off to representing the debilitating effects *in toto* of poverty. Orwell's poor and working class are often moral and decent almost in direct proportion to the level of hardship they face. This holds for Conrad and Carlyle as well. But the proles do not live in a fully rationalized world and the vitality they get from their Work almost goes without saying. Satisfying Work continues to survive in Winston's world only because Work is an aberration in the text. It is not treated as part and parcel of rationalism, even though it epitomizes rationalism. Writing fiction, even what is arguably science fiction, does not affect the way in which Orwell writes about work. Winston's work might be the only glimpse of an indulgence in nonrationalized feeling in the completely rationalized world.

The mixed values of Orwell's fiction are the result of a polarized or nonconfrontational attitude towards moral and pragmatic interests, between Work and labour. Orwell writes in the naturalist genre but fails to maintain an attack on society because he trusted in 'decency' – that the individual could be responsible for his or her own codes – and because he was made uneasy by popular anger or even the average person's political consciousness. Since the amorality of pragmatic compromise could be sequestered off or held in abeyance by a self-sufficient moralist, and since Orwell saw a profound morality in the ordinary Joe's social adaptation, he did not imagine a contest between Work and economic reality. In fact, naturalism never achieved the same kind of success or popularity in Britain as it did in continental Europe because of a deep-seated belief in moralism – the power to do good despite the bad, the ability and imperative to will yourself a wholly ethical identity – an equally rooted belief in pragmatism, and a tendency to split the two so that they do not cancel each other out. Orwell encompasses the tendencies of Carlyle and Conrad in his antipodal positioning of freedom and economics. Value, finally, is located in intransitive activity, and the individual himself or herself is elevated over a disparaged and disparaging reality.

EPILOGUE

Postindustrial and Postmodern Work

Despite derision from postmodernism on the one hand and the anti-work manifestoes of slackers on the other, the idea of Work continues to survive into the present day. And despite the rhetoric of postindustrial utopians and cyber-enthusiasts who downplay poverty and economic domination, issues surrounding labour continue to overwhelm us. If we are witnessing a substantial and widespread increase in the standard of living, and the 'if' is a big one, it still does not follow that the interests which our labour serves today have undergone any kind of substantial revision. And if we are witnessing the end of industry – a revolution of 'flexible' work, task-based work, de-differentiated work, and the possibility of shop-floor innovations – it does not follow that contemporary versions of work are intrinsically (or extrinsically) satisfying for the many.

What has changed is that for the first time ever the dominant mode of self-conscious and deliberate cultural activity, postmodernism, corresponds to and ratifies the concurrent mode of work. The relationships between Victorian literature and utilitarianism or modernism and neo-classical consumerist theory, for example, were ambiguous, notwithstanding significant points of collusion. The theoretical principles of postmodernism are nearly identical to those lying behind the definition of postindustrialism, and the bond between the two worldviews is for the most part solid and friendly. Postmodernist enthusiasts embrace the idea, and the structure, of postindustrialism, and vice versa. This is despite the fact that most postmodernists reject the concept of Work and most postindustrialists confidently boast that Work is a present-day reality. In this brief epilogue I ask questions about what postmodern and postindustrial theory embrace. I am not suggesting that everyone who accepts that postmodernism and postindustrialism are palpable realities accepts that each or both are suffused with enormous value, but I do want to examine the popularity of the theories in light of their respective devaluation or dismissal of Work *and* labour. I am interested in the assumptions behind postindustrialism and postmodernism concerning work, especially when the paths cross, and I am interested in the politics of post- or anti-work rhetoric. But this is an epilogue: I am merely touching upon immense topics, observing from the historical and dialectical perspective I have used throughout this discussion, and in a necessarily cursory manner, critiquing generally and liberally. This is not a conclusion: it is not a summary of my argument and in some ways I am abandoning the themes discussed and even the parameters used in the book. I am, for example, no longer focused on Carlyle, Conrad, or Orwell, or indeed on England.

Daniel Bell first ushered in the idea that the West was becoming postindustrial in *The Coming of Postindustrial Society* (1973). He asks us to abandon the image of the factory when we talk about work and envision in its place professionals, advisers, experts, technocrats, educators, and a technical 'elite' in the service sector. His society is wealthy, fair, full of convenient amenities, and 'communal.' Having matured beyond a 'mode of life modeled on economics ... [on] maximization and optimization' in industrial society, postindustrialism represents a real 'change in the *social structure*' (127, 114). Bell does not speak of a problem-free society, but the tenor of his theory emphasizes social amelioration, justice and equal opportunity, wealth and health, and happiness for all. At the centre of the postindustrial society are the rewards accrued by advances in the dissemination of information. Postindustrial theory highlights that information, fast technology, and fast information technology. Bell argues that 'information and theoretical knowledge are the strategic resources of the postindustrial society just as the combination of energy, resources, and machine technology were the transforming agencies of industrial society' ('Social' 545). It would be difficult to deny that the West has seen a shift from manual to mental work. Though statistics about the current state of work are difficult to interpret, as they often seem to be corresponding to and shamelessly promoting sundry political and theoretical objectives, it is clear that more and more people work in service and information sectors and fewer and fewer in 'industrial' fields of work. There are, however, at least six major problems with postindustrial theory.

The first problem with postindustrial theory is its basis in Enlightenment reasoning: its belief in progress, human reason, and 'man,' and its optimism or flat-out utopianism. As Jean-François Lyotard says in *The Postmodern Condition* (1979), the idea of the information society 'fails to challenge the general paradigm of progress in science and technology, to which economic growth and the expansion of sociopolitical power seem to be the natural complements' (7). The development of knowledge and reason in itself is said to correspond to freedom and a better world. The implied faith in progress is coupled with an explicit belief in beneficent technology. Technology, as Fredric Jameson argues, is understood to be the 'ultimate determining instance' of social life (*Postmodernism* 37). Tom Stonier and Yoneji Masuda, self-declared postindustrial utopians, argue that the mechanisms of the information society enhance democracy (by diffusing information), and that the Internet and TV liberate (Kumar 14). They contend that the information society will wipe out the need for war because wars are fought over resources. But it seems apparent that an increased supply of information (not to mention contending ideologies) does not reduce the demand for, say, oil.

The second, probably the most significant, problem with postindustrial theory is that it deliberately ignores, downplays, or conceals the fact that with the shift from manual to mental forms of work there have been no coincidental shifts in the distribution of workplace (or structural) power and authority. The dynamic of the workplace – or the division of labour between conception and execution – has not changed. The deadening, paper-pushing routines of information channelling, tracking, and circulating are not that different from Taylorism on the factory floor. Taylorism and Fordism were not primarily about efficiency and productivity. As Stephen Marglin has shown, one of the basic uses of the division of labour was to prevent workers from acting for and by themselves: data processing for the sake of data processing is only a slight variation on domination for domination's sake (15–17). James Beniger convincingly argues that the structure of the information society demands 'increases in the speed of material processing and of flows through the material economy' in the same way as assembly line rationalism did a century ago (435). The fact that the material basis of the production has changed does not mean that the organization of the production has changed. New technologies, the electronic panopticon, only augment the potential for increased surveillance, domination, and control, and the insistence on an orderly, rational, set manner of production.

That postindustrial theory downplays the fact that no shift in workplace domination has occurred can be further divided into two categories, the third and fourth shortcomings of the theory: the 'new' global division of labour and the old matter of class. Unendurable labour, low wages, child labour, and the kind of working conditions that England saw during the worst years of the 'industrial revolution' exist today all over the world. If Western multinational corporations – Disney and Nike are often used as examples – exploit resources (human and natural) in other nations while creating nonindustrial jobs at home, then they only enable parts of the world to be postindustrial. Globalization and free trade create a demarcated postindustrialism. Certain segments of the world's population have always been postindustrial, which takes us to the fourth point.

Not only does postindustrial theory ignore non-Western industry, it ignores and denies industry, poverty, and class within the West. It builds its social and economic models on the idea that all are enjoying and have equal access to an era of plenty, leisure, learning, and happiness. By emphasizing technology, efficiency, automation, abundance, and consumer freedom, postindustrialism obscures issues surrounding economic domination and class. Stanley Aronowitz and colleagues document the growth of sweatshops, child labour, underpaid and 'contingent' work, underground labour, and economic disparity in Europe and the United States (31–6). They also show that people in postindustrial societies are working longer now than ever before (37). Though it is true that it has become extremely difficult to rely on traditional demographic variables such as consumption habits to identify the classes, as individuals from all classes more and more seem to piece themselves together from various mass media images, it is not true that the division between the rich and the poor has decreased in terms of economic, political, or social power (Gorz, *Critique* 66).

Following Orwell, we cannot deny that the proliferation of consumer goods has led to a real improvement in the overall standard of living for the once-identifiable working class. For some workers, not only has the ability to possess easily been taken for granted, they themselves have become 'wealthy' through unions or stock options. Herbert Marcuse critiques this 'good way of life' on the grounds that it 'militates against qualitative change,' that the 'new technological work-world thus enforces a weakening of the negative position of the working class: the latter no longer appears to be the living contradiction to the established society' (*One* 12, 31). Though Marcuse's case is vitiated by an antidemocratic, ascetic snobbery and an assumption of the disappearance of poverty, he is right to point out that an increase in the availability of goods does not 'compensate for the fact that the decisions over life and death, over personal and national security are made at places over which the individuals have no control' (*One* 32). Postindustrial theory denies that the relations of production have not changed; that poverty is rampant and critical in the West (though effectively ghettoized); that, as E.F. Schumacher says, 'wants will always rise faster than the ability to meet them' (25); that information technology is in part responsible for bigger and bigger corporations and more and more centralization (and thus less and less direct control by the worker over the object of work); and that if some material needs have been met for workers it does not follow that 'higher-order' needs at the workplace, or beyond it, have been met. A great deal of industrial work still takes place: the kind of work that enables postindustrial activity to make millionaires (just as with the global division of labour or as Orwell's miners enable intellectuals to have their insights).

The fifth pitfall of the theory, then, again related to its assumptions, has to do with its super-categories – the flexibility of the term 'postindustrialism.' Postindustrial theory groups nearly everyone who is not working in a factory as a 'professional.' It is one thing to show that our world is more oriented towards mental than physical labour by showing increases in the number of jobs in education or administration, but it is another to imply the disappearance of physical work by calling janitors 'sanitation experts' and thus grouping them as professionals. Moreover, to class service-sector jobs – retail, restaurant work, parking attendants – in the same category as expert professionals, as do John Naisbitt and Patricia Aburdene (26) as well as Vladislav Inozemtsev (96–7), for example, is to ignore that those jobs have more akin with industrial factory work (being paid by the hour, having a physical nature) than with information technology. The implication of a world where routine has been done away with, where everyone enjoys the same dignity of work, is ideological nonsense. Working in a factory can be easier than waiting tables: less people to boss you about, less people to judge how you do your job, less people to deny you are an 'expert.'

The assumption of a classless, professional society is based on or fortified by the idea of a knowledge theory of value, the sixth shortcoming of postindustrial theory. To begin with, postindustrial theorists treat knowledge and information as a brand new thing, as if before the computer value was determined only by labour, land, or capital. The *combination* of knowledge, labour, land (or inherited power), and capital has always been that which leads to value, generated growth, made riches. That we privilege knowledge today is in effect to conceal that labour takes place (whether making the product or selling it), that capital is needed to make money, and that power is remaining in the hands of those who have always had it. Perhaps knowledge is more accessible today and innovation now open to a wider spectrum of people. But that a handful of computer whiz-kids made it big by designing websites for insurance companies does not mean that we should ignore the thousands of Asian women putting the hardware together. It does not mean that domination has disappeared or made the myths of equal opportunity and rags to riches in any way actual. The emphasis on knowledge as that which determines value is analogous to the liberal dictum that value or social wealth accrues from the abstract movement of the market and not the labour – and I mean the effort or the capital – that enables the market. The assumption of a knowledge theory of value – along with the misleading super-categories of postindustrial experts and professionals, the downplaying of class, the denial of the global division of labour, the misconstrued idea about freedom and the distribution of power in the workplace, and the throwback to a general Enlightenment utopianism – is an attempt to bypass or conceal what I have been calling *labour*.

A more popular counterpart to postindustrial theory is postmodernism. As a description of contemporary life, postmodernism is often accepted by intellectuals and social observers, though it remains loosely and dubiously defined. I am only interested in postmodernism as it relates to theories of work. In some ways, postmodernism surveys the shift from an economy based on production to one based on consumption, the same shift that modernists were faced with and which Orwell feels 'torn both ways' about. Instead of being put off by consumerist culture, however, postmodernists tend to support it as a relation to or a sign of the healthy transgression of boundaries between 'high' and 'low' culture. Still, the foremost meaning of postmodernism comes from Lyotard. Postmodernism, following him, campaigns against 'grand narratives.' Lyotard especially argued that after Auschwitz and Stalin, the ideas of Progress, rationality, and science must be discredited: postmodernism today disparages any and all meta-narratives, including Work. Claiming to be more interested in the local (though not the specific) than the universal; maintaining that knowledge and truth are temporary and shifting; positing that there is no centre from which to steadily view, interpret, or know the world; arguing the multi-directionality of information, a kind of hypertextual world-text and the lack of a steady origin and destination of knowledge; and confirming another lack – of deep structures or final causes – the postmodern attitude does not tolerate concepts of Work: at best it might express amusement. The idea of Work involves all of the centring, universalizing, essentializing schemata that are anathema to postmodernism's image of itself. The 'work' of art, an expression of personal style or freedom (in Ruskin's sense), has been replaced by the 'text,' with its 'dead author' (Jameson, *Postmodernism* 77). The idea of Work, as we have seen, encompasses a strict valorization of the past, vitality, earnestness, activity, humanist notions of subjectivity, and the fixity of nature. Postmodernism, to put it bluntly, does not. Postmodern (and postindustrial) theory would undo the idea that the worker objectifies himself or herself in the object of the work, thereby grounding, discovering, or solidifying a sense of identity. If the keyword for postmodernism is irony, then that irony turns to cynicism when applied to Work.

There are several points of theoretical contention between post-industrialism and postmodernism in the context of work. Postmodernism refuses to accept that the 'new' world has a privileged carrier of change whereas postindustrialism trumpets high-tech. Lyotard in fact argues that the computer age equals the mercantilization of knowledge. But the greatest disagreement between the two theories must be that whereas postindustrial theory adopts a neo-Enlightenment faith in reason, science, and progress, postmodernism calls itself a 'post-science,' wishing to leave the totalizing unity of science in its wake and spearheading an anti-Enlightenment, post-humanist trend. Yet the two theories also agree with each other in such a way as to create a self-contained frame of reference. Both theories claim to favour and proceed through hybridized, decentralized, yet self-reflexive mechanisms. And both theories celebrate the multivalence and multiplicity of theoretical knowledge in itself. Because postmodernism stands adamantly against meta-narratives, its advocates often accept the fragmentation or 'flexibility' of postindustrial society. Both postindustrial and postmodern theories see the censure of social fragmentation as a modernist refusal of difference. Stewart Clegg, though not a fan of either theory, argues that 'Where modernist [work] was rigid, postmodern organization is flexible ... Where modernist organization and jobs were highly differentiated, demarcated, and de-skilled, postmodernist organization and jobs are highly de-differentiated, de-demarcated, and multi-skilled' (181). The new emphasis on contract and subcontract work, networking, or loyalty to the job and not to transient co-workers is represented as an alternative to job stagnation, repetition, and de-skilling. That job definitions have been atomized and wage scales have been problematized according to postmodern multiplicity or that work is now task-based, as opposed to being time-based, does not necessarily indicate intrinsic job satisfaction or extrinsic justice. Such work organization can also be the means by which employers try to squeeze the most out of employees while avoiding pension payments and allowing themselves the flexibility to downsize at whim. Again I refer to Aronowitz et al.'s documentation of the recent increase in white-collar working hours (37). 'Flexibility' is most significantly the rhetoric of hyper and very successful – not late – capitalism.

Marxist scholars, including Jameson, have been quick to point out that postmodernism is the ideology of the postindustrial (or post-Fordist) society. They argue that postmodernism is the crutch globalism or multinational capitalism leans on just as modernism was the cultural trend during the heyday of industrial capitalism. Marxism, in turn, is accused of employing a totalizing narrative revolving around industrial workers, class, and capitalism. But Marxism's critique, and especially Jameson's critique, should not go undervalued: nearly alone they attempt to identify causes and initiate political discussions. In *Postmodernism* (1991), Jameson wonders not only what has become of history in postmodernism, but also why postmodern images of ubiquitous commodification are meant to titillate or exhilarate, not cause anxiety or anger. Both postindustrialism and postmodern theories go out of their way to show themselves as if transcending politics, especially in their assumption of a world rising above class and poverty. In this way they resemble modernism and its attitude of having outgrown *issues*. Postmodernism's emphasis on endless contingency and deferral, its knee-jerk rejection of binaries, and its focus on reflexivity strip themselves of political content. Postindustrial theorists often reject notions of left and right politics because they themselves, largely the right wing, have been by and large victorious in achieving their goals of global free enterprise and minuscule government. One has to wonder about declarations of a postindustrial world where, as Daniel Bell famously argues, the game against nature is now a game between people just as environmentalism becomes a popular political movement. One also must wonder about postmodern declarations that irony reigns supreme just as NGO-based, anti-capitalist, drop-the-debt, anti-multinational protests are shaking up the West.

The effect of the alliance between postindustrial and postmodern theory is to undermine both the issues surrounding labour and the idea of Work, which, as I will suggest in a moment, is in effect to further entrench rationalism. First, however, I will continue to discuss modern organizations of work in order to argue that the West is not a postindustrial or a postmodern society in a meaningful way except in the most isolated and rarefied quarters. Sar Levitan and Clifford Johnson contend that 'Despite an enormous decrease during this century in the amount of human labour required to produce given quantities of goods, no corresponding decrease in the number or relative proportion of workers has taken place' (1). André Gorz shows that only a privileged few have gained from postindustrial work and that the clear majority of Westerners continue to live on the brink of unemployment, working de-skilled jobs (*Critique* 66). But it is not my intention here to reproduce statistics. It is difficult to gauge whether or not the idea of Work has decreased because higher absenteeism, the desire for early retirement, and shorter workweeks might mean an increase in the desire for Work outside of employment. The current do-it-yourself home improvement craze seems to suggest a desire for Work, though watching Martha Stewart putter about is also a good reminder that to enjoy Work one needs money. The taking of second jobs and working longer employment hours, on the other hand, might only suggest an increase in a 'labour ethic' and not a 'work ethic.' I tend to agree with Michael Rose that despite the representation of a postmodern society and the discourse of a postindustrial one, 'what is striking is how stable some work values seem to have remained' (92). Rose argues, without dislodging history, that the idea of Work is 'not being abandoned because of a move towards "postindustrialism"' (93).

This is not to suggest that 'flexible capitalism' or the postindustrial workplace fosters intrinsic job satisfaction. Inozemtsev, however, sees nothing but roses in current organizations of work: 'Today's corporation unites people, not as simple sources of physical energy or the appendages of machines and mechanisms, but primarily as creative individuals' (186). He argues and refers to hundreds of others who argue that modern corporations are now driven by non-economic goals, not only profit, and that a 'whole new work ethic is emerging under which the product carries the imprint of the personality of its creator' (182). Barry Jones comes close to confirming this Work point of view by suggesting that the West is moving from 'time-saving' principles (trying to minimize the labour time of workers in order to decrease costs and increase profits) to 'time-absorbing' principles (careers in research, administration, information services, and so on, where people do not punch the clock). He is correct to point out that time-absorbing work has historically been done by 'those for whom work and existence were inextricably linked, unaffected by "division of labour"' (82). Time-absorbing work, however, does not necessarily entail the kind of cottage economics advocated by the Schumacher/Jeremy Rifkin school (which attempts to bring a spirit of Work to economics and labour), even if resituated in electronic and information-based technologies. More often it would simply mean having employees exhaust themselves for the company brass.

For every backer of postindustrial theory there is a critic who takes into consideration the deepening economic inequalities associated with the rise of high-tech. Richard Sennett suggests that 'the new language of flexibility implies that routine is dying in the dynamic sectors of the economy,' but that 'at least two-thirds ... of modern jobs ... are repetitive in a way which Adam Smith would recognize as akin to those in his pin factory' (44). 'Flexibility' can be read as an ideological ruse instilling values that tolerate the fragmentation and accept the risks, unsteadiness, lack of community and loyalty, and validation of opportunitism easily linked to short-term work. Sennett underlines the uncertainties bred into today's short-term contract job market, arguing that 'What's peculiar about uncertainty today is that it exists without any looming historical disaster; instead it is woven into the everyday practices of a vigorous capitalism. Instability is meant to be normal' (31). He also shows that job insecurity is nothing new, but that now it is not only manual workers who suffer its effects, but postindustrial 'professionals' as well. As said, the language of 'time-absorbing' or 'task-based' activity can be read as a ploy to squeeze the most out of the worker for the least amount of pay or for very controlled pay. Just as the only mechanism to gauge whether Carlyle's aggrandizement of work was complete in itself, or if it was on loan to businessmen in order to mobilize their economic machines, is to confront his rhetoric of Work with matters surrounding labour (what he himself does not do), the current moral elevation of the organization of work, the supposed fusing of 'work' and 'life' under postmodernism, must be seen in reference to the group who profits most. Flexible capitalism allows corporations to treat the workforce as a reserve army, calling up workers when it suits their needs and unilaterally controlling the labour supply – keeping it high by endlessly fluctuating the demand.

The idea that rationalism in work has been reduced in the transition from the factory to the office or the computer terminal or from modernist to postmodernist society is absurd. The idea that in moving from a dominant ideology of deferred gratification to one of 'spend now' we have radically changed our politely hedonistic 'make a living ethic' is equally as absurd. In *Critique of Economic Reason* (1989), Gorz argues that even leisure has become organized by rationalist economics, that economic logic has colonized all aspects of life. '*Technical culture*,' he holds, '*is lack of culture in all things non-technical.* Learning to work means unlearning how to find, or even look for, a meaning to non-instrumental relations with the surrounding environment and with other people' (86). Postindustrialism and the computer, as Krishan Kumar argues, have ushered in more standardization and a greater division of labour in the contemporary workplace than scientific management ever did (19). The dot.com organization of the information society entails the maximization of information for its own sake, quantity and now speed over quality, and the elevation of methods above the end (where it garners support from postmodernism). In other words, the formal rationality of the means is substantially irrational in the same way that Weber, Marx, Marcuse, Schumacher, and many others have defined the formal rationality of economic maximization – maximization or profit-seeking for its own sake – as substantially irrational or empty. If contemporary workers find Work in such environments it only shows that rationalization comes as something external to them.

In certain fields the workplace may have been restructured to include employee innovation (which, everything else being just, would probably mean employee satisfaction), but such restructuring takes place only when it promises to be efficient and increase profit for employers. This is also the reasoning of slackers as they interpret the postindustrial rhetoric of work. (To clarify, postindustrialists claim a new organization of work that fosters intrinsic satisfactions, though they nonetheless continue to maintain that work is a disutility and that people seek and desire leisure. Postmodernists denounce Work wholesale.) Slackers are proud to be social dropouts. In order to reject society – its laws, its conventions, its underlying kill-or-be-killed mentality – they wholly reject work. Having been around for about twenty years now, they have taken to computers but generally insist that since they do not put effort into anything, their links and so forth might not work. Their creed includes procrastinating, stealing paper clips from the companies they work unambitiously for (as clerks or mailroom attendants – some of them *have* to work), watching TV, and being unproductive in as many ways as they can. They are urban, subversive for its own sake, and young. They target Work, but in fact reject the world of labour: Work is refuted because it is understood to be the ideology of capitalism. Bob Black, one of their heroes, argues against

Work because it is a tool used to promote the self-interested society, though he also rejects unions and what's left of the pro-Work rhetoric of the Marxist school. However, though he preaches in *The Abolition of Work* (1985) the need to turn work into play, declares himself to be half nihilist and half ludist, he ends up by affirming something akin to William Morris's values. Work, he suggests, should be creative, fun, community-based, irreverent (as with artisanal stubbornness), and as multidirectional as his own prose. Slackers, Black, and Morris all believe that in capitalism there can be no truly meaningful work. From that, slackers and Black argue that work is not a good source of social or personal identity. They avoid being accused of a hypocritical or full-bellied attitude by happily relying on the welfare system and trying to reverse the stigma associated with it. Their nihilism is understandable in a world where Work is constantly appropriated for the greed of the few. In many ways, Orwell foresees slackerism when trying to understand Henry Miller in 'Inside the Whale' (1940):

> The passive attitude will come back, and it will be more consciously passive than before. Progress and reaction have both turned out to be swindles. Seemingly there is nothing left but quietism – robbing reality of its terrors by simply submitting to it. Get inside the whale – or rather, admit that you are inside the whale (for you *are*, of course). Give yourself over to the world-process, stop fighting against it or pretending that you control it; simply accept it, endure it, record it. That seems to be the formula. (*CEJL* 1: 526)

Slackers are a clear minority, but the anti-work or 'post-work' attitude has become increasingly widespread. Slackerism is in one way an extreme variation of postmodernism in its belief that one thing is as good as another, that any lifestyle (or interpretation) is valid, that irony is the only defence, and that the categories of 'good and bad' have to be transgressed. Slackerism is only more comfortable with the nihilism and violence that would follow than are postmodern academics. Other 'post-work' movements, as expressed by Gorz or by Aronowitz et al. in 'The Post-Work Manifesto' (1998), call for shorter working hours (as adopted in Scandinavian countries) and less emphasis on the needs of the market. Again, the attack is consistently aimed at the conditions of labour, not Work – though it is expressed as a case against Work. The case for shorter working hours, for example, is not made on the basis that work is inherently undesirable, but that shorter hours would create higher levels of employment.

Carlyle preached Work while he scorned but accommodated labour. Today, notwithstanding slackers, Work is scorned while labour – economic activity – is preached. In Carlyle's day Work was preached just as industrial technology made it worthy of scorn. Today work is a source of stress, fear, and competition just as postindustrial high-tech guarantees its satisfying flexibility. We often imagine that at one time workers did not consider their efforts a commodity and did not seek to maximize their incomes. Instead of social or financial mobility, and other extrinsic gains, work provided the opportunity for creative satisfaction, a sense of identity, and community spirit (along with the festive pleasures associated with groups). Such a narrative, however, must be incomplete as it begins to ignore need. Postindustrial theory continues to deny the realm of necessity by assuming an era of abundance, of met needs. Postmodernism then offers a narrative displacing Work. The idea of a world without origin, of actions that refer only to other actions, would satisfy only the nouveau riche and geek chic few who have others working and building things for them.

But the most harm that postindustrial theory can have is to diminish or obfuscate matters surrounding labour, specifically domination – precisely the damage that the rhetoric of Work causes. Postindustrial society, where and when it exists, has done nothing to lessen the way people with (and sometimes without) power treat those working for or beside them. In today's world of computer-oriented work the mode of domination has become less personal, more like bureaucratic bullying. Instead of a single, suspiciously surveying power centre, a boss, productivity is impersonally measured by central computers. As surveillance increases so does the assumption that workers are lazy, that they will do anything to avoid work, and that the role of management is thus to ensure people are busy for the sake of busyness. This assumption justifies the surveillance. Marcuse, who does not forgo the idea of Work but understands that 'the mode of work' matters, suggests that in the history of work there has been one constant, domination. He argues that work has been '*imposed* upon individuals – first by mere violence, subsequently by a more rational utilization of power ... [and] no matter how useful this rationality was for the progress of the whole, it remained a rationality of *domination*' (*Eros* 33). Rationality, he argues, can have positive value when

> derived from knowledge and confined to the administration of functions and arrangements necessary for the advancement of the whole. In contrast, domination is exercised by a particular group or individuals in order to

sustain and enhance itself in a privileged position. Such domination does not exclude technical, material, and intellectual progress, but only as an unavoidable by-product while preserving irrational scarcity, want, and constraint. (33–4)

By dismissing domination as a master narrative – only pure Work is free of domination and there is no such thing as pure Work – the postindustrial/postmodern alliance is attempting to undermine ways to rethink labour, and by dismissing Work as a master narrative it is attempting to undermine ways to enable Work. The result is not the same as we have seen with the undialectical approach to work, which eases the tension between Work and labour: in this case, attention is drawn away from those who would Work and those who need to labour. There has to be tension between Work and labour. A dialectical approach to work might blur the dialectic and initiate the kind of cross-hybridization that so titillates postmodernists. For example, as feminist theorists argue, earning a living (negotiating labour) can itself contribute to a sense of identity, accomplishment, and all the intrinsic benefits that we associate with Work. Though there will always be some conflict between Work and labour – that is, as long as one works for the gain of others – they need not be treated as frozen, polar opposites. The reform of labour should include measures to guarantee the conditions of Work, and the discourse of Work should include the recognition that it is inextricably connected – and that means dialectically connected – to labour. Our tendency to compartmentalize moral and pragmatic concerns speaks of what is feared: a resolution and the process of achieving a resolution.

Speaking about the division between labour, or the need for specific reforms, and Work, or 'the great Romantic criticism of Utilitarianism,' E.P. Thompson makes the point that 'After William Blake, no mind was at home in both cultures, nor had the genius to interpret the two traditions to each other.' He goes on to say that 'In the failure of the two traditions to come to a point of junction, something was lost. How much we cannot be sure, for we are among the losers' (*Making* 915). Blake was a great dialectician, perhaps *the* great dialectician, but reading Carlyle, Conrad, and Orwell does not make one a loser. Thompson, however, is right: the spirit of change, whether or not born from radical artisans, and the spirit of Work, whether or not articulated by Romantics or those negotiating that inheritance, has to be brought together if the fight against Economic man – businessmen – is going to succeed.

Works Cited

Ambrosini, Richard. *Conrad's Fiction as Critical Discourse.* Cambridge: Cambridge UP, 1991.
Applebaum, Herbert. *The Concept of Work: Ancient, Medieval, and Modern.* Albany: State U of New York P, 1992.
Arendt, Hannah. *The Human Condition.* 1958. Chicago: U of Chicago P, 1989.
Aronowitz, Stanley, Dawn Esposito, William DiFazio, and Margaret Yard. 'The Post-Work Manifesto.' *Post-Work: The Wages of Cybernation.* Ed. Stanley Aronowitz and Jonathan Cutler. New York: Routledge, 1998. 31–80.
Beckett, Samuel. 'Ding-Dong.' *More Pricks than Kicks.* 1934. London: Calder and Boyars, 1973. 39–49.
– *Proust.* 1931. New York: Grove Press, 1957.
– *Quad.* 1984. *The Complete Dramatic Works.* London: Faber and Faber, 1986. 449–54.
Behnken, Eloise M. *Thomas Carlyle: Calvinist without the Theology.* Columbia: U of Missouri P, 1978.
Bell, Daniel. *The Coming of Post-Industrial Society: A Venture in Social Forecasting.* New York: Basic Books, 1973.
– 'The Social Framework of the Information Society.' *The Microelectronics Revolution: The Complete Guide to the New Technology and Its Impact on Society.* Ed. Tom Forester. Oxford: Basil Blackwell, 1980. 500–49.
Bellamy, Ron. 'Victorian Economic Values.' *In Search of Victorian Values: Aspects of Nineteenth Century Thought and Society.* Ed. Eric M. Sigsworth. Manchester: Manchester UP, 1988. 43–55.
Beniger, James R. *The Control Revolution: Technological and Economic Origins of the Information Society.* Cambridge: Harvard UP, 1986.
Benjamin, Walter. 'The Storyteller.' *Illuminations.* 1955. Trans. Harry Zohn. Ed. Hannah Arendt. New York: Schocken Books, 1968.

Bentham, Jeremy. 'Deontology, A Table of the Springs of Action, and Article on Utilitarianism.' 1817. *The Collected Works of Jeremy Bentham*. Ed. Amnon Goldworth. Oxford: Clarendon, 1983.

Bhabha, Homi K. 'Signs Taken for Wonders.' *The Post-Colonial Studies Reader*. Ed. Bill Ashcroft, Gareth Griffiths, and Helen Tiffin. London: Routledge, 1995. 29–35.

Biernacki, Richard. *The Fabrication of Labour: Germany and Britain, 1640–1914*. Berkeley: U of California P, 1995.

Birken, Lawrence. *Consuming Desire: Sexual Science and the Emergence of a Culture of Abundance, 1871–1914*. Ithaca: Cornell UP, 1988.

Black, Bob. 'The Abolition of Work.' *The Abolition of Work and Other Essays*. Port Townsend: Loompanics Unlimited, n.d. 15–33.

Boos, Florence S. 'Narrative Design in *The Pilgrims of Hope*.' *Socialism and the Literary Artistry of William Morris*. Ed. Florence S. Boos and Carole G. Silver. Columbia: U of Missouri P, 1990. 147–66.

Bourdieu, Pierre. 'The Disenchantment of the World.' *Algeria 1960*. Trans. Richard Nice. Cambridge: Cambridge UP, 1979. 1–94.

– *The Logic of Practice*. Trans. Richard Nice. Stanford: Stanford UP, 1990.

Bradshaw, David J., and Suzanne Ozment, eds. *The Voice of Toil: Nineteenth-Century British Writings about Work*. Athens: Ohio UP, 2000.

Brantlinger, Patrick. *The Spirit of Reform: British Literature and Politics, 1832–1867*. Cambridge: Harvard UP, 1977.

Bruss, Paul. *Conrad's Early Sea Fiction*. Lewisburg: Buckwell UP, 1979.

Burke, Kenneth. *A Grammar of Motives*. Berkeley: U of California P, 1969.

Burnett, John, ed. *Useful Toil: Autobiographies of Working People from the 1820s to the 1920s*. London: Allen Lane, 1974.

Campbell, Beatrix. *Wigan Pier Revisited*. London: Virago P, 1984.

Campbell, Ian. *Thomas Carlyle*. London: Hamish Hamilton, 1974.

Carlyle, Thomas. 'Chartism.' 1839. *English and Other Critical Essays*. London: J.M. Dent, 1950. 165–238.

– *The Collected Letters of Thomas Carlyle and Jane Welsh Carlyle*. Vol. 23. April 1848–March 1849. Ed. Clyde de L. Ryals et al. Durham: Duke UP, 1995.

– *Past and Present*. 1843. Ed. Richard Altick. Boston: Riverside, 1965.

– *Reminiscences*. 1881. Oxford: Oxford UP, 1997.

– *Sartor Resartus*. 1833. Ed. Kerry McSweeney and Peter Sabor. Oxford: Oxford UP, 1991.

– 'Signs of the Time.' 1829. *Scottish and Other Miscellanies*. London: J.M. Dent, 1950. 223–45.

Chesterton, G.K. *William Cobbett*. London: Hodder and Stoughton, 1925.

Clegg, Stewart R. *Modern Organizations: Organization Studies in the Postmodern World*. London: Sage Publications, 1990.

Conrad, Joseph. 'The Ascending Effort.' 1921. *Notes on Life and Letters*. London: J.M. Dent and Sons, 1949. 71–5.
- *Chance*. 1913. Harmondsworth: Penguin, 1974.
- *The Collected Letters of Joseph Conrad*. Ed. Frederick Karl. 6 vols. Cambridge: Cambridge UP, 1986.
- 'Confidence.' 1919. *Notes on Life and Letters*. London: J.M. Dent and Sons, 1949. 202–8.
- *Heart of Darkness*. 1902. Ed. Paul O'Prey. London: Penguin, 1989.
- *Lord Jim*. 1900. New York: Signet, 1981.
- *The Mirror of the Sea and A Personal Record*. 1906, 1912. Ed. Zdzisław Najder. Oxford: Oxford UP, 1988.
- *The Nigger of the 'Narcissus.'* 1897. New York: Penguin, 1976.
- 'Tradition.' 1918. *Notes on Life and Letters*. London: J.M. Dent and Sons, 1949. 194–201.

Cooper, Thomas. '"Merrie England" – No More!' 1845. *The Literature of Struggle: An Anthology of Chartist Fiction*. Ed. Ian Haywood. Aldershot: Scolar Press. 1995. 53–9.
- 'Seth Thompson, the Stockinger.' 1845. *The Literature of Struggle: An Anthology of Chartist Fiction*. Ed. Ian Haywood. Aldershot: Scolar Press. 1995. 46–52.

Crick, Bernard. *George Orwell: A Life*. Harmondsworth: Penguin, 1980.
- 'Orwell and English Socialism.' *George Orwell: A Reassessment*. Ed. Peter Buitenhuis and Ira Nadel. New York: St Martin's, 1988. 3–19.

Danon, Ruth. *Work in the English Novel: The Myth of Vocation*. London: Croom Helm, 1985.

Dentith, Simon. '"The Journalists Do the Shouting": Orwell and Propaganda.' *New Casebooks George Orwell*. Ed. Graham Holderness, Bryan Loughrey, and Nahem Yousaf. New York: St Martin's, 1998. 203–27.

Dickens, Charles. *Bleak House*. 1852–3. Ed. Norman Page. Harmondsworth: Penguin, 1971.
- 'The Chimes.' 1844. *Christmas Books*. London: The Folio Society, 1988. 83–160.
- *David Copperfield*. 1849–50. Ed. Trevor Blount. Harmondsworth: Penguin, 1982.
- *Dombey and Son*. 1848. Ed. Peter Fairclough. Harmondsworth: Penguin, 1974.
- *Hard Times*. 1854. Ed. George Ford and Sylvère Monod. New York: Norton, 1966.
- *Letters Of Charles Dickens* Vol. 7. *1853–1855*. Ed. Graham Storey, Kathleen Tillotson, and Angus Easson. Oxford: Clarendon, 1993.
- 'On Strike.' 1854. *Dickens' Journalism* Vol. 3. London: J.M. Dent, 1998. 196–210.
- *Our Mutual Friend*. 1864–5. Ed. Stephen Gill. Harmondsworth: Penguin, 1984.

Disraeli, Benjamin. *Sybil or The Two Nations*. 1845. Harmondsworth: Penguin, 1954.

Dobb, Maurice. *Political Economy and Capitalism*. London: Routledge, 1944.

Eagleton, Mary, and David Pierce. *Attitudes to Class in the English Novel*. London: Thames and Hudson, 1979.

Eagleton, Terry. *Criticism and Ideology: A Study in Marxist Literary Theory*. London: NLB, 1976.

– *Exiles and Émigrés: Studies in Modern Literature*. London: Chatto & Windus, 1970.

Eliot, George. *Essays of George Eliot*. Ed. Thomas Pinney. New York: Columbia UP, 1963.

Engels, Friedrich. *The Condition of the Working Class in England*. 1845. Ed. Victor Kiernan. London: Penguin, 1987.

– 'The Origin of the Family, Private Property, and the State.' 1884. *The Marx-Engels Reader*. Ed. Robert C. Tucker. 2nd ed. New York: Norton, 1978. 734–59.

Fleishman, Avrom. *Conrad's Politics: Community and Anarchy in the Fiction of Joseph Conrad*. Baltimore: Johns Hopkins P, 1967.

Forster, E. M. *Howards End*. 1910. Ed. Oliver Stallybrass. London: Penguin, 2000.

Frankel, Boris. *The Post-Industrial Utopians*. Cambridge: Polity Press, 1987.

Freud, Sigmund. *Civilization and Its Discontents*. 1930. Trans. James Strachey. New York: Norton, 1989.

– *The Future of an Illusion*. 1927. Trans. James Strachey. New York: Norton, 1989.

Frye, Northrop. *Anatomy of Criticism: Four Essays*. 1957. Princeton: Princeton UP, 1973.

Galbraith, John Kenneth. *Economics in Perspective: A Critical History*. Boston: Houghton, 1987.

Gaskell, Elizabeth. *Cranford*. 1853. London: J.M. Dent, 1973.

– *Mary Barton*. 1848. Ed. Edgar Wright. Oxford: Oxford UP, 1987.

– *North and South*. 1855. Ed. Angus Easson. Oxford: Oxford UP, 1998.

Gaston, Paul. 'The Gospel of Work According to Joseph Conrad.' *The Polish Review*. 20.2–3 (1975): 203–10.

Glyn, Andrew. 'Contradictions of Capitalism.' *The New Palgrave Marxian Economics*. Ed. John Eatwell, Murray Milgate, and Peter Newman. New York: Norton, 1990. 104–9.

Gorz, André. *Critique of Economic Reason*. Trans. Gillian Handyside and Chris Turner. London: Verso, 1989.

– *Farewell to the Working Class: An Essay on Post-Industrial Socialism*. Trans. Michael Sonenscher. London: Pluto Press, 1987.

Graff, Gerald. *Literature against Itself*. Chicago: U of Chicago P, 1979.

Gramsci, Antonio. *Selections from the Prison Notebooks.* 1971. Trans. and ed. Quintin Hoare and Geoffrey Nowell Smith. New York: International Publishers, 1997.

Grennan, Margaret R. *William Morris: Medievalist and Revolutionary.* New York: Russell and Russell, 1970.

Guild, Nicholas. 'In Dubious Battle: George Orwell and the Victory of the Money-God.' *Critical Essays on George Orwell.* Ed. Bernard Oldsey and Joseph Browne. Boston: G.K. Hall, 1986. 144–50.

Harvey, Charles, and Jon Press. *Art, Enterprise and Ethics: The Life and Works of William Morris.* London: Frank Cass, 1996.

Harvie, Christopher. *Political Fiction in Britain from Disraeli to the Present.* London: Unwin Hyman, 1991.

Haywood, Ian. *Working Class Fiction from Chartism to* Trainspotting. Plymouth: Northcote House, 1997.

Hegel, Georg. *The Philosophy of History.* 1840. Trans. J. Sibree. New York: Dover, 1956.

Himmelfarb, Gertrude. *The Idea of Poverty: England in the Early Industrial Age.* New York: Alfred K. Knopf, 1984.

Hitchens, Christopher. *Why Orwell Matters.* New York: Basic Books, 2002.

Hobsbawn, Eric. *The Invention of Tradition.* Cambridge: Cambridge UP, 1983.

Hoggart, Richard. 'Introduction to *The Road to Wigan Pier.*' 1965. *George Orwell: A Collection of Critical Essays.* Ed. Raymond Williams. Englewood Cliffs: Prentice-Hall, 1974. 34–61.

– *The Uses of Literacy: Aspects of Working-Class Life with Special Reference to Publications and Entertainments.* New York: Oxford UP, 1957.

Holderness, Graham. *D.H. Lawrence: History, Ideology, and Fiction.* Goldenbridge: Gill and Macmillan, 1982.

Holloway, John. *The Victorian Sage.* 1953. New York: Norton, 1965.

Horkheimer, Max, and Theodor W. Adorno. *Dialectic of Enlightenment.* 1944. Trans. John Cumming. New York: Continuum, 1987.

Houghton, Walter. *The Victorian Frame of Mind.* New Haven: Yale UP, 1957.

Huizinga, Johan. *Homo Ludens: A Study of the Play Element in Culture.* 1950. Boston: Beacon, 1955.

Ingle, Stephen. *George Orwell: A Political Life.* Manchester: Manchester UP, 1993.

– *Socialist Thought in Imaginative Literature.* London: Macmillan, 1979.

Inozemtsev, Vladislav L. *The Constitution of the Post-Economic State: Post-Industrial Theories and Post-Economic Trends in the Contemporary World.* Aldershot: Ashgate, 1998.

Jacobson, Dan. 'The Invention of Orwell.' Review of *George Orwell: The Complete Works,* Ed. Peter Davidson. *Times Literary Supplement* 21 August 1998: 3–5.

James, Henry. 'Preface to The Princess Casamassima.' *The Art of the Novel.* 1907. New York: Charles Scribner's Sons, 1937. 59–78.

Jameson, Fredric. *Marxism and Form: Twentieth-Century Dialectical Theories of Literature.* Princeton: Princeton UP, 1971.

– *The Political Unconscious: Narrative as a Symbolic Act.* Ithaca: Cornell UP, 1981.

– *Postmodernism, or, the Cultural Logic of Late Capitalism.* 1991. Durham: Duke UP, 1999.

Jardine, Lisa, and Julia Swindells. 'Homage to Orwell: The Dream of a Common Culture, and Other Minefields.' *Raymond Williams: Critical Perspectives.* Ed. Terry Eagleton. Boston: Northeastern UP, 1989. 108–29.

Jewsbury, Geraldine. *Marian Withers.* 3 vols. London: Colburn, 1851.

Jones, Barry. *Sleepers, Wake: Technology and the Future of Work.* Melbourne: Oxford UP, 1982.

Joyce, Patrick, ed. *The Historical Meanings of Work.* Cambridge: Cambridge UP, 1987.

Karl, Frederick. *A Reader's Guide to the Contemporary English Novel.* Rev. ed. New York: Farrar, Straus, and Giroux, 1972.

Keating, P.J. *The Working Classes in Victorian Fiction.* London: Routledge, 1971.

Knapp, James F. *Literary Modernism and the Transformation of Work.* Evanston: Northwestern UP, 1988.

Kubal, David. *Outside the Whale: George Orwell's Art and Politics.* Notre Dame: U of Notre Dame P, 1972.

Kumar, Krishan. *From Post-Industrial to Post-Modern Society: New Theories of the Contemporary World.* Oxford: Blackwell, 1995.

Lafargue, Paul. *The Right to Be Lazy.* Trans. Charles H. Kerr. Chicago: Charles H. Kerr and Company Co-operative, 1907.

Lawrence, D.H. *Sons and Lovers.* 1913. New York: Viking, 1965.

Le Quesne, A.L. *Carlyle.* Oxford: Oxford UP, 1982.

Levine, George. *The Boundaries of Fiction: Carlyle, Macaulay, Newman.* Princeton: Princeton UP, 1968.

Levitan, Sar, and Clifford Johnson. 'The Survival of Work.' *The Work Ethic – A Critical Analysis.* Ed. Jack Barbash, Robert Lampman, Sar Levitan, and Gus Tyler. Bloomington: Industrial Relations Research Association Series, 1983. 1–25.

Lowe, Donald. *The History of Bourgeois Perception.* Chicago: U of Chicago P, 1982.

Lukács, Georg. *The Historical Novel.* 1955. Trans. Hannah and Stanley Mitchell. Harmondsworth: Penguin, 1981.

– *History and Class Consciousness.* 1923. Trans. Rodney Livingstone. London: Merlin, 1971.

– *The Theory of the Novel.* 1915. Trans. Anna Bostock. London: Merlin, 1988.

Lutchmansingh, Lawrence. 'Archaeological Socialism: Utopia and Art in William Morris.' *Socialism and the Literary Artistry of William Morris.* Ed. Florence S. Boos and Carole G. Silver. Columbia: U of Missouri P, 1990. 7–25.

Lyotard, Jean-François. *The Postmodern Condition: A Report on Knowledge.* Trans. Geoff Bennington and Brian Massumi. Minneapolis: U of Minnesota P, 1984.

Marcuse, Herbert. *Eros and Civilization: A Philosophical Inquiry into Freud.* 1955. New York: Vintage, 1962.

– *One-Dimensional Man: Studies in the Ideology of Advanced Industrial Society.* 1964. Boston: Beacon, 1970.

Marglin, S. A. 'What Do Bosses Do?' *The Division of Labour: The Labour Process and Class-Struggle in Modern Capitalism.* Ed. André Gorz. New Jersey: Humanities P, 1976. 13–54.

Marx, Karl and Frederick Engels. 'Economic and Philosophic Manuscripts of 1844.' *The Marx-Engels Reader.* Ed. Robert C. Tucker. 2nd ed. New York: Norton, 1978. 66–125.

– *The German Ideology.* 1846. *The Marx-Engels Reader.* Ed. Robert C. Tucker. 2nd ed. New York: Norton, 1978. 146–200.

– *Karl Marx: Early Writings.* Trans. and ed. T. B. Bottomore. New York: McGraw-Hill, 1964.

McKibbon, Ross. *The Ideologies of Class: Social Relations in Britain, 1880–1950.* Oxford: Clarendon Press, 1990.

Meakin, David. *Man and Work: Literature and Culture in Industrial Society.* London: Methuen, 1976.

Mendilow, Jonathan. *The Romantic Tradition in British Political Thought.* London: Croom Helm, 1986.

Meyers, Jeffrey. *Orwell: Wintry Conscience of a Generation.* New York: Norton, 2000.

Mill, J.S. 'Bentham.' 1838. *Utilitarianism.* Ed. Mary Warnock. Glasgow: Fount, 1962. 78–125.

– 'The Negro Question.' *Fraser's Magazine* 41 (1850): 27.

Morris, William. 'Art and the People.' 1883. *William Morris: Artist, Writer, Socialist.* Vol. 2. Ed. May Morris. Oxford: Basil Blackwell, 1966. 382–406.

– 'The Hopes of Civilization.' 1888. *News from Nowhere and Other Writings.* Ed. Clive Wilmer. London: Penguin, 1993. 307–28.

– 'The Lesser Arts.' 1877. *News from Nowhere and Other Writings.* Ed. Clive Wilmer. London: Penguin, 1993. 233–54.

– *News From Nowhere.* 1890. Ed. Clive Wilmer. London: Penguin, 1993.

– 'The Pilgrims of Hope.' 1886. *Three Works.* London: Lawrence and Wishart, 1968. 115–78.

– 'The Revival of Handicraft.' 1888. *The Collected Works of William Morris.* Vol. 22. London: Longmans Green and Company, 1914. 331–41.

– 'Useful Work *versus* Useless Toil.' 1888. *News from Nowhere and Other Writings.* Ed. Clive Wilmer. London: Penguin, 1993. 285–306.

Naisbitt, John, and Patricia Aburdene. *Megatrends 2000: Ten New Directions for the 1990s.* New York: Avon, 1990.

Najder, Zdzisław. *Joseph Conrad: A Chronicle.* Trans. Halina Carroll-Najder. New Brunswick: Rutgers, 1983.

Nietzsche, Frederic. *The Dawn of Day.* 1881. Trans. J.M. Kennedy. Ed. Oscar Levy. New York: Russell and Russell, 1964.

– *A Nietzsche Reader.* Trans. and ed. R.J. Hollingdale. London: Penguin, 1977.

Norman, Richard. *The Moral Philosophers.* Oxford: Oxford UP, 1998.

O'Brien, Conor Cruise. 'Passion and Cunning: An Essay on the Politics of W.B. Yeats.' 1965. *Passion and Cunning: Essays on Nationalism, Terrorism and Revolution.* New York: Simon and Schuster, 1988. 8–61.

Orwell, George. *A Clergyman's Daughter.* 1935. Harmondsworth: Penguin, 1966.

– *The Collected Essays, Journalism and Letters of George Orwell* (Volume I, *An Age Like This: 1920–1940*; Volume II, *My Country Right or Left: 1940–1943*; Volume III, *As I Please: 1943–1945*; Volume IV, *In Front of Your Nose: 1945–1950*). Ed. Sonia Orwell and Ian Angus. London: Secker & Warburg, 1968.

– *Coming Up for Air.* 1939. Harmondsworth: Penguin, 1979.

– *Down and Out in Paris and London.* 1933. Harmondsworth: Penguin, 1981.

– *Keep the Aspidistra Flying.* 1936. Harmondsworth: Penguin, 1975.

– *Nineteen Eighty-Four.* 1949. London: Penguin, 1989.

– *The Road to Wigan Pier.* 1937. Harmondsworth: Penguin, 1981.

Pahl, R.E. 'Editor's Introduction.' *On Work.* Oxford: Basil Blackwell, 1988.

Patai, Daphne. *The Orwell Mystique.* Amherst: U of Massachusetts P, 1984.

Perkin, Harold. *The Origins of Modern English Society: 1780–1880.* 1969. London: Routledge, 1978.

Polanyi, Karl. *The Great Transformation.* New York: Farrar and Rinehart, 1944.

Rai, Alok. *Orwell and the Politics of Despair.* Cambridge: Cambridge UP, 1988.

Rees, Richard. *George Orwell: Fugitive from the Camp of Victory.* Carbondale: Southern Illinois UP, 1962.

Reilly, Jim. 'The Novel as Art Form.' *Literature and Culture in Modern Britain, Volume One: 1900–1929.* Ed. Clive Bloom. London: Longman, 1993. 55–75.

Reilly, Patrick. *George Orwell: The Age's Adversary.* New York: St Martin's, 1986.

Rieff, Philip. 'George Orwell and the Post-Liberal Imagination.' *George Orwell.* Ed. Harold Bloom. New York: Chelsea House, 1987. 45–62.

Rodden, John. 'Orwell and the London Left Intelligentsia.' *New Casebooks George Orwell.* Ed. Graham Holderness, Bryan Loughrey, and Nahem Yousaf. New York: St Martin's, 1998. 161–81.

Rose, Michael. *Re-working the Work Ethic.* London: Batsford, 1985.

Rosenberg, John D. *Carlyle and the Burden of History*. Oxford: Clarendon, 1985.
Rosenberg, Philip. *The Seventh Hero: Thomas Carlyle and the Theory of Radical Activism*. Cambridge: Harvard UP, 1974.
Ruskin, John. *The Works of John Ruskin*. 39 vols. London: George Allen, 1903–12.
Russell, Bertrand. 'In Praise of Idleness.' 1932. *In Praise of Idleness and Other Essays*. New York: Simon and Schuster, 1972. 9–29.
Russell, Norman. *The Novelist and Mammon*. Oxford: Clarendon, 1986.
Sandison, Alan. *The Last Man in Europe: An Essay on George Orwell*. London: Macmillan, 1974.
Sanders, Charles Richard. *Lytton Strachey: His Mind and Art*. New Haven: Yale UP, 1957.
Sayers, Sean. 'The Need to Work: A Perspective from Philosophy.' 1987. *On Work: Historical, Comparative, and Theoretical Approaches*. Ed. R.E. Pahl. Oxford: Basil Blackwell, 1988. 722–41.
Scarry, Elaine. *Resisting Representation*. New York: Oxford UP, 1994.
Schumacher, E.F. *Good Work*. New York: Harper and Row, 1979.
Sennett, Richard. *The Corrosion of Character: The Personal Consequences of Work in the New Capitalism*. New York: Norton, 1998.
Shaw, George Bernard. 'Introduction.' *Hard Times*. By Charles Dickens. New York: Norton, 1966. 332–9.
Smith, Adam. *An Inquiry into the Nature and Causes of the Wealth of Nations*. 1776. Vol. 1. Oxford: Claredon, 1976.
Stearns, Peter, N. *Be a Man: Males in Modern Society*. New York: Holmes and Meier, 1979.
Strachey, Lytton. 'Carlyle.' *The Shorter Strachey*. Ed. Michael Holroyd and Paul Levy. Oxford: Oxford UP, 1980. 99–105.
– *Eminent Victorians*. 1918. Garden City: Garden City Publishing, n.d.
Thomas, Keith. Ed. *The Oxford Book of Work*. Oxford: Oxford UP, 1999.
Thompson, E.P. *The Making of the English Working Class*. 1963. London: Penguin, 1980.
– *The Poverty of Theory and Other Essays*. London: Merlin, 1980.
– *William Morris: Romantic to Revolutionary*. London: Lawrence and Wishart, 1955.
Trela, D.J. and Rodger L. Tarr, eds. 'Magazine of Domestic Economy and Family Review.' 1843. *The Critical Responses to Carlyle's Major Works*. Westport: Greenwood, 1997. 143–6.
Tressell, Robert. *The Ragged Trousered Philanthropists*. 1914. London: Paladin, 1991.
Trotter, David. *The English Novel in History: 1895–1920*. London: Routledge, 1993.

Tyler, Gus. 'The Work Ethic: A Union View.' *The Work Ethic – A Critical Analysis.* Ed. Jack Barbash, Robert Lampman, Sar Levitan, and Gus Tyler. Bloomington: Industrial Relations Research Association Series, 1983. 197–210.

Ure, Andrew. *The Philosophy of Manufactures.* 1835. London: Frank Cass, 1967.

Vanden Bossche, Chris R. *Carlyle and the Search for Authority.* Columbus: Ohio State UP, 1991.

Veblen, Thorstein. *The Theory of the Leisure Class: An Economic Study of Institutions.* 1912. New York: Funk and Wagnalls, 1967.

Vicinus, Martha. 'Chartist Literature and the Development of a Class-Based Literature.' *The Socialist Novel in Britain: Towards the Recovery of a Tradition.* Ed. H. Gustav Klaus. Brighton: The Harvester Press, 1982. 7–25.

Wadhams, Stephen. *Remembering Orwell.* Markham, ON: Penguin, 1984.

Watt, Ian. *Conrad in the Nineteenth Century.* London: Chatto & Windus, 1980.

– *The Rise of the Novel.* Berkeley: U of California P, 1965.

Webb, Beatrice. *My Apprenticeship.* 1926. New York: AMS Press, 1977.

Webb, Igor. *Custom to Capital: The English Novel and the Industrial Revolution.* Ithaca: Cornell UP, 1981.

Weber, Max. *Economy and Society: An Outline of Interpretive Sociology.* 1914. Vols. 1 and 2. Trans. Ephraim Fischoff et al. Ed. Guenther Roth and Claus Wittich. Berkeley: U of California P, 1978.

– *The Protestant Ethic and the Spirit of Capitalism.* 1904–5. Trans. Talcott Parsons. New York: Charles Scribner's Sons, 1958.

Wells, H.G. *Experiment in Autobiography.* New York: Macmillan, 1934.

– *The History of Mr. Polly.* 1910. Ed. Gordon N. Ray. Cambridge: Riverside, 1960.

– *Tono-Bungay.* 1909. London: Collins' Clear-Type P, n.d.

Wheeler, Thomas Martin. *Sunshine and Shadow.* 1849–50. *Chartist Fiction.* Ed. Ian Haywood. Aldershot: Ashgate, 1999. 65–200.

Wiener, Martin J. *English Culture and the Decline of the Industrial Spirit, 1850–1980.* Cambridge: Cambridge UP, 1981.

Williams, Raymond. *Culture and Society: 1780–1950.* London: Chatto and Windus, 1958.

– *The English Novel from Dickens to Lawrence.* London: Chatto and Windus, 1970.

– Introduction. *Dombey and Son.* By Charles Dickens. Harmondsworth: Penguin, 1974. 11–34.

– *Keywords: A Vocabulary of Culture and Society.* Rev. ed. New York: Oxford UP, 1976.

– *Orwell.* 3rd ed. Hammersmith: Fontana P, 1984.

– *William Morris: Romantic to Revolutionary.* London: Lawrence and Wishart, 1995.

Woodcock, George. *The Crystal Spirit: A Study of George Orwell.* New York: Minerva, 1968.
– 'George Orwell, 19th Century Liberal.' *George Orwell: The Critical Heritage.* Ed. Jeffrey Meyers. London: Routledge and Kegan Paul. 1975. 235–46.
Woolf, Virginia. 'Mr. Bennett and Mrs. Brown.' 1924. *Collected Essays.* Ed. Leonard Woolf. Vol. 1. London: Hogarth, 1980. 319–37.
– *Orlando.* 1928. London: Granada, 1982.
– *A Writer's Diary.* 1954. Ed. Leonard Woolf. San Diego: Harvest, 1981.

Index

Aburdene, Patricia, 216
Adorno, Theodor, 25
alienation, 4, 20, 23, 24, 38, 40, 41, 56, 86, 158
Alison, William, 75
Ambrosini, Richard, 106
Anderson, Perry, 18
anti-utilitarianism and anti-rationalism, 5, 18, 20, 21–2, 23, 25, 28, 29, 42, 49, 66–7, 70, 76, 79, 81–2, 85–6, 96, 107, 114, 122, 123, 127, 145, 147, 153, 165, 167, 169, 209, 210
Arendt, Hannah, 20–1, 24, 40, 55, 90, 94, 106, 116; *The Human Condition*, 20–1
Arnold, Matthew, 58, 123–4
Arnold, Thomas, 141
Aronowitz, Stanley, 215, 219, 223; 'The Post-Work Manifesto,' 223
artisans and artisanship, 40, 47–8, 50, 52, 57, 70, 84, 93, 109, 159, 131, 134, 223
authoritarianism, 34, 45–7, 53, 79, 87, 110–11, 122, 139, 207

Bakhtin, Mikhail, 181
Barthes, Roland, 25
Beckett, Samuel, 137, 144; *Quad*, 144
Beever, John, 166
Behnken, Eloise, 38–9
Bell, Daniel, 213, 219; *The Coming of the Postindustrial Society*, 213
Bellamy, Edward, 91; *Looking Backward*, 91
Bellamy, Ron, 25
Beniger, James, 214
Benjamin, Walter, 108–9; *Illuminations*, 108
Bennett, Arnold, 147, 149
Bentham, Jeremy, 42, 78, 87, 123; 'Deontology, A Table of the Springs of Action,' 42
Benthamism, 42, 63–5, 78, 122
Biernacki, Richard, 29
bildungsroman, 81, 83, 149, 161
Birken, Lawrence, 134, 135, 137; *Consuming Desire*, 134
Black, Bob, 222–3; *The Abolition of Work*, 223
Blackwood, William, 105
Blair, Charles, 11
Blake, William, 225
Bobrowski, Thaddeus, 9, 10, 97
Booth, Charles, 34

Bourdieu, Pierre, 18–20, 47, 53–4, 66, 160; *The Logic of Practice*, 18–20
Bradshaw, David J., 26; *The Voice of Toil: Nineteenth-Century British Writings about Work*, 26
Brown, Ford Madox, 49
Bruss, Paul, 100–1
Burke, Kenneth, 61
Burnett, John, 159
Butler, Samuel, 139–40, 141; *The Way of All Flesh*, 139–40

Calvin, John, 3
Calvinism, 39, 60
camaraderie, 11, 70, 162, 163–4
Campbell, Beatrix, 154, 186
Campbell, Ian, 9
Camus, Albert, 137
Captains of Industry, 38, 40, 43, 48, 55, 56, 59–60, 64, 80–1, 87, 90
caritas, 16, 66, 71, 78, 163
Carlyle, James, 9
Carlyle, Jane, 80
Carlyle, Thomas, 4, 6, 7–9, 10, 11–13, 14–17, 22, 23, 30–1, 32, **34–69**, 70, 72, 74, 75, 79, 80, 82, 83, 86, 88–90, 93, 94, 99, 100, 106, 109–10, 111–13, 120, 121–2, 123, 124, 132, 133, 134, 136, 139, 141, 143, 144, 145, 147, 148–9, 150, 151–2, 153, 156, 157, 159, 164–5, 169, 174, 175, 176, 178–9, 181, 187, 188, 203, 204, 207, 209, 211, 213, 221, 223, 225; 'Chartism,' 34, 46, 55; *Latter-day Pamphlets*, 35; *Past and Present*, 34, 35, 37–8, 43–7, 51, 54–9, 68, 75, 99, 112, 145; *Reminiscences*, 9; *Sartor Resartus*, 10, 37–8; 'Signs of the Time,' 45, 57

Chartism and Chartists, 40, 44, 47, 54, 55, 80, 84
Chesterton, G.K., 56
classical economics, 16, 28–9, 134–5, 178, 187
Clegg, Stewart, 218
Cobbett, William, 8, 56
Coleridge, Samuel Taylor, 78
'Condition-of-England Question,' 34, 76
Conrad, Joseph, 4, 6, 7–8, 9–10, 11–13, 14, 15, 21, 23, 30–1, 32, 43, 51, **94–118**, 119, 120–1, 122, 123, 124, 128, 133, 134, 137, 138–9, 143, 145, 147, 150, 151–2, 153, 156, 159, 169, 174, 175, 181, 203, 207, 209, 211, 213, 225; 'The Ascending Effort,' 106; *Chance*, 99–100; *Heart of Darkness*, 97–105, 114, 117, 196; *Lord Jim*, 99, 103–4, 107–8, 120; *The Mirror of the Sea*, 97; *The Nigger of the 'Narcissus,'* 98, 107, 109–15, 117; *The Secret Agent*, 106; 'The Secret Sharer,' 110; 'Tradition,' 98–9; *Youth*, 99
conservatism and radical conservatism, 5, 7–8, 11, 15, 29, 31, 44, 69–70, 75, 95, 109, 117, 127, 133–4, 153, 172, 174, 190
Cooper, Thomas, 37, **82–5**, 86, 129, 133; '"Merrie England" – No More!,' 84, 85; 'Seth Thompson, the Stockinger,' 84–5, 133
Crick, Bernard, 11, 152, 167, 177, 200

Danon, Ruth, 27; *Work in the English Novel*, 27
Defoe, Daniel, 121; *Robinson Crusoe*, 68
Dentith, Simon, 183

deus ex machina, 39, 83, 84, 133
Dickens, Charles, 10, 31, 34, 36–7, 58, **69–76**, 79, 81, 82, 106, 119, 138, 161, 164, 173, 177, 179–80, 193; *Bleak House*, 72–3, 75; *The Chimes*, 69; *A Christmas Carol*, 69; *David Copperfield*, 3, 75, 177; *Dombey and Son*, 69, 71–2, 73; *Hard Times*, 70–1, 72, 74, 145; *Our Mutual Friend*, 119
Disraeli, Benjamin, 73, 79, 82; *Sybil*, 73, 79
disutility, 4, 5–6, 29–30, 43, 45, 86, 134, 139, 173, 222
division of labour, 4, 5, 41, 47, 64, 86, 110, 119, 214–15, 216, 221, 222
Dobb, M.H., 66

Eagleton, Mary, 126–7
Eagleton, Terry, 11, 25, 55–6, 78, 97, 116–17, 154, 196, 198, 202, 207–8; *Criticism and Ideology*, 97
economism, 7, 13, 18–19, 25, 28, 64–8, 70, 151, 172, 173, 187, 204
efficiency, 7, 44, 64, 104, 105, 111, 118, 121, 214, 215, 222
Ekevall, Kay, 160
Eliot, George, 68, 199; *Middlemarch*, 199
Eliot, T.S., 137, 138, 139, 143–4, 145, 148–9, 206; 'Sweeney Erect,' 145; 'The Waste Land,' 143
Emerson, Ralph Waldo, 17
Engels, Friedrich, 39, 158, 170–1; *The Condition of the Working Class in England*, 158, 171
Englishness, 9, 10, 12–13, 15, 30, 43–4, 48, 51, 74, 79, 156, 176
English socialism, 152, 161, 177
existentialism, 99, 104, 111, 185

Fabians and Fabianism, 25, 92, 122–3
fin de siècle, 107, 133, 138
Fleishman, Avrom, 115, 116
Forster, E.M., 8, 97, **123–8**; *Howards End*, 71, 126–8; *A Passage to India*, 137
Foucault, Michel, 25
Freud, Sigmund, 12, 124–5, 140; *Civilization and Its Discontents*, 124; *The Future of an Illusion*, 124
Froude, James, 60

Galsworthy, John, 147
Gaskell, Elizabeth, 36, 73, 75, **76–82**, 126; *Cranford*, 77–8; *Mary Barton*, 73, 77, 78–9; *North and South*, 77, 78–82, 126
Gaston, Paul, 100–1
Gordon, Charles, 142
Gorz, André, 220, 222, 223; *Critique of Economic Reason*, 222
Gosse, Edmund, 183
Gosse, Philip Henry, 183
Graff, Gerald, 26
Graham, Cunninghame, 117
Gramsci, Antonio, 45
Green, Henry, 32
Greg, W.D., 78
Grennan, Margaret, 91
Guild, Nicholas, 201

Hardy, Thomas, 32
Harvey, Charles, 92–3; *Art, Enterprise and Ethics*, 92–3
Harvie, Christopher, 125; *Political Fiction in Britain*, 125
Haywood, Ian, 129, 132, 133
hedonism, 5, 29, 45, 140, 164, 166, 199, 222

Hegel, Georg, 23, 37–9, 63
Herbert, Sidney, 142
Himmelfarb, Gertrude, 40, 58, 70, 73
Hitchens, Christopher, 8
Hoggart, Richard, 154, 168; *The Uses of Literacy*, 168
Holderness, Graham, 125; *D.H. Lawrence: History, Ideology, and Fiction*, 125
Holloway, John, 49
homo economicus, 14, 29, 35, 45, 59, 61, 63, 65–7, 94, 135, 140
homo faber, 14, 23, 24, 35, 37, 46, 59, 86, 135, 140, 187
Horkheimer, Max, 26
Houghton, Walter, 6–7, 68–9; *The Victorian Frame of Mind*, 68–9
Huizinga, Johan, 51–2, 114
Hulme, T.E., 144, 148
humanism, 61

ideals and Idealism, 14, 37, 57–8, 60, 66, 94, 95, 97, 99, 104–5, 117, 154, 167
idleness, 4, 39, 43, 45, 74, 81, 140
inconsistency, 86, 95, 152–3, 155–6
Ingle, Stephen, 152, 154, 200
Inozemtsev, Vladislav, 220
intellectualism, 13, 39, 152, 161, 168, 176, 179

Jacobson, Dan, 153
James, Henry, 137, 144, 146, 199; *The Portrait of a Lady*, 199
Jameson, Fredric, 25, 31, 103–4, 107–8, 214, 218, 219; *The Political Unconscious*, 107–8; *Postmodernism*, 219
Jardine, Lisa, 167
Jewsbury, Geraldine, 80–1, 82; *Marian Withers*, 81

Johnson, Clifford, 220
Jones, Barry, 220
Jones, Ernest, 84
Joyce, James, 137, 197; *Ulysses*, 137, 144, 147, 197, 205
Joyce, Patrick, 162, 170

Kafka, Franz, 137
Karl, Frederick, 161, 195
Keating, P.J., 30, 193
Kipling, Rudyard, 117–18, 137; 'The Glory of the Garden,' 117–18; 'McAndrew's Hymn,' 118; 'Mrs. Bathurst,' 137; 'A Truthful Song,' 118
Kirwan, Celia, 153
Knapp, James, 143–4; *Literary Modernism and the Transformation of Work*, 143–4
Korzeniowski, Apollo, 9
Kumar, Krishan, 222

Lafargue, Paul, 93, 163
laissez-faire, 15, 26, 45, 55, 61–4, 75, 100, 101–2, 122, 185
Laski, Harold 180
Lawrence, D.H., 124–5, 137, 157, 185–6; *Lady Chatterley's Lover*, 125; *Sons and Lovers*, 125
leisure, 4, 6, 29–30, 62, 130, 140, 165–6, 173, 215, 222
Le Quesne, A.L., 12
Levitan, Sar, 220
liberalism, 6–7, 15, 17, 30, 36, 42, 47, 59–60, 62–5, 69–70, 74, 80, 95, 114–15, 122, 164, 196–7, 216
Locke, John, 65
Lukács, Georg, 16–17, 18, 25, 59, 68, 72, 95, 148, 208
Lutchmansingh, Lawrence, 88–9

Luther, Martin, 3
Lyotard, Jean-François, 214, 216, 218; *The Postmodern Condition*, 214

machines and technology 4, 39–42, 81, 86, 91, 103, 108, 118–19, 121–2, 144, 153, 169, 181, 186–9, 213–17, 220–2, 224
Malthus, Thomas, 82
Malthusianism, 60, 69
Manchester, 78, 81
Manchester School, 64
Manning, Henry Edward, 141–2
Marcuse, Herbert, 61–2, 215–16, 222, 224
marginal economics, 96, 124, 134–5, 146
Marglin, Stephen, 214
Martineau, Harriet, 60, 82; *Illustrations of Political Economy*, 60
Marx, Karl, 18, 20, 23–5, 26, 37–8, 80, 86, 88, 91–2, 100, 124, 134, 136, 148, 149, 157–8, 222; *Capital*, 24; *The German Ideology*, 24; *Philosophical Manuscripts*, 86
Marxism and Marxists, 25, 39, 86, 92, 93, 158, 160, 163, 171, 172, 174, 176, 184, 187, 219, 222
masculinity and manliness, 5, 16, 35, 87, 111–14, 157–9, 175, 184–9, 204
Masuda, Yoneji, 214
Maurice, F.D., 49
Mayhew, Henry, 34, 183
Meakin, David, 27, 90; *Man and Work*, 27
Merrie, England, 12, 44
Meyers, Jeffrey, 155
Mill, J.S., 42–3, 78, 82, 123, 134
Miller, Henry, 223

mining and miners, 39, 72, 157–62, 170, 173, 207, 216
modernism, 97, 107, 108, 117, 123, 124, 127, **133–49**, 150, 212, 218, 219
moral economy, 4, 7, 70, 114, 134
moral individualism, 15–16, 28, 31, 71, 73, 101, 105, 117, 120–1, 143, 150, 151, 168, 178, 186, 191–3, 197–8, 202, 205, 206, 208, 209, 210–11
Morley, John, 26; *Critical Miscellanies*, 26
Morris, William, 37, 56, 67, **88–93**, 131, 181, 195, 223; 'The Lesser Arts,' 89; *News From Nowhere*, 91–2; 'The Pilgrims of Hope,' 90; 'The Revival of Handicraft,' 90

Naisbitt, John, 216
Najder, Zdzisław, 10, 97
nationalism, 12–13, 39, 45, 56, 59–60, 76, 151
naturalism, 34, 149, 194, 195, 204, 205, 207–8, 211
neoclassical economics, 16, 28–9, 134–5, 137, 145, 212
Newman, John Henry, 142
Nietzsche, Frederic, 140, 141
Nightingale, Florence, 141–2

O'Brien, Conor Cruise, 188
observer and participant, 11, 13, 32, 49–50, 52, 101, 109, 159, 161, 163, 171, 175, 179, 181, 183, 191, 204, 207
'only connect,' 24, 28, 66, 71, 75, 78–80, 125–7
organicism, 5, 34, 44, 45, 64, 66, 75, 87, 95, 97, 109–10, 115–17, 133, 169, 207

Orwell, George, 4, 6, 7–8, 10–13, 14, 15, 22, 23, 30, 31, 32, 34–5, 49–50, 52–3, 58, 67, 70, 73–5, 87–8, 90–1, 95, 98, 101, 106, 109, 111–13, 115, 118–19, 122, 138–9, 143, 145, 146, 149, **150–211**, 213, 215, 216, 217, 223, 225; *Animal Farm*, 192, 193; *Burmese Days*, 192, 193; 'Charles Dickens,' 73–5, 173; *A Clergyman's Daughter*, 192–3, **193–9**, 200, 201, 208, 210; *Coming Up for Air*, **203–8**, 210; *Down and Out in Paris and London*, 155, 162–4, 173–5, 177–8, 179, 181–2, 184–6, 191; 'The English People,' 189; 'The English Tradition,' 174; *Homage to Catalonia*, 207; 'Inside the Whale,' 138–9, 189, 205–6, 208–9, 223; *Keep the Aspidistra Flying*, 155, 174, 192–3, **199–203**, 208, 210; 'A Nice Cup of Tea,' 183; *Nineteen Eighty-Four*, 162, 180, 192, 193, 202, **208–11**; *The Road to Wigan Pier*, 157–62, 166–75, 177–8, 179, 183, 184–90, 191, 192; 'Some Thoughts on the Common Toad,' 199; 'Such, Such Were the Joys,' 183; 'Why I Write,' 180, 183
Ozment, Suzanne, 26; *The Voice of Toil: Nineteenth-Century British Writings about Work*, 26

Pahl, R.E., 44
participant. *See* observer
Patai, Daphne, 154, 184
Pater, Walter, 140
paternalism, 30, 34, 37, 40, 43, 45, 61, 69, 70, 79, 87, 113, 114, 133, 153, 159, 177, 205, 207
Pierce, David, 126–7
Polanyi, Karl, 60, 136
political economy, 22, 23–4, 29, 36, 43, 45–6, 48, 49, 54, 60–4, 71, 77–9, 110
positivism, 25, 61
postindustrialism, 212–17, 218–20, 221–2, 224–5
postmodernism, 212–13, 217–25
Pound, Ezra, 137, 144
pragmatic realism, 16, 31, 176, 191, 192–3, 199, 205, 206–9
praxis, 18, 23, 25, 56
Press, Jon, 92–3; *Art, Enterprise and Ethics*, 92–3
Protestantism, 3, 5, 15, 22, 27, 30, 76, 90, 164, 197
Puritanism, 5, 22, 164, 189

Rai, Alok, 154
rational actor theory, 16, 19–20, 28–30, 61, 64–7, 95, 135, 136
rationalism, 4, 6, 14–17, 21–3, 26, 28, 29, 36, 42, 61–7, 69, 72, 76, 81, 94, 99, 101, 108, 114–15, 135–7, 143–5, 146, 148–9, 153–4, 156, 162, 172, 174, 185, 189–90, 199, 205, 207, 209, 224–5
Rees, Richard, 172, 201
Reilly, Jim, 108; 'The Novel as Art Form,' 108
Reilly, Patrick, 205
rhetoric of work and labour, 32, 35, 49–53, 58, 62–5, 88, 107–9, 114, 159, 174, 178–84
Ricardo, David, 25, 82, 134
Rieff, Philip, 196–7
Rifken, Jeremy, 221
Rodden, John, 183
Romantics, 5, 28, 34, 37, 39, 43, 48, 195, 225
Rose, Michael, 220

Rosenberg, Philip, 58
Ruskin, John, 25, 30, 37, 49, 68, 70, **85–8**, 89, 90, 93, 95, 103, 127, 132, 155–6, 183, 218; *The Crown of Wild Olive*, 87; *The Stones of Venice*, 86–7
Russell, Bertrand, 140, 141; 'In Praise of Idleness,' 140

sailing and sailors, 8, 9–10, 12, 97, 99, 108, 112, 114, 115–16, 118
Sandison, Alan, 164, 197
'satisficing,' 29, 77, 162
saving illusion, 98, 104–5, 196
Sayers, Sean, 166
Scarry, Elaine, 52
Schumacher, E.F., 216, 221, 222
self-reliance and the self-made man, 6, 16, 22, 27, 37, 81–2, 84–5, 177, 192
Sennett, Richard, 221
Shaw, Bernard, 32, 34, 70, 74, 123
slackers, 119, 212, 222–3
Smiles, Samuel, 6, 177
Smith, Adam, 64, 77, 134, 221; *The Wealth of Nations*, 64
social exploration, 34
Stearns, Peter, 188
Stephen, Leslie, 26; *The History of English Thought in the Eighteenth Century*, 26
Stewart, Martha, 220
Stonier, Tom, 214
Strachey, Lytton, 141–3; *Eminent Victorians*, 141–3
St Simonism, 60
stupidity and simplicity, 30, 35, 47, 51, 113–14, 129–30, 175–8
Swindells, Julia, 167

Tawney, R.H., 22, 164

Thomas, Keith, 26; *The Oxford Book of Work*, 26
Thompson, E.P., 18, 25, 35–6, 41–2, 44, 47–8, 91–2, 225; *The Making of the English Working Class*, 47–8
Tolstoy, Leo 17
Tom Jones, 16
tragic sensibility, 31, 46, 88, 112–13, 115, 168, 170, 173, 189, 204, 206, 207
Tressell, Robert, 97, **128–33**; *The Ragged Trousered Philanthropists*, 129–33
Trotter, David, 135, 137
Tyler, Gus, 159

underdog, 15–16, 30–1, 73, 76, 81, 133, 163, 164, 176, 188, 190, 192, 194
unemployment, 35, 85, 154, 157, 159, 164–6, 167, 173, 177–8, 179, 186, 187
Ure, Andrew, 34, 42, 56, 67; *The Philosophy of Manufactures*, 42
utilitarianism, 5, 25, 41, 42–3, 45, 49, 52, 55, 60–1, 63–5, 71, 73, 76, 78, 95, 114, 123, 154, 172, 212, 225
utopianism, 7, 16, 77, 90–1, 93, 95, 120, 154, 205, 212, 214, 216

Vanden Bossche, Chris, 48
Veblen, Thorstein, 135–7; *The Theory of the Leisure Class*, 135–7
Vicinus, Martha, 84

Watt, Ian, 68, 102
Webb, Beatrice, 34, 122–3
Webb, Igor, 70
Weber, Max, 21–3, 60, 136, 164, 222
Wells, H.G., 97, **118–23**, 147, 148;

246 Index

'Experiment in Autobiography,' 118; *The History of Mr. Polly*, 119–20, 200; *Men Like Gods*, 140; *The Time Machine*, 119; *Tono-Bungay*, 119, 120–2, 135

The Westminster Review, 69

Wheeler, Thomas Martin, 83, 84

Wiener, Martin, 27–8; *English Culture and the Decline of the Industrial Spirit*, 27–8

Wilde, Oscar, 140; 'The Soul of Man under Socialism,' 140

Williams, Raymond, 20, 21, 25, 48–9, 55, 56, 65, 68–9, 73, 94, 123, 154, 160, 177, 183–4, 191, 200, 208; *Culture and Society*, 21, 48, 68–9, 183; *Keywords*, 65; *Orwell*, 183–4

Wilson, Edmund, 178

Woodcock, George, 10, 58, 73–4, 152, 153, 164, 166, 167, 179

Woolf, Virginia, 137, 144, 146, 147–8, 149; *Orlando*, 149

work, meanings of, 4, 5–6, 8, 11, 19, 20–1, 22, 24, 26, 29, 35, 37, 38–43, 48, 52, 55, 67–8, 75, 76, 86, 98–9, 112, 116, 149, 157, 161, 162, 197, 204, 210, 221, 224

Work (Ford Madox Brown), 49

'Work' (John Ruskin), 87

work ethics, 5–6, 22, 27, 30, 35, 44, 46, 67, 72, 73, 76, 85, 101, 102, 105, 139, 141–2, 149, 159, 163, 172–5, 196, 220

working-class culture and character, 6, 8, 11–12, 18, 13, 20, 28, 29, 30–1, 33, 35, 43–4, 46–8, 70, 75, 82–3, 86–8, 123, 127, 129, 130, 145–6, 148–9, 151, 152–3, 156, 160, 162–5, 166–72, 175, 177, 181, 184, 189, 191, 195, 204, 207

work rationalization, 4, 5, 6, 13, 14, 16, 17, 22, 31, 36, 63, 72, 76, 77, 78, 83, 85–6, 94, 101, 106, 132–3, 144, 145, 154, 156, 165, 178, 186, 210–11, 214, 221

writing as work, 32, 49–53, 106, 161, 179

Wuthering Heights (Emily Brontë), 71

Yeats, William Butler, 137, 143, 145, 188; 'Meditations in Time of Civil War,' 145

Zola, Emile, 157